Mothers on the Move

Mothers on the Move

Reproducing Belonging between Africa and Europe

PAMELA FELDMAN-SAVELSBERG

The University of Chicago Press
Chicago and London

The University of Chicago Press, Chicago 60637
The University of Chicago Press, Ltd., London
© 2016 by The University of Chicago
All rights reserved. Published 2016.
Printed in the United States of America

25 24 23 22 21 20 19 18 17 16   1 2 3 4 5

ISBN-13: 978-0-226-38974-5 (cloth)
ISBN-13: 978-0-226-38988-2 (paper)
ISBN-13: 978-0-226-38991-2 (e-book)
DOI: 10.7208/chicago/9780226389912.001.0001

Library of Congress Cataloging-in-Publication Data

Names: Feldman-Savelsberg, Pamela, 1958– author.
Title: Mothers on the move : reproducing belonging between Africa and Europe /
     Pamela Feldman-Savelsberg.
Description: Chicago : The University of Chicago Press, 2016. | Includes
     bibliographical references and index.
Identifiers: LCCN 2016005825 | ISBN 9780226389745 (cloth : alk. paper) |
     ISBN 9780226389882 (pbk. : alk. paper) | ISBN 9780226389912 (e-book)
Subjects: LCSH: Cameroonians—Germany—Berlin. | Cameroonians—Germany—
     Berlin—Ethnic identity. | Immigrant families—Germany—Berlin—Psychological
     aspects. | Belonging (Social psychology)—Cameroon. | Motherhood—
     Psychological aspects.
Classification: LCC DD867.5.C3 F45 2016 | DDC 305.48/896711043155—dc23 LC record
     available at http://lccn.loc.gov/2016005825

Dedicated to the next Cameroonian-German generation:
Mmeughaiy, Yessigheh, Kayisaiy, Nursseg, and Borzenghen
Yaje and Afanyu
Willy

Contents

Preface and Acknowledgments

Many Cameroonians took time out of their busy schedules to tell me about their lives, hopes, and struggles. I am forever grateful for their warmth and openness. Out of respect for their anonymity, they must remain unnamed. In almost all cases, they have chosen their own pseudonyms, at times with enormous wit. I remember many instances of raised eyebrows, winks, and rolling laughter when a woman said, "Aw, then let me be called . . . ."

The stories these Cameroonians share among themselves and with me connect tellers and listeners to people, places, and ideas. They also help me tell a story, one among many possible stories about African migration and family making in Europe. I have striven to attend to diversity among "Cameroonian migrant mothers," to the uniqueness of their life histories and desires, all patterned by a common set of conditions.

Other stories have been told about migration and the search for well-being. Most anthropologists aim to show the humanity and agency of those most disadvantaged and marginalized. Anthropologists make a strong moral argument for deservingness of basic rights and services in the face of overwhelming global inequalities. In migration research, this has led many scholars to focus on the plight of irregular migrants, those who move across international borders without the security of visas, residence permits, and work permits. I have been inspired by much of the nuanced, sensitive work on "access denied" in the anthropologies of migration and health care. Unwittingly, though, this research may be marginalizing other types of migrants from the master narrative. The danger is that a well-intended research focus may end up reinforcing stereotypes of the migrant, especially the African migrant, as illegal(ized), impoverished, and in need of help.

My Cameroonian interlocutors are keenly aware of this narrative, and hoped for a different story. They complain bitterly about being buffeted by what anthropologists would term structural violence, but also narrate rich lives of family connection, community activism, and educational achievement. They detail lives infused by law and different stances toward it, ranging from awe, to navigation of a complex state apparatus, to avoidance. Mothers talk about law when they evoke what it feels like to be foreign, demonstrating the significance of law for legal as well as illegal migrants. The story my Cameroonian interlocutors hope for includes the condition of illegality as only one among many other migrants' lived experiences.

Following their lead, I may surprise some readers by including among my Cameroonian interviewees a physician, an engineer, a specialist in comparative literature, a historian of science, numerous doctoral and masters students, and even the doctoral advisee of a member of the German constitutional court. I also interviewed and spent time with secretaries, accountants, home health aides, hotel housekeeping staff, housewives, and the unemployed, some of them refugees. Some Cameroonians I met have experienced extended periods of irregular immigration status and its concomitant trauma, while others have arrived and remained legal immigrants or have become German citizens. Shaped by their diverse biographies and circumstances, each of these women manages in her own way commonly shared predicaments of belonging, reproduction, and connection engendered by migration. They remind us not only that "a story is always situated" (Abu-Lughod 1993, 15), but also that there are many stories to be told. This reminder seems to have become ever more urgent during 2015 and 2016, with massive refugee movements into Europe.

I have tried to be careful to distinguish the stories individual women have told me about their lives, and the story I am telling by finding patterns in this rich variation. I use typeface to distinguish verbatim and remembered speech. I render verbatim quotations taken from audio-recorded interview transcriptions in italics, and quotations written in field notebooks in regular typeface.

I particularly thank Elizabeth Beloe, Marie Biloa Onana, and Victoria Yiwumi Faison for urging me to speak to these different stories. My discussions with them and with fellow researchers in Berlin—Hansjörg Dilger, Susann Huschke, Annett Fleischer, and Heide Castañeda—have helped me reflect upon the ethics of anthropological representations. My hosts and colleagues during a generous fellowship year at the Käte Hamburger Center for Advanced Studies in the Humanities "Law as Culture" in Bonn—in particular Werner Gephart, Nina Dethloff, Raja Sakrani, Joachim Savelsberg, Maurizio Ferraris,

Elizabeth Suzanne Kassab, and Greta Olson—thought through with me ways that stories about law participate in the work of migrant self-presentation and anthropological representation.

These are just some of the many individuals who have contributed to the making of this book, in addition to several institutions. Because the underlying research spans over three decades of engagement with Cameroon, these include teachers, hosts, and funding agencies that have made my work in Bangangté, Yaoundé, and Berlin both possible and enjoyable. In these acknowledgments, I concentrate on the Berlin leg of my research.

I am grateful to the Wenner-Gren Foundation for Anthropological Research for awarding me a Post-PhD Research Grant and Osmundsen Initiative Supplement in support of field research in Berlin during 2010–2011. Carleton College generously supported exploratory research in summer 2009 with a Small Faculty Development Grant, and my research during 2010–2011 with a Hewlett Mellon Fellowship, supplementing my sabbatical leave. During the writing process, the college provided a Humanities Center Student Research Assistance Grant (2013) for explorations in the field of legal anthropology, a leave of absence supplement, and, through the Broom Chair in Social Demography and Anthropology, a contribution to the German translation.

I thank the Max Planck Institute for Social Anthropology in Halle, especially its LOST (Law, Organization, Science and Technology) research colloquium, and the Institute of Social and Cultural Anthropology, Freie Universität Berlin, and its Working Group on Medical Anthropology for hosting me in 2010–2011. The intellectual stimulation and encouragement they provided during my fieldwork were invaluable. Then and during subsequent visits to Berlin and Halle, I have particularly benefited from long discussions with my main hosts—Richard Rottenburg and Hansjörg Dilger—as well as Katharina Schramm, Andrea Behrends, and Astrid Bochow in Halle; and Elizabeth Beloe, Susann Huschke, Dominik Mattes, Caroline Meier zu Biesen, Britta Rutert, and Mustafa Abdullah at the Freie Universität Berlin. For introducing me to initial contacts in 2009 and for her continuing interest in my project, I thank Annett Fleischer, then just completing her PhD at the Freie Universität Berlin. For further contacts and interest, I thank Hervé Tchemeleu of the Afrika Medien Zentrum as well as Drs. Anatole and Flaurance Kenfack.

While in Berlin I was able to learn about the institutional settings of migrant family making from a number of organizations. I thank first and foremost Rosaline M'Bayo and her coworkers at ViA (Verein für interkulturelle Arbeit), as well as anonymous individuals at Balance, ProFamilia, Malteser Migranten Medizin, MediBüro Berlin, Deutsche AIDS-Hilfe, and the Zentrum für Flüchtlingshilfen und Migrationsdienste, Berlin. Like my Cameroonian interlocutors, these individuals gave generously of their time and expertise. In addition, I am thankful to Carolyn Sargent for inviting me to visit her fieldsite in Paris, thus awakening me to the importance of scale in studying African migrations to Europe.

I could not have written this book without a generous residential fellowship from the Käte Hamburger Center for Advanced Studies in the Humanities "Law as Culture" at the Friedrich-Wilhelm Universität in Bonn. I owe great thanks to its leadership, especially Werner Gephart, Nina Dethloff, and Raja Sakrani, as well as to its academic and support staff for providing just the right combination of intellectual stimulus and protection from distraction. My fellow Fellows—from five disciplines, eight countries, and six continents—asked just the right questions, helping me to articulate my thoughts for an interdisciplinary audience.

I presented parts of this research in numerous professional venues, including annual meetings of the American Anthropological Association and Council for European Studies; the Working Group on Anthropology and Population, Department of Anthropology, Brown University; the Rockefeller Bellagio Center; the joint colloquium of the Seminar für Ethnologie (Martin Luther Universität-Halle) and the Max Planck Institute for Social Anthropology; the Colloquium on Law, Organizations, Science and Technology, Max Planck Institute for Social Anthropology; the Working Group on Medical Anthropology, Freie Universität Berlin; the Institute of Social and Cultural Anthropology colloquium, Freie Universität Berlin; the Kölner Ethnologisches Kolloquium, University of Cologne; the workshop "Trust and Intimacy in Relationships of Health and Healing: Perspectives from Africa, Past and Present," Freie Universität Berlin; the Dialogos faculty lecture series, Humanities Center and Learning Teaching Center, Carleton College; Angelina Weld Grimké Lecture in African and African American Studies, Carleton College; Department of Anthropology, Macalester College; the Minnesota Population Center, Center for German and European Studies, and Department of African-American and African Studies, University of Minnesota; the International Roundtable Series, Hamline University; the workshop "Rethinking Care: Anthropological Perspectives on Life Courses, Kin-Work and Their Trans-Local Entanglements," IKG Work and the Human Lifecycle in Global History, Humboldt University, Berlin; the Marriage and Family Therapy Program, St. Mary's University of Minnesota; and a series of conferences and workshops at the Käte Hamburger Center for Advanced Study "Law as Culture," including the Fellows colloquium, the Forum "Law as Culture," and the conferences "Globalization and Documentality: à propos 'Documentality' by Maurizio Ferraris" and "The Normative Complex: Legal Cultures, Validity Cultures, Normativities." At each of these occasions I received helpful suggestions, deserving criticism, and lively debate that furthered my writing. I cannot name all of these interlocutors here, but would particularly like to mention Caroline Bledsoe, Heide Castañeda, Cati Coe, Hansjörg Dilger, Maurizio Ferraris, Marie-Claire Foblets, Kristine Krause, Jessaca Leinaweaver, Elizabeth Suzanne Kassab, Martin Ramstedt, Richard Rottenburg, Carolyn Sargent, Daniel Jordan Smith, and Bruce Whitehouse.

I am grateful for the feedback I have received from colleagues and friends who have read all or parts of the manuscript, including Jennifer Cole and Christian Groes, who introduced me to the concept of affective circuits, and Erdmute Alber, Elizabeth Beloe, Heike Drotbohm, Alma Gottlieb, Flavien Ndonko, and the two anonymous reviewers.

Numerous research assistants and student workers have helped in the preparation of the manuscript. First and foremost, Elizabeth Beloe provided invaluable research assistance in the field, initiating a process in which we became both friends and colleagues. Julia Baumhauer and Claire Spilker used their multilingual talents and ethnographic experience to transcribe the Berlin interviews. At Carleton College, Rafadi Hakim and Anna Morrison coded my trilingual interview transcripts with care and enthusiasm. Their work was prepared by the efforts of Elizabeth Durham, Leah Eby, and John Trevino. Lyssa Searcy and Emily Scotto provided invaluable bibliographic assistance. Mary Buswell, Emily Rifkin, Katie Shaffer, Isaac Shapiro, and Lindsey Walters have double-checked demographic data and bibliographic citations; Katie and Isaac prepared the maps. My hearty thanks go to all these future scholars, as well as to Heidi Eyestone for her help with the photographs.

This book has benefited greatly from the fine editorial wisdom of the editors and staff of the University of Chicago Press. I am grateful to David Brent for his early advice and for skillfully shepherding the book through the review and production process, to his wonderful assistant Ellen Kladky, and to Ryo Yamaguchi. I thank Louise C. Kertesz for her excellent copyediting, and Michael Taber for work on the index.

Finally, I must thank my husband, Joachim, and daughters, Anna and Rebecca. Joachim Savelsberg's wit and patience has enriched our life together on three continents. As colleague, friend, and husband, he has known when to provide frank critique or an encouraging word. Our discussions over many years, and particularly on long walks along the Rhine during our fellowship year in Bonn, have sharpened my argument. Joachim is and will always remain my most important interlocutor. He and our daughters have helped me experience some of the joys and challenges of transnational family making. During fieldwork and writing, we overcame geographic distance while our family experienced the joyful birth of our granddaughter, Mara, as well as sickness and death among those closest to us. I am deeply grateful to them all.

Cast of Characters

Character Name, alphabetized	Chapters of Appearance
Gisèle	Chapters 1, 3, 4
Happi	Chapters 4, 5, 6
Hortense	Chapters 1, 2
Iris	Chapters 1, 3, 4, 5, 6
James	Chapters 3, 4
Josiane	Chapter 2
Jucal	Chapters 1, 3, 4, 6
Justine	Chapters 3, 4, 5
Kelvin	Chapter 4
Kemayou	Chapter 6
KemKarine	Chapters 1, 3, 4, 5
Lily	Chapters 1, 3, 4, 5, 6
Lola	Chapters 1, 5
Magni	Chapters 1, 3, 4, 5, 6
Maimouna	Chapters 1, 6
Maria Mar	Chapters 3, 5, 6
Marthe	Chapters 1, 3, 4, 5
Mrs. Black	Chapters 3, 5, 6
Nanette	Chapter 2
Nya	Chapters 3, 6
Olivia	Chapter 4

Character Name, alphabetized	Chapters of Appearance
Paulette	Chapters 1, 2
Placide	Chapter 4
Princess	Chapter 5
Rose	Chapters 1, 5, 6
Solange	Chapters 4, 5
So'nju	Chapters 1, 3, 4, 5, 6
Sophie	Chapters 3, 5
Tamveun	Chapter 2
Tessy	Chapters 3, 4
Yvonne	Chapters 4, 5

1

Introduction

> We are always on the move, for ourselves and for our children.
> MAGNI, Berlin 2009

Toward the beginning of our multiyear friendship and year of intense collaboration regarding maternity, mobility, and belonging, my Cameroonian research assistant leaned her head toward mine, coffee from a Berlin university library café steaming up our glasses. A migrant mother herself, Magni[1] confided, "We are always on the move, for ourselves and for our children." Like many of my interlocutors, this young woman embodies the rushing movement of a working mother getting through her day, the bureaucratically regulated physical movement across international boundaries, and the upwardly mobile movement of an international student. Like many other Cameroonian women, Magni had migrated to Germany in search of better conditions in which to raise her family.

Ironically, Cameroonian women often find that their migration creates challenges to the social and emotional connections that constitute belonging—a complex mix of recognition by, and attachment to, a particular place or group. Like many others we spoke with, Magni found her relations, her things, and her loyalties stretched between Cameroon and Germany. In the course of our work together, Magni and I heard many stories regarding migrant women's difficulties with respect to reproduction and belonging, summarized in their recurrent exclamation that "it's hard being a mother here." Their difficulties were emotional and social, medical and legal. Despite their complaints, clearly it was through their children that our Cameroonian interviewees managed to overcome the burdens of exclusion and forge new layers of belonging. Through their children, young women strengthened connections to kin in Cameroon and built new connections to Cameroonian diasporic communities and to German officials. Having and raising children in Berlin may have been hard and lonely for these recent immigrants, but it also helped young mothers adjust to a new place.

This book explores how Cameroonian women in Germany seek to establish their belonging through birthing and caring for children and what happens to their ties in places of origin and places of migration in the process. It is partly a tale about immigrant integration—belonging in Germany—but also a story about belonging in new ways with fellow migrants in Berlin and with Cameroonians back home.

Cameroon is a small country with a land mass approximately the size of California, nestled between West and Central Africa. A century ago, Cameroon was still a German colony; split between French and British rule following World War One, Cameroon gained political independence in 1960. As more and more of its approximately 22 million inhabitants (World Bank 2013) are seeking education, jobs, and new lives in Europe, Cameroonian migration to Berlin represents one variation of a larger phenomenon of African migration to the global north.

Africans are migrating to Europe more than ever before, migrating as families, to sustain families, and to found new families. In a world of movement, what does it mean to belong? How do migrant mothers create a sense of belonging for themselves, for their children, and through their children? A decade after the turn to the new millennium, this tension among mobility, rootedness, and reproduction was palpable in my interactions with Cameroonian mothers in Berlin. Each woman narrated different hardships about motherhood "on the move," simultaneously revealing how those hardships prompted them to extend and intensify their social networks while occasionally putting other connections on hold. From the tender phase of mother-infant care through the turbulent teen years, mothers deploy their children to forge connections across a variety of social networks.

Belonging to these social networks—kin groups and households, ethnic or migrant community associations, and states—encompasses a range of statuses and feelings. Through their children, women may maintain or gain their citizenship status, national or ethnic identity, emotional connection, and feelings of recognition, acceptance, and comfort. Women's and their children's belonging can be felt (an interior state), performed (by behaving according to certain codes), or imposed (e.g., when a bureaucrat categorizes a woman as deserving of assistance). In interaction with family members stretching from Cameroon to Germany, with migrant associations, and with German officials, migrant mothers variably enact belonging through rights, duties, and expectations regarding financial transactions (remittances, fees, taxes); decision making (voting, advice); physical presence (residence and visits); bodily care (of

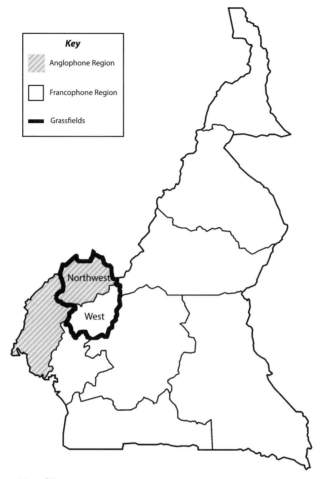

FIGURE 1.1. Map of Cameroon.

mothers and infants); and use of symbols, including language choice and naming practices).

Migration complicates belonging, stretching some connections to the
breaking point while facilitating new ones. This is particularly so in the highland Grassfields area, spanning two Cameroonian provinces and bearing a long
history of labor migration and political opposition to the central state within
Cameroon. Spanning two Cameroonian provinces, Grassfields peoples include
the French-speaking Bamiléké of the West Region and their ethnic cousins
from the English-speaking Northwest Region (see figure 1.1). Bamiléké make up
30 percent and Anglophones 20 percent of Cameroon's population of 22 million. A series of economic and political crises in Cameroon since the 1980s

sharpened and politicized ethnic boundaries, a phenomenon that scholars term the "politics of belonging" (e.g., Geschiere 2009).

Cameroonians from this area—the focus of my research—migrate to improve the conditions in which they regenerate families. In the Cameroonian cities where Bamiléké and Anglophones move, locals consider them ethnic strangers; discrimination and corruption (Transparency International 2014) make accessing health care and supporting a family difficult. Hard labor, poor nutrition, and disease render women's fertility fragile. Indeed, the statements I heard in Berlin about the difficulties of motherhood in the diaspora reminded me of previous encounters with mothers in both rural and urban Cameroon, a recurrent gesture of hands clapped together then opened, palms up, indicating, "We have nothing"—not enough children, not enough food or material goods or the conditions to grow healthy families.

These conditions of reproductive insecurity in Cameroon motivate many to search for well-being through transnational migration (see also Stoller 2014). Cameroonians call migration to seek one's fortune abroad "bushfalling." In this case, "bush" denotes an unknown place simultaneously full of rich potential and mysterious danger. To "fall bush" literally means to hunt or to cultivate distant fields, but in contemporary Cameroon it refers to migration to Europe, North America, and occasionally the Middle East and Asia (Alpes 2011; Fleischer 2012; Nyamnjoh 2011; Pelican and Tatah 2009; Pelican 2013). The predicaments that Bamiléké and Anglophone women face in Cameroon motivate bushfalling and tell us why young Cameroonian mothers find themselves in Berlin.

Although transnational migration is one way Cameroonian women seek to overcome Cameroonian impediments to growing and supporting their families, transnational migration renders women's reproduction and belonging even more insecure. Through migrating, African women make "choices for their future children and for their children's future" (Shandy 2008, 822), based on legal, economic, cultural, and emotional logics. These choices entail sacrifice as mothers leave the embrace of their families and familiar ways of being behind to face the material, social, and emotional challenges of starting anew in a strange place. While moving across space is one way to be *socially* mobile and realize middle-class aspirations, migration necessitates managing new sets of expectations about belonging-through-children that emanate from kin back home as well as from laws and bureaucratic procedures in Germany.

Women seek to manage these often contradictory expectations by forging connections that support them as mothers and allow them to care for others. Finding partners, being pregnant, giving birth, and rearing children—in other words, practices of physical and social reproduction—tie mothers to families, to communities, and to states. For example, when parents care for their children, they fulfill family expectations while drawing upon help from extended kin or entitlements from community associations and government social service agencies. Such exchanges embed mothers in overlapping fields of social relationships and thus form the basis of their multilayered belongings.[2] Mothers purposefully build, maintain, and manage networks through their reproductive practices. And mothers shape their reproductive decisions in part because they are striving for the sense of positive value and recognition that comes with belonging.

Mothers negotiate belonging through exchanges of care, money, goods, and words within these networks. Later in this chapter, I will imagine these ties as electrical circuits along which exchanges flow in discontinuous ways that respond simultaneously to external constraints and to the emotions of mothers' network of relationships. I draw inspiration from Jennifer Cole and Christian Groes's recent conceptualization of *affective circuits* in their work on personhood and the pursuit of regeneration in African migration to Europe (2016). In this book, we will see that mothers juggle multiple, sometimes contradictory, expectations by making, dropping, and picking up again ties established through kinship, community organizations, and state actors. By situationally cultivating certain affective circuits and letting other circuits temporarily "rest," Cameroonian migrant mothers manage the contingent nature of belonging for mothers who are "always on the move."

Examining motherhood and child-rearing among Cameroonians in Berlin invites us into a larger world of African migrations and transnational family-making. Much of the literature on transnational families examines how women create and manage connections to others through the circulation of children, including fostering, adoption, and other forms of distributed parenting (e.g., Alber, Martin and Notermans 2013; Coe 2013; Leinaweaver 2008, 2013; Parreñas 2005; Reynolds 2006). But it neglects the role child*bearing* plays in mothers' webs of belonging. And what happens when mothers and children move together, or when children born in the country of migration stay with their immigrant mothers?

This book focuses on childbearing and child-rearing as processes of belonging and not-belonging for Cameroonian migrant mothers in Berlin. By soliciting care from multiple directions, the young child helps its mother with her transition to a new place. Sending older children to school and commiserating with other mothers about the challenges of raising tweens provides migrant mothers further opportunities to reflect upon what it means to be African while becoming established in Europe. Furthermore, by sharing experiences about their encounters with the state apparatus and bureaucracy in Berlin, mothers develop a migrant legal consciousness, common orientations about getting along in a new land. Women resolve, manage, and reproduce the challenges of migration through their efforts to forge networks with kin, with community organizations, and with authorities. Along these affective circuits, migrant mothers circulate emotions, support, and ideas that orient them to a new cultural, reproductive, and juridical landscape. Although Cameroonian mothers repeatedly lament that "It's hard being a mother here," they recognize that their children create opportunities as well as difficulties for their new lives in Germany.

Concepts

Four concepts frame my argument: reproductive insecurity, belonging, affective circuits (i.e., emotion-laden social networks), and legal consciousness. I take reproductive insecurity as a motivator to movement, including young Cameroonians' drive toward both physical and social mobility. Mobility complicates belonging, which encompasses both jural-political and affective aspects. Jural incorporation and emotional belonging condition forms of relatedness and the exchanges that flow along and form affective circuits within Cameroonian women's social networks. Stories about belonging and exclusion, about encounters with neighbors, teachers, physicians, and public officials, circulate along these same social ties, sedimenting into forms of legal consciousness and political subjectivity. Affective circuits and legal consciousness are the tools through which mothers on the move navigate the tricky seas of reproduction and belonging.

REPRODUCTIVE INSECURITY

Connections between reproduction and belonging are sharply revealed by instances in which reproduction goes awry. I propose the term "reproductive insecurity" to address the conditions and anxieties surrounding such reproductive challenges. Reproductive insecurity encompasses social and cultural reproduction (e.g., the reproduction of social inequalities among culturally defined groups) as well as biological reproduction (creating people to populate those groups). While my Berlin interlocutors tell me that "all reproduction in the diaspora is a challenge," some examples from my work among the Bamiléké in Cameroon illustrate instances when biological and social reproduction become short-circuited in communities of origin (what migration researchers call "sending communities"). A woman may face infertility

(Feldman-Savelsberg 1999) or repeated miscarriages (Feldman-Savelsberg, Ndonko and Yang 2006), putting her marriage and community belonging at risk. By seeking an abortion, she may break one set of cultural proscriptions to maintain culturally appropriate models of motherhood (Feldman-Savelsberg and Schuster n.d.). Her reproduction may become part of ethnic stereotyping in the context of autochthony movements that seek to exclude Bamiléké migrants from full Cameroonian citizenship (Feldman-Savelsberg and Ndonko 2010; Geschiere 2007). These and other challenges to reproduction and belonging occur frequently in the medically and politically treacherous context of sub-Saharan Africa.

These Cameroonian examples reveal the important interrelations among biological reproduction, cultural notions of procreation, and social reproduction. Human biological reproduction occurs in the context of social institutions that shape patterns of sexual partnerships and the physical health necessary for conception, gestation, and childbirth. Just as important for reproductive insecurity are the ways participants understand these processes, where children come from and how they are made (Delaney 1991). To illustrate, let's visit the Bamiléké paramount chieftaincy (called "fondom" in Cameroonian Pidgin English and in English-language scholarship on Cameroon) where I began my long research encounter with Cameroon. During the 1980s in Bangangté, parents understood procreation through rich culinary metaphors of hot sex, gendered ingredients, and cooking-pot wombs. Thirty years later their children, now cosmopolitan migrant mothers in Berlin, framed procreation in biomedical terms but retained their mothers' concerns regarding the effects of social discord on fertility. Cameroonian ideas about procreation, while changing over time, clearly place biological reproduction within the realm of social relationships.

The circumstances of birth create multiple layers of social relationships, as a child is born into a lineage, strengthens its parents' conjugal and affinal ties, and gains citizenship either on the basis of genealogy (jus sanguinis) or place of birth (jus soli). Sustaining these relationships and their associated values, norms, and potential inequalities over time constitutes social reproduction (Bourdieu 1977; Edholm, Harris and Young 1978). As Colen points out in her work on "stratified reproduction" (1995), both biological and social reproductive labors are processes distributed among multiple actors—mothers, fathers, siblings, aunts, grandmothers, and non-kin caregivers (cf. Laslett and Brenner 1989; Goody 2008; Coe 2013). Distributed reproductive labors forge a number of relationships that can be rendered insecure—through colonial and postcolonial intrusions, through structured misunderstandings between reproductive health providers and immigrant clients (Sargent 2011), and through the "exclusionary incorporation" (Partridge 2012) that greets African migrants on European shores.

We can see that numerous material, cultural, and social conditions render human reproduction, cultural belonging, and social reproduction problematic. Reproductive insecurity encompasses the conditions and social experience of these difficulties and linkages (Feldman-Savelsberg, Ndonko, and Yang 2005). The *conditions* rendering biological and social reproduction insecure (e.g., social determinants of health inequalities such as poverty, infectious disease, social disruption, violence) are primarily political and economic, often linked to domestic and transnational labor migration. These conditions generate personal and collective anxiety, the *affective aspect* of reproductive insecurity. The emotional force of reproductive insecurity is revealed and (re)produced through speech and bodily practices expressing fear of reproductive mishaps from infertility and pregnancy loss to "demographic theft" (Castañeda 2008) as well as through concerns about the ability to maintain—or reproduce—a particular form of social organization and sense of cultural distinctiveness.[3]

BELONGING

Belonging is one way of expressing relatedness, key to anthropology from its earliest studies of kinship to more recent work on reproduction and migration (e.g., Leinaweaver 2008, 2011). Nothing could be more central to anthropology than the constitution and continuity of culturally defined groups and ways in which group membership is established and experienced for individuals. Despite the de facto permeability of their boundaries, these groups—based on such attributes as kinship, residence, gender, ethnicity, religion, or citizenship—are the building blocks of social organization. The process of creating and maintaining group membership—belonging—for oneself and for one's dependents is an important part of reproductive labor. Indeed, social reproduction is not only about reproducing structured relationships among individuals and groups; it is also about reproducing emotional commitment—an emotional sense of belonging—to those groups and positions.

Belonging is an expansive term, encompassing relatedness based on (1) social location, (2) emotional attachment through self-identifications, and (3) institutional, legal, and regulatory definitions that simultaneously grant recognition to and maintain boundaries between socially defined places and groups (Yuval-Davis 2006, in Krause and Schramm 2011, 118). Looking a bit more closely at these three bases of relatedness, we see that belonging can be felt, performed, or imposed.

Cameroonian migrant mothers "belong" to social locations at the intersection of class, race, gender, and citizenship status (e.g., being an educated black woman with Cameroonian citizenship). Often, social locations become regulatory categories, imposed on migrant mothers and thus constraining their actions. Migrant mothers are not only identified, but also self-identify, with various social categories and groups. Thus they feel an emotional sense of belonging. They may yearn toward "belonging" to the middle class and the comforts and prestige of this status, through deep emotional commitment to ideals of companionate marriage (Hirsch 2003; Hirsch and Wardlow 2006) and raising their own children (Coe 2013). By acting according to socially recognized codes of behavior, mothers perform their belonging to specific groups. Mothers perform different kinds of belonging when they claim rights (e.g., to help from kin following a birth), fulfill duties (e.g., sending remittances to family members, and paying taxes to governments), and participate in decision making (e.g., by voicing their opinions at hometown association meetings). Mothers also perform belonging by being physically present (e.g., to care for family members, or to fulfill visa obligations), and by choosing to teach their children either a Cameroonian national language (French or English) or German. These various ways of belonging may either complement or contradict each other, and are context-specific. Depending on the situation, migrant mothers may identify with all fellow mothers, with other black African immigrants of any gender, with those from their hometown, or with members of their extended family.

A century ago, when their children left for labor migration, village grandmothers urged them to "remember where their umbilical cord is buried," meaning to remember the family and the soil from whence they came and to which they owed fealty. Using this same idiom, migrant mothers raise their children to maintain emotional attachment to their extended families and their place of origin. They teach their children—with varying success—to identify with blackness, with Africa, with Cameroon, and with the home area of their ancestors. Fostering the emotional attachment of belonging is a tricky task, for at least two reasons. First, mothers also want their children to succeed and integrate in Germany, demanding of their little ones refined skills at switching from Cameroonian to German behavioral codes. Second, even within Cameroon, the identities toward which one can direct emotional attachment are multiple, overlapping, and often the subject of political conflict.

Struggles over boundary drawing, boundary maintenance, and split loyalties are at the core of the "politics of belonging" approach that dominates scholarship on Cameroon (e.g., Eyoh 1998; Fonchingong 2005; Geschiere 2009; Jua 2005; Ndjio 2006; Nyamnjoh and Rowlands 1998; Page, Evans, and Mercer

2010). This scholarship frames belonging in terms of the politics of primary patriotism in multiethnic states characterized by internal migration and disputes—sometimes violent ones—over rights and recognition (e.g., Broch-Due 2005; Evans 2010; Geschiere and Gugler 1998). Do individuals "belong" more to their place of origin or their place of residence? Are they more loyal to their ethnic polity (e.g., a local chiefdom) or to the nation-state? And where, in the context of internal migration, do people enjoy basic rights to residence, employment, and political representation?[4]

In contemporary Cameroon, these questions are posed not only about individuals, but also about groups. State actors and media question the loyalty of ethnic groups and regions with a history of opposition politics. They mobilize resentments toward internal migrants within receiving communities (urban and plantation areas in the southern third of the country), using the terminology of "autochthons" and strangers. Autochthony, being "born from" or of "the soil" (Geschiere 2009, 2) seems to naturalize place-based belonging for first-comers, defining them "*against* strangers" or late-comers (Whitehouse 2012, 13, emphasis in the original). Autochthony discourse thus negates the socially and culturally based belonging of refugees, migrants, and their descendants (Malkki 1992; Ong 2003). Attention to blood quantum likewise naturalizes genealogically based belonging, whether in "ethnobranding" to capitalize on ethnicity among Native Americans (Comaroff and Comaroff 2009, 92, 108) or in citizenship regimes based on jus sanguinis (as in Germany). German laws denying dual citizenship for people from countries other than the European Union or Switzerland seem to deny the lived reality of African migrants' simultaneous belonging in terms of both political and cultural subjectivities (Krause and Schramm 2011). Not only does the powerful state—whether Cameroonian or German—deny simultaneous belonging; in Berlin, Cameroonian hometown association membership rules based on genealogical connection to a home place do the same, albeit on a smaller scale.

The fixation on belonging in terms of place and kinship has shallow historical roots in Africa (Whitehouse 2012, 210), but carries considerable emotional force. Cameroonian transnational migrants despair that long-term residence and even German citizenship do not confer acceptance *as German*; at the same time they worry that their German-born offspring will lose their culture and language, so they take pains to keep host-society influences in check. The anguish of exclusion is never far from the warmth of moral conviviality, identified by Mercer, Page, and Evans as the "quieter" form of belonging; conviviality expresses ways that "loyalty to 'home' can provide the language, ideas and values to enable cooperation . . . and to establish the right way to live comfortably together within a place" (2008, 232). Thus we see that

belonging has many sides, from the political belonging of elites exploiting affinity for political ends, to legal incorporation through citizenship and state
regulation, to the affective side of acceptance, identification, and loyalty. While
noting their mutual production, here I concentrate on emotional belonging,
shaped by families, community organizations, and jural structures.

AFFECTIVE CIRCUITS

The affective side of belonging for Cameroonian mothers on the move is
much more than the individual's emotions of loyal identification and comfortable acceptance when included, or painful misrecognition when excluded. This kind of belonging is produced, reproduced, and challenged in
social relationships. Emotional belonging is thus part of being embedded in
social networks, whose malleable structure of ties creates conduits that are
maintained by ongoing interaction and exchange. We can picture the ties
mothers forge as circuits through which flow money, goods, and medicines;
fostered children and visitors; love, moral support, and demands (Cole and
Groes 2016). Indeed, these financial, advisory, physical, and symbolic exchanges are the very means for enacting belonging that we identified above.
Imagining electrical currents, short circuits, and circuit breakers, we realize
that these flows are not continuous but can be slowed, dropped, blocked, and
picked up again, for example, when pregnant women with shaky residence
status avoid communicating the hardships of migrant life with their mothers.
To push the metaphor further, the currents do not only vary in speed and
strength, but also occasionally shift to direct current rather than alternating
current. In other words, the exchanges at times flow mostly in one direction
despite an ethos of long-term reciprocity—at least among kin. I follow Cole
and Groes (2016) in calling this variety of social networks *affective* circuits,
because the things that move along them are so intertwined with—and indeed express—the emotive and loving elements of belonging to families and
communities.

State policies engender networks between authorities—who enforce regulations—and migrants. State policies thus create one type of circuit, or circuit-
breaker, that shapes who moves, who belongs, and how, and consequently the
success or failure experienced by African migrants to Europe. Like any visit
to a consulate or Foreigners Office (*Ausländeramt*), situations such as relatives being denied visas to provide perinatal care for their migrant sister or
daughter reveal the intensity of emotions electrifying state-based circuits of
belonging. Hometown associations, kin, peers, and lovers, more or less linked
in social networks, generate other types of affective circuits. Each of these

affective circuits exerts political and social control (and motivation) regarding migrant mothers' lives and families. Echoing discussions about whether social capital is epiphenomenal to social networks or is actively created by social agents (Astone et al. 1999), I argue that affective circuits are more than external constraints or motivators to migrant mothers' reproductive practices. Instead, affective circuits are created as women seek, perform, and produce belonging by purposefully embedding themselves and their children in overlapping, multileveled social networks.

These networks enable intimate economies of care that connect migrant mothers with African relations and German "others" (immigration agents, child-protection caseworkers, neighbors, teachers, doctors). They become acutely relevant when migrant mothers face reproductive challenges—from conception to birth, infant care to schooling. For obstetric and pediatric care, groups of kin, friends, and acquaintances—what medical anthropologists call "therapy management groups" (Janzen 1978, 1987)—emerge from these networks to define the issue, choose remedies, and offer solace. When these functions are taken over by networks spread across the European and African continents, we refer to them as transnational therapy networks (Krause 2008). Because the work of reproduction extends beyond the medical, the metaphoric notion of affective circuits captures particularly well the highly gendered labor, responsibility, and emotions that migrant mothers undertake to grow and anchor children—and themselves—in uncertain circumstances (Whyte 1997). Engaging in affective circuits is what makes Cameroonian migrant mothers belong and what helps them overcome reproductive insecurity.

LEGAL CONSCIOUSNESS

A very immediate source of insecurity for Cameroonian migrant mothers is the law, because German legal institutions affect so many aspects of daily life (Breyer 2011). Cameroonians interact with authorities for momentous, status-changing actions that mark international border-crossing, such as getting visas or becoming naturalized. Like all German residents, they also interact with public officials for such ordinary occurrences as registering and deregistering one's address to move to a new apartment, upon which a myriad of transactions from opening a bank account, obtaining a phone contract, or getting a library card depend. As we will discover in this book, reproductive processes of birthing and raising children likewise are framed by law and interaction with authorities, from getting a birth certificate for a new child to obtaining a health certificate to register a child for school. Immigration status is decisive, because it determines the ease, and even possibility, of the tasks that constitute daily life and livelihood. The force of law thus can be felt independently of people's understandings of it.

In light of my concern with Cameroonians' emotional *sense* of belonging, rather than examining the law per se, I focus on legal consciousness—how law is experienced and understood (Merry 1990) by ordinary Cameroonian migrants. In shaping belonging, and in creating or ameliorating reproductive insecurity, what matters most is not what the law *is*, but what actors *think* it is. Like belonging and reproductive insecurity, legal consciousness is not an individual attribute or attitude, but rather a stream of shared sociocultural knowledge that emerges through social interaction. Legal consciousness is a process through which "actors construct, sustain, reproduce, or amend the circulating (contested or hegemonic) structures of meanings concerning law" (Silbey 2005, 334). The stories Cameroonians tell each other about moments of acceptance and exclusion, about encounters with neighbors, teachers, physicians, and public officials, sediment into collectively held ideas about getting along with and in spite of the law in a new place. It is here that culture, including legal cultures (Friedman 1975; Nelkin 2004; Silbey 2010), are formed, contested, and interwoven.

A focus on legal consciousness reveals that "law" is found not only in bureaucratic legal institutions, but rather infuses daily life. In this way, legal consciousness and affective circuits are the means through which Cameroonians manage the interrelated challenges of reproductive insecurity and belonging. Legal consciousness also connects the interactional levels of family, community organizations, and the state. Telling stories of everyday joys and sorrows, including encounters with German officials, is an important element of Cameroonian migrants' sociality; migrants exchange stories in family settings and at community meetings, within the same affective circuits along which they provide care and forge belonging. Understandings of the law emerge through interactions with authorities and their retellings—commentary on how law affects such socially reproductive practices as binational marriage (Fleischer 2012) and disciplining children toward academic success (Kamga 2014). Several Cameroonian mothers I spoke with were convinced that their children could have them arrested if they merely threatened a light spanking, making mothers despair about how to "teach [their] children manners."

As we will see in chapter five, through its process of social interaction and meaning-making, Cameroonians' legal consciousness creates situationally specific units of belonging, distinguishing among home/not-home and we/them (Feldman-Savelsberg and Ndonko 2010; Kohlhagen 2006a). Within hometown associations, patterns of trust, mistrust, and dispute resolution are shaped by interactions between those with and those without regularized immigration status (Kohlhagen 2006b). And as we will see in chapter six, migrant mothers with greater financial, symbolic, and informational resources can use the law, or at least identify with following its rules. Those more precariously placed may avoid interacting with authorities of all sorts, trying to get out of law's way (Castles 2007). The "shadow of the Leviathan" sometimes motivates the most vulnerable migrants—those with irregular immigration status—to use alternative mechanisms of regulation and dispute resolution (Spittler 1980). At other times, especially in cases of intimate partner violence, Cameroonian mothers make use of the legal and social services provided by the German state and local nongovernmental organizations (NGOs) in Berlin.

While social status thus shapes orientations to the law, the law likewise affects migrants' social status. Labor law for immigrants combines with misrecognition to devalue migrants' qualifications in destination countries, causing migrants to lose social status in their destinations even while symbolically gaining status in sending communities from the mere fact of being "bushfallers." For example, by migrating to Berlin, a multilingual secretary or specialized pediatric nurse's aide trained in Cameroon may become merely an unemployed mother attending a mandated course in German as a second language. Migrant mothers are wary that the gossip of their fellow migrants may expose this "status paradox of migration" (Nieswand 2011) to their kin and friends back home in Cameroon. Women thus manage their insecurity by following patterns of trust and mistrust in community organizations to slow or speed up, drop and pick up again selected affective circuits. These examples demonstrate that attending to legal consciousness allows us to braid together the other conceptual poles of reproductive insecurity, belonging, and affective circuits, revealing how they—and the law—infuse interactions within and across spheres of family, community, and the state.

Researching Mothers on the Move: Methods and Data

I have investigated the interweaving of reproductive insecurity, belonging, attitudes toward the law, and the networks undergirding affective circuits through scaffolded projects following a community over three decades in multiple locales—from the Cameroonian countryside, to its capital city, and then to Berlin. In each subsequent locale, the scale of "community" increased. This book draws from my research in all three locales. As I moved from one research locale and project to the next, my personal experiences with motherhood—and transnational motherhood—inflected my relationships with Cameroonian mothers, the things we confided in each other, and undoubtedly the ways I have understood and interpreted the particularity of their lives and stories.[5]

Just after college, in 1980, I joined the Peace Corps to work on a health education project in rural Cameroon. Attending a birth for the first time, holding a frightened teenage mother's hand as she struggled through labor, was both a moving and life-changing experience for me. I began to think about my future as an anthropologist as well as my potential future as a mother in new ways. This was the beginning of a pattern, in which each visit to Cameroon and each research project raised questions that became the basis of the next project.

Three years after my Peace Corps experiences, I began my research in Bangangté, a rural Bamiléké kingdom (referred to by Cameroonians as fondom),[6] starting with a summer collecting stories about women rendered infertile through witchcraft. Through several subsequent years of archival research and fieldwork, I found that women and men used infertility as an idiom expressing their gendered unease regarding belonging to and reproducing lineages, threatened as they saw it by the fondom's political incorporation into the Cameroonian state (Feldman-Savelsberg 1999). As a participant-observer living in the king's (fon's) palace grounds from December 1985 through December 1986, I engaged in countless conversations about what it takes and what it means to become a mother in Bangangté and as a Bamiléké woman. To answer my interlocutors' astonishment that I was still childless at the ancient age of 28, I needed to explain how my peculiar cultural ideal of completing graduate school before childbearing, as well as living on a different continent from my spouse, delayed my own entry into motherhood. I heard mothers reprimand migrating youths, "Don't forget where your umbilical cord is buried!" thus alerting me to the importance of emigration in local imaginaries of reproductive danger. Archival work revealed this to be a Bamiléké and indeed Grassfields-wide phenomenon over the past century. Accompanying a fon's wife to southern Cameroon as she appealed to the urban Bangangté diaspora inspired my next project in Yaoundé, the capital city and metropolis of some 2.5 million inhabitants.

In Yaoundé during the 1990s and early 2000s, women's management of reproductive events was deeply inflected by their experiences as ethnic strangers at the height of the "autochthony debates." The autochthony debates, the autochthon-*allogène* problem, were arguments about whether internal migrants within Cameroon really "belonged" to their places of residence or their places of ethnic origin, discussed above regarding the politics of belonging. Cameroon had recently transitioned to a multiparty political system,

FIGURE 1.2. Cameroonian newspaper headline: "*Il n'y a pas de problème Bamiléké au Cameroun*" (There is no Bamiléké Problem in Cameroon), ironically indicating the contested nature of belonging for Bamiléké peoples living in Cameroon. *Le Patriote* no. 391, June 4–10, 2001, 1.

Credit: Heidi Eyestone

reawakening discourse from Cameroon's colonial past and struggle toward independence that links state politics with both reproduction and belonging.

Once a German colony, during WWI Cameroon was divided between Britain and France in a League of Nations mandate, gained independence in 1960, and became a bilingual federal republic in 1961. The loyalty of Francophone Bamiléké (30 percent of the Cameroonian population) has been questioned ever since they became involved in armed resistance to the party in power in the years surrounding independence (1956–1973). This Bamiléké history of political opposition combines with their reputation for entrepreneurial drive and high fertility to create ethnic stereotypes regarding the so-called "Bamiléké Problem" (Geschiere and Nyamnjoh 2000; Geschiere 2007; Kago Lele 1995).[7] Anglophone Cameroonians (20 percent of Cameroon's population) share a similar reputation for entrepreneurial drive, as well as a history of labor migration and domestic diaspora formation as "come no goes" (a Pidgin expression describing labor migrants who come to stay rather than returning to their places of origin). Anglophones have their own "Anglophone Problem" (Konings and Nyamnjoh 2003), facing political and linguistic marginalization in a Francophone-dominated country. During the transition to multiparty rule in the 1990s, Cameroon's major opposition party was launched in the English-speaking part of the greater Grassfields area. Cameroonian public discourse associates both the Northwest (Anglophone Grassfields) and West (Bamiléké) Regions with opposition politics; facing official states of emergency, public violence, and the continual questioning of their loyal belonging in the national arena has led many Bamiléké and Anglophones to seek refuge first in urban areas, and then overseas.

When I conducted my research (1997–2002) on ways Bamiléké women in Yaoundé, the nation's capital, manage reproductive events through networks formed in their hometown associations, a constitutional change had only recently introduced multiparty politics. The new political parties quickly became associated with particular ethnic groups and regions. In this context, interest politics promoted favoritism along ethnic lines in the provision of Cameroonian government services—to the detriment of Bamiléké and Anglophone citizens. Since then, ethnic divisions in Cameroon have only sharpened with repeated economic crises. Discrimination, high unemployment, and expensive fees and bribes make accessing health care difficult. Anglophone and Bamiléké youth complain that corruption and lack of future perspectives—what Jua terms the loss of transitional pathways (2003)—impede founding and supporting families. Current material conditions combine with emotionally charged collective memories. Bamiléké and Anglophone Grassfielders invoke memories of the violence surrounding independence when they worry about state plots against their fertility through such rumored technologies as sterilizing vaccines (Feldman-Savelsberg, Ndonko, and Schmidt-Ehry 2000).[8]

I found that Bamiléké women's hometown associations provided the social capital for women to get along (*se débrouiller*) in the face of the triple burdens of reproductive challenges, ethnic discrimination, and—for many—urban poverty (Feldman-Savelsberg and Ndonko 2010). My Yaoundé research built upon ties established in Bangangté, and combined participant observation, a two-round network survey of the 166 members of six Bamiléké women's hometown associations, and follow-up in-depth interviews with fifty women.

This research also built upon shared experience. Many of the women I spoke with in Yaoundé had suffered miscarriage, stillbirth, or neonatal death related to at least one of their pregnancies. In addition, several had suffered their losses when either their spouse or another significant support person was overseas, pursuing educational and business opportunities. Only a few years before, my husband and I had suffered the death of our first daughter, just barely five days old. When this tragedy struck, we had just made an international move and were establishing ourselves in a new city thousands of miles from any relatives or old friends who could provide support. When my interviewees asked me about my own experiences with motherhood, despite the differences in our contexts, we could easily empathize about the joys and sorrows of transnational maternity. Their empathetic curiosity extended to what it was like being a continent away from my young children while conducting fieldwork. That my husband would travel with the children to visit relatives in his native Germany during my absence seemed like a familiar and meaningful pattern to my Cameroonian friends in Yaoundé. Through such personal discussions and my collection of reproductive histories among Yaoundé's emerging middle class, I discovered that periods of transnational migration played an increasingly important role in family formation for Bamiléké women in Cameroon. Because my interlocutors found that anti-Bamiléké discrimination closed avenues to middle-class prosperity, husband and wife of the emerging educated elite spent time pursing opportunities abroad—often taking turns by leaving one spouse at home to take care of their young family.

I was curious if the sometimes painful cultural and political divisions I had earlier witnessed in Cameroon were replicated in the transnational diaspora, and how such divisions might affect families. This led me to spend over twelve months during 2010–11 undertaking research with Cameroonian mothers in Berlin. I chose Berlin for several reasons. Since the history of the Holocaust, debates about race, foreignness, and belonging have held a prominent spot in German public culture. As the cosmopolitan capital of a reunited Germany, Berlin is often at the center of these debates (Mandel 2008). In addition, Germany has a special relationship to Cameroon. Germany had been Cameroon's first colonial power, and currently has an active foreign aid and cultural presence in Cameroon. But, Germany ended its colonial domination of Cameroon during the First World War. Thus, in a twist of history, young Cameroonians find Germany an attractive migration goal exactly because it is not one of Cameroon's two most recent colonial powers—England or France. Germany's standing as the most successful economy in the eurozone makes it additionally attractive, as does—ironically—Germany's exacting bureaucracy. Several Cameroonians in Berlin told me that German immigration rules may be tough, but they are also predictable.

Because of the difficulty of university admission in Cameroon—particularly to coveted courses of study, and particularly for Bamiléké (who face discriminatory quotas) and Anglophones (who face linguistic discrimination)—the pursuit of higher education looms large in Cameroonians' migration rationales. Berlin hosts three prestigious universities and several other institutions of postsecondary education. An early migratory path from Cameroon to these universities emerged in the mid-1980s, before German unification, when scholarships targeted at Cameroonians were established by both Germanies (the Federal Republic, or West Germany, and the German Democratic Republic, or East Germany) (GTZ 2007, 7). With its nearly-free university education, Berlin is one of the most popular destinations among Cameroon's emerging middle class (Fleischer 2012).

Many Cameroonian migrant mothers arrive in Berlin as students or come to join a student spouse, gaining legal residency through laws governing family reunification. Indeed, family reunification and educational migration are the most frequent forms of legal migration from Cameroon to Germany. In 2012, slightly over two thousand Cameroonians migrated to Germany, of whom 1,044 arrived with temporary residence permits following the new residency law. Of these, 636 Cameroonians came as students, 250 via family reunification, 219 as asylum seekers, and only 53 with work permits. The total number of Cameroonian students registered in Germany in 2012 was 6,016, representing 27.2 percent of all students from sub-Saharan Africa. (Rühl 2014; Dick 2014).

These migrant pathways shape the composition of the Cameroonian diaspora population in Germany, which is young, of childbearing age, relatively well educated, and disproportionately Bamiléké and/or Anglophone. Cameroonians continue to migrate to Germany in increasing numbers even when migration from other sub-Saharan African countries is declining. By 2012, over sixteen thousand Cameroonians were legally registered in Germany, well over two-fifths of whom are women (Statistisches Bundesamt 2013; Schmid 2010, 147). Some young Cameroonian couples migrate together, others form new relationships in Germany, and many establish families; between 2005 and 2012, 8,961 Cameroonian births were registered in Germany (Rühl 2014). Berlin itself hosts a sizable Cameroonian immigrant population, with 1,928 documented (and probably several times more undocumented) migrants geographically dispersed[9] in the 3.5 million metropolis (Amt für Statistik Berlin-Brandenburg 2013, 22).

I preceded and followed my fieldwork year in Berlin with rolling ethnography during summer and winter-break visits. During these periods of fieldwork stays, I expanded my focus beyond migrants from Bangangté to include both French-speaking Bamiléké and Anglophone Grassfields women migrants and their families. Despite their different colonial histories on the "French" and "British" sides of what is now an interior border in Cameroon, Bamiléké and Anglophone Grassfielders share cultural and social structural features in their fondoms, a history of labor migration and associational life within Cameroon's southern cities, and sociopolitical marginalization within the current politics of belonging. Both groups are disproportionately represented among Cameroonian migrants to Germany.

FIGURE 1.3. Map of Cameroonians distributed across the 12 districts (or boroughs) of Berlin.

In Berlin, I attended meetings of the hometown association of my original village fieldsite. I also conducted participant observation in homes, at life-cycle events, in daycare centers, social service agencies, and medical clinics, as well as over fifty interviews with transnational Cameroonians. The vast majority of in-depth semistructured interviews were undertaken in women's homes, a few in hallways of city government offices, a quiet corner of a shopping mall, a coffee shop, a community center, and a private physician's office. I interviewed mostly Cameroonian immigrant mothers and mothers-to-be, as well as a few women struggling with infertility, two couples, and seven men. My Cameroonian interviewees ranged in age from eighteen to forty-three, and their children ranged from newborns to age fifteen.

Curious about how Cameroonian mothers' experiences intersected with German discourse and management of migrant family formation, I also interviewed German authorities at sites where Cameroonian mothers sought social services and fulfilled bureaucratic obligations as they established themselves and their families in Berlin. These "German others" were staff in family planning centers, clinics for the uninsured, social service and immigration offices, a training center for migrant youth, a home for asylum seekers, and the African-led community- based organization in which I volunteered. This organization counseled and engaged in HIV prevention work among recently arrived African migrants. My language skills as a speaker of English, German, and Cameroonian French, as well as the knowledge about interpersonal etiquette that I had gained through my many years in Cameroon, helped me in my volunteer work as an interpreter and escort when clients needed to visit welfare offices or clinics. Through volunteering, I met Maimouna, a young woman seeking asylum on humanitarian grounds, whose journey through the German bureaucracy I describe in chapter six.

Migrant status creates vulnerabilities even for the most legally, economically, and professionally secure, rendering work with immigrants ethically and interpersonally delicate. Magni—my research assistant whose remarks open this chapter—worked closely with me to identify Cameroonian women with a wide range of migration experiences, and to identify particular sites where I would be likely to meet people and observe how Cameroonians raise their children in the diaspora.[10] In choosing whom to talk to, we considered key axes of diversity (including ethnicity, occupation, education, migration history, and family status, composition, and residential scattering). We were sensitive to our respondents' expressions that migrant communities are misrepresented by public and social-science focus on illegality. Magni was also keenly aware of the ethical conundrums she faced doing research in her own community (Beloe 2014). We could not avoid following lines of trust and interlocutors' friends of friends, despite the risks that came with our unintended resort to snowball sampling. We knew that individual migrant gatekeepers are most likely to suggest people in similar positions holding similar ideas, just as institutional gatekeepers lead one toward their clients, and thus people in particular categories of "neediness." But trust (or rather mistrust) was a common theme for my interlocutors within their own communities and social networks (see also Cole 2014), making contacts through friends of friends a necessary precondition to conducting research among a diasporic population. Trust and mistrust also affected women's relation to me as a researcher (Feldman-Savelsberg 2011). On the one hand, sharing confidences about my own periods of transnational mothering made our exchange of stories more reciprocal and thus, I believe, richer. On the other hand, my knowledge of things Cameroonian—at times including shared acquaintances—made confiding in me seem risky to my interviewees. How could they be certain that I would not spread gossip about them to friends and family in Cameroon? To mitigate their vulnerability and mistrust, I let my interlocutors choose their own pseudonyms for both recorded and nonrecorded interviews. My interlocutors also chose their interview locale, and chose whether or not to let me participate in family dinners, life-cycle events, or association meetings. Throughout the research process, I was careful not to talk about my interviews with others within the relatively small, and thus easily exposed, Cameroonian "community" in Berlin. To further protect privacy, in my writing I have occasionally altered inconsequential but potentially identifying details.

The three interlinked projects informing this book follow women's experiences becoming mothers in three locales at different historical moments when ethnicity and belonging were highly politicized issues. Some of the differences we perceive in village, urban, and transnational settings include variations over time. The migrant mothers I met in Berlin were young children when I was working in Bangangté, and were teens when I conducted research in Yaoundé. Bringing their stories together helps us understand that the predicaments that Cameroonian women face in Cameroon inform how these mothers on the move forge ties that help them create and grow families in Germany.

Connecting the lives of mothers in Cameroon with those of Cameroonian mothers in Germany also has broader implications for creating dialogue among anthropological subfields. Rarely have anthropologists examined the intersection of the politics of belonging with the politics of reproduction (Kanaaneh 2002). Likewise, research on domestic diasporas (stranger communities within national boundaries) is seldom brought into conversation with transnational diaspora studies (Coe 2011; Mercer, Page, and Evans 2008). In the next section I sum up the argument of the book and introduce you to the themes and characters to come.

SUMMING UP THE ARGUMENT: BUILDING CIRCUITS
AND FORGING BELONGING THROUGH CHILDREN

Whether in their highland villages of the greater Grassfields region, in urban Yaoundé, or in cosmopolitan Berlin, Bamiléké and Anglophone Cameroonian mothers' lives are full of movement. Even before becoming mothers, Cameroonian women may be more experienced in moving than in staying put. I invite you to take your own journey through this book to learn how Cameroonian women with roots in the English- and French-speaking Grassfields imagine future lives and families, manage locale-specific reproductive insecurities through migration, and forge and drop network ties along the way. We will explore affective circuits in the various locales through which migrant mothers move and in which they seek to anchor themselves. You will be introduced to several Cameroonian women whose migration histories are tied to how they live in and build families. These migrant mothers emerge as individuals, with unique biographies, struggles, and strategies to make and grow families. They share stories with each other, as well as with me, thereby refining their family repertoires (Coe 2013; Swidler 1986), their orientations toward the law, and their ideas about belonging. Direct quotations from interviews and participant observation, rendered in italics,[11] let us understand something of the tone of their lives and expressions.

You will learn that Hortense moved within her village as a young girl to be fostered in a family that could feed her and send her to school, and then moved again when opportunities seemed more enticing in the capital. Hortense's friend Paulette moved into and out of the village setting, following the contours of an ill-fated marriage. Come along with me from Cameroon to Berlin to meet Lily, who as a teen followed her mother to France and later joined her husband in Germany; Lily crossed continental and national boundaries to seek better conditions in which to earn a livelihood and raise a family. We will see that Marthe and Rose both gave up nascent careers to reunite with their husbands and start families in Germany. Marthe is highly educated and married to a Cameroonian with a permanent German residency permit, while Rose suffered a period of irregular (illegal) residence following marital abandonment and divorce. We will learn that Marthe and Rose thus faced drastically different consequences for family formation, connection to Cameroonian diasporic networks, and integration into German legal categories. We will also meet Bih, who told me, *"Oh, I have big dreams, but the problem is how to accomplish it. Everyone dreams, right?"* Academically gifted, Bih, who was orphaned, migrated to Berlin on scholarship and to join her husband who had preceded her in migrating for graduate studies in Germany. A sophisticated cosmopolitan who values the traditions of her homeland, Bih's quest to give birth "the right way" brought her across the ocean to North America, weaving a complex, transcontinental web of connections among female kin in a growing Cameroonian diaspora.

Paradoxically, the very movement that women undertake to make reproduction and belonging-through-reproduction possible also puts belonging at risk, entailing new movement. Although Cameroonian women have long sought to establish their belonging through their babies, their migration to Germany complicates this process. On the one hand, migration permits these young women to adopt "novel orientations toward their social worlds" (Cole 2010, xi) within their transition to motherhood. On the other hand, it is tough to maintain loving relationships over great distances, to learn whom to trust within one's diasporic community, and to submit to a dizzying array of regulations in the country of migration. Migration makes it difficult to maintain the statuses (e.g., citizenship) and feelings (e.g., comfortable acceptance) that constitute belonging.

From finding a spouse through the periods of birth, infant care, and the rearing of school-aged children, Cameroonian migrant mothers forge connections with kin, with fellow migrants, and with German institutional actors. Such connections help mothers deal with the difficulties surrounding reproduction. Simultaneously, these interwoven relationships undergird mothers' belonging, solving the problems that make it so "hard being a mother here." Women carefully manage these connections to adapt to their changing circumstances as young mothers within the Cameroonian diaspora, switching affective circuits on and off. They try to control what kinds of information, goods, money, and emotions flow back and forth between them and three sets of actors: kin, who either remain in Cameroon or are scattered in other migration destinations; fellow migrants organized into hometown associations; and German state and humanitarian actors.

We will see that while these three spheres of interaction may influence one another, each has a different underlying logic and a distinct set of circulating items. When we focus on affective circuits among transnational families, examining the nature and content of delayed reciprocity shows us that intergenerational exchanges shift over time. One woman we will meet, Eveline, temporarily lost contact with her family while she was applying for asylum in Germany. Once Eveline achieved refugee status, she was able to pick up the dropped circuit of exchanges with her mother. But Eveline was still too poor to send gifts or money to Cameroon; instead, Eveline's mother helped support her migrant daughter and grandson by sending gifts that express love and connection. Eveline hoped that over time the direction of flow in this affective circuit would reverse, once she became more established in Germany and could send her mother remittances, consumer items, and care. By engaging in a circuit of reciprocal care, Eveline and migrant mothers like her simultaneously fulfill duties to their elders, strengthen their ties and social standing vis-à-vis their families, and forge future-oriented connections of belonging for their children. Observing transformations in the content, direction of flow, and emotional valence of such exchanges teaches us not only about Cameroonian migrants to Berlin. These observations entail broader lessons about how the "developmental cycle" (Goody 1958) and historical political-economic contexts of affective circuits shape relations between spouses and changing gender roles (Boehm 2012; Hirsch 2003) as well as global care chains (Hochschild 2000; Parreñas 2000) among transnational migrants.

Congruent with emerging research regarding community life among African migrants to Europe (Cole 2014; Mercer, Page, and Evans 2008), we will learn that migrant community life cuts two ways for Cameroonian migrants to Berlin. Year-end parties of migrant associations and life-cycle ceremonies such as celebrations introducing a new baby to the community (D'Alisera 1998) create feelings of warm conviviality when people share recipes from home and friendly banter. But not all verbal exchanges are friendly. Belonging to associations, and thus to the right to share in what one interviewee called "*islands of home*," is regulated by by-laws regarding descent, fees, and regular attendance at monthly meetings. Those who do not or cannot follow these rules become the objects of public debate. Likewise, parents whose children become "too German" may find that fellow migrants scrutinize their parenting styles. At the same time that Cameroonian mothers seek out other migrants from home, they become fearful of gossip, and even of betrayal to German authorities. The complicated nature of affective circuits in Cameroonian migrant civic life serves as a cautionary tale against romanticizing "community," the retention of "traditional" legal forms in a new setting (Kohlhagen 2006b; Spittler 1980), and hometown associations' potential contribution toward economic development (Beloe n.d.; Mercer, Page, and Evans 2008, 49–54). The stories of Cameroonian mothers' encounters with and avoidance of their fellow migrants leads us not to an unrelentingly dark picture of abjection (Ferguson 2006, 192–93), but rather to a differentiated vision of the forms and consequences of African migrants' community life.

Both family life and community life happen in the shadow of the state, and Cameroonian mothers' narratives about raising families in Berlin reveal the formalistic logic of their affective circuits with German state and humanitarian actors. As happens with other migrant groups in other European and North American countries (e.g., Coutin 2000), German bureaucrats enforce norms that place Cameroonian mothers into categories of citizen/noncitizen, legal/illegal, self-sufficient or needy. Cameroonian women learn to fit themselves into categories of deservedness (Fassin 2011; Ticktin 2011). They pay their taxes, bear children with the "right" kind of citizen or permanent resident father, and live up to German codes of good parenting. Some perform a needy or vulnerable role to help them secure a more favorable immigration status, along with the right to work, receive social services, and have access to quality medical care. Others either reject being labeled as "needy," or somehow fail to convince those in power of their deservedness. Tragedy can strike, such as when a woman loses custody of her child or gets deported. But the threatening shadow of the state can also become protective shade, as happened when a woman's shelter shielded Fanny from an abusive husband and prevented her deportation. Less dramatically but affecting many more migrant families, the widespread nature of state-mandated inexpensive and high-quality child care in Berlin allows working mothers to keep their children with them rather than fostering them out to poorer relatives in Africa (see also Coe 2013). Such observations, grounded in the particularities of Cameroonian mothers in Berlin, have wider implications for understanding policies that affect migrant families throughout the European Union.

In Berlin, the implementation of some policies (e.g., rules about who "counts" as family for family reunification purposes) makes it difficult for Cameroonian mothers to maintain rich exchanges with kin—particularly direct caregiving at moments of great reproductive significance—and thus to raise and socialize their children in ways they see fit. The implementation of other policies, however, results in a dense network of social services that makes it possible for migrant mothers to attend school, earn a living, *and* raise their children in Berlin. Because children stay with their mothers, children become essential players in their mothers' social integration following migration to Germany. Children elicit the care and interest of several types of actors, stimulating exchanges that flow along affective circuits. The needs of infants and the status they give their mothers sometimes overcome the circuit breakers of distance, mistrust, and law that threaten to interrupt these flows. Cameroonian mothers in Germany use their children to manage these complex, emotionally charged circuits of exchange and thus to struggle through the dual difficulties of reproduction and belonging in the diaspora. By no means do I imply that deploying children in this way is a self-serving strategy. Instead, migrant mothers sacrifice the companionship, social support, comfort, and familiarity of belonging in Cameroon to seek social mobility "for the children," as they say, by coordinating their reproductive lives and relationships with the effort of being "always on the move."

Each of the following chapters details a different aspect of the affective circuits migrant mothers forge *through* their children and *for* their children to manage the many predicaments they face. Chapter two, "Cameroonian Predicaments," reveals how a century of challenges surrounding belonging, reproduction, connection, and movement *in* Cameroon motivate migration *within* and *beyond* Cameroonian borders. Building upon notions of horizon, contradiction, and expectations (Johnson-Hanks 2006; Graw and Schielke 2012), the chapter ends with an exploration of how women cultivate themselves (and their children) to be "emigratable," asks why they migrate, and why they migrate *now*. Chapters three and four explore the stop-and-start nature of kinship-based affective circuits for migrant women at different points in their reproductive life courses, or mothering careers. Chapter three, "Starting Cameroonian Families in Berlin," focuses on mothers creating connections (and thus belonging) for themselves, through their marriages and through bearing children. Chapter four, "Raising Cameroonian Families in Berlin," focuses on the efforts mothers undertake to forge connections for their children, anchoring them simultaneously in a network of social relations and in a set of attitudes toward culture and identity. Chapter five, "Civic Engagement," examines how affective circuits formed through migrant associations initiate and deepen connections within the diasporic community, but do not necessarily breed trust and intimacy. It explores the possibilities and limits of migrant civic engagement through a series of scenes: a routine association meeting, a year-end party, a celebration introducing a new baby to the community, programming to teach children about their culture, and a Cameroonian grandfather's wake. Drawing together the themes of the book, and evoking what it feels like to be foreign, chapter six, "In the Shadow of the State," demonstrates that by building networks and sharing orientations toward the legal climate of their new land, migrant mothers partly resolve and partly replicate Cameroonian predicaments of reproductive insecurity and problems of belonging when they move to Berlin.

2

Cameroonian Predicaments

Then we were many, as many as the blades of grass that now grow in the royal compound.
CHE'ELOU, Bangangté, 1986

The sun slanted toward us as Che'elou and I sat together on a small grassy hillock one day in 1986. I was a young American anthropologist, not yet a mother, researching how women expressed their anxieties about social and political change through an idiom of complaints about infertility. Che'elou was one of the many wives of the fon of Bangangté, a prominent Bamiléké paramount chieftaincy in the French-speaking highland Grassfield region of the Republic of Cameroon. A vital elderly woman in her mid-eighties, Che'elou had never managed to bear children but had served as the current fon's nurse-maid. Che'elou was well respected among her cowives as an intelligent and hard-working farmer, full of wisdom regarding Bamiléké traditions and the most effective ways to resolve personal disputes. Che'elou was also my adopted grandmother—rather, Che'elou had generously adopted *me* as her granddaughter. Che'elou had taught me through words and example, and chided me when I asked questions about things that just seemed self-evident to her; often we just sat together, enjoying one another's presence.

That mournful October day, we were watching Che'elou's younger cowives dance slowly around a fresh grave, intoning the mourning song "*O ne na ya, mama?* Where are you going, mama?" Earlier that week, three of Che'elou's elderly cowives had died, a tragic coincidence of old age and inadequate health care. Che'elou was sad and exhausted after publicly mourning her cowives over the past three days. As she clutched her bamboo staff—a marker of her honored status as a postmenopausal woman—Che'elou quietly lamented the passing not only of a cherished companion but also the more vital palace life of her young adulthood. Married shortly after King (fon) Njiké II had acceded to the throne in 1912, Che'elou had experienced the palace compound as a lively and well-organized village, filled with some 150 royal wives, their

FIGURE 2.1. Cheʹelou, an elderly wife of the Fon of Bangangté, on a grassy hillock watching the funeral of a cowife, Bangangté 1986. Her lament, "*Then we were many, as many as the blades of grass that now grow in the royal compound,*" comments on predicaments of belonging, reproduction, connection, and movement facing Bamiléké and other Grassfields people in Cameroon.
Credit: Pamela Feldman-Savelsberg

children, notables, and "servants" of the king. As inhabited, "civilized" space, the palace grounds were always kept clear of grass, with pounded earthen paths and courtyards. The palace grounds of Che'elou's old age were much less populous, and Che'lou's thirteen cowives were not nearly as fastidious as she in keeping their yards free of weeds. With only sixteen adults (including me, the resident anthropologist) and twenty-three children living in the palace compound, many of the sites inhabited during Che'elou's youth were overgrown with savanna grass or reverting to forest.

Che'elou's nostalgic lament, *"Then we were many, as many as the blades of grass that now grow in the royal compound,"* was a poignant indication of an elderly woman's feelings about the physical and social decline of palace life, and of Bangangté in general. As Che'elou complained about the depopulation of the palace, her fellow Bamiléké reiterated Che'elou's concerns regarding declining fertility, rural flight, and the difficulties of reproducing a Bamiléké way of life, given the economic and political challenges that Cameroon continued to face (Feldman-Savelsberg 1999, 175–77). For their part, young people bemoaned the lack of rural opportunities to make a living, raise the funds to get married and start a family, and put their newfound educations to use. When seeking these opportunities elsewhere in Cameroon, young Bamiléké and their English-speaking Grassfields compatriots faced discrimination as ethnic strangers. Che'elou's lament reminds us that family-making and belonging have long been challenging for women of Bamiléké and Grassfields origins, and that migration within and beyond Cameroon is part of that challenge.

Predicaments of Belonging: Historical and Political Roots

At the time Che'elou married fon Njike in 1912, Cameroon had been a German colony for nearly thirty years. Neither Njike's royal retainers nor the local colonial officers anticipated that World War I would soon break out, and that Cameroon would soon fall under a new set of colonial rulers, continuing a long history of dramatic change. Even before the colonial era, the area now comprising the Republic of Cameroon was shaped by over two thousand years of African population movements. Numerous peoples migrated through and sometimes settled in what would become Cameroon, located where the West African coast makes a sharp bend, geographically and culturally at the borderland between West Africa and Central Africa. As a result, Cameroon boasts a rich cultural diversity as well as a long history of shifting ethnic boundaries and loyalties.

Within this culturally diverse context, the highland Grassfields plateau has had a particularly dynamic history. Nestled between dry savanna and Sahel to the (now) predominantly Muslim north and rain forest to the (now) predominantly Christian south, the Cameroonian Grassfields stretches across two provinces of contemporary Cameroon—the English-speaking Northwest Region (referred to as "western Grassfields") and the French-speaking West Region (referred to as "eastern Grassfields"). The Grassfields is one of the most densely populated areas of Cameroon. According to estimates from Cameroon's National Institute of Statistics, in 2013 Cameroon's total population was 21,143,237, with an average population density of 45.4 people per square kilometer. In contrast, average population density in the two provinces of the Grassfields region was 134.28/km2 (West Region) and 109.9/ km2 (Northwest Region) (Republic of Cameroon 2013, 86–87). People of Grassfields *origin*—in urban areas as well as rural homelands—make up roughly 40 percent of the total Cameroonian population. Bangangté, where Che'elou spent most of her life, is one of some one hundred Bamiléké kingdoms of the eastern Grassfields.

The earliest Bamiléké kingdoms (also referred to as paramount chieftaincies or fondoms) emerged during the sixteenth century, when population movements in the northern savanna region of Adamoua pushed the "pre-Tikar" Ndobo into the Bamiléké plateau (Notué and Perrois 1984, 10–14). The "hunter-king" founding legends of many Bamiléké dynasties reflect a historical process in which "strangers" employed a combination of conquest, ruse, and forging of new alliances to become the rulers of original, "autochthonous" populations. Succession disputes, the search for new territories to hunt and grow crops, and movements of refugees fleeing interkingdom warfare continued to transform the number and boundaries of Bamiléké kingdoms up through the nineteenth century (Feldman-Savelsberg 1999, 43–48). As a result, the very constitution of Bamiléké and similar Grassfields polities (the Bamoun sultanate and the fondoms of the western Grassfields) has long created predicaments of belonging for its populace. Questions of origins, border crossing, and allegiance emerge over and over again in personal biographies.

These questions of belonging and allegiance were tied to long-distance trade in goods (ivory, palm oil, wood, iron implements) and people (slaves and pawns) that connected Grassfields kingdoms with other African polities and with emerging European powers (Warnier 1985). Mystifying use of "medicines" and deception surrounded the slave trade, especially when heads of households—perhaps overwhelmed by obligations, or searching for wealth and prestige—allegedly sold their young relatives in secret (Argenti 2007; Warnier 1985). Such actions repeated a recurring process of large-scale "forms of violence and mass destabilization that were originally of exogenous origin" (Argenti 2007, 242) and were taken over by smaller-scale betrayals and power plays by local elites (Bayart 1979, 1993). European slave trade, initiated after Portuguese traders arrived on the Cameroon coast in 1472, established a cultural legacy of fears regarding external and internal forces that drains the wealth, health, and people of Grassfields kingdoms and the families that populate them. These fears found expression in newly emerging beliefs in anthropophagic witchcraft that sent zombies to work in a parallel world, as well as in analogous discourses of the state, like a sorcerer, "eating" the people (Ardener 1970; Geschiere 1997, 2013; Hours 1985).

During the colonial era, regulations regarding labor recruitment and health care reinforced these fears while establishing new forms of belonging. Cameroon's colonial period began on July 12, 1884, when coastal Duala kings made a treaty with the German Empire. German colonial officials, traders, and missionaries made their way into the mountainous Grassfields territory by the 1890s. There they found a densely populated and richly cultivated territory, crisscrossed by paths and markers indicating active commercial and interchiefdom diplomatic relations (Hutter 1892; Kaberry 1952; Nkwi 1987; Tardits 1960, 66). Working through local fons, colonial officials began recruiting forced labor to build the roads, railroads, and ports so necessary to the colonial project. Indigenous rulers were rewarded with markers of prestige— e.g., two-story colonial-built stone palaces—and the ability to skim off any taxes collected for the colonial administration. Census-taking established who was registered as a subject of which chiefdom or subchiefdom, attaching people more firmly to a particular place or group than had previously been the case (Kuczynski 1939). Grassfields peoples "belonged" simultaneously to their kingdom and to the colonial government, in a form of nested, double-citizenship.

The German colonial period was short-lived (Rudin 1938). During World War I, between 1914 and 1916, the German colony of Kamerun was gradually conquered by French and British forces. A League of Nations mandate divided the colony between France and Britain, with roughly 80 percent of the territory falling under French rule. The mandates of British Cameroon and French Cameroun, established in 1920, continued as UN Trusteeships following World War II (LeVine and Nye 1974). The boundary between French and British Cameroon ran right through the Grassfields, solidifying a terminological distinction between the Bamiléké (and Bamoun) in the French-dominated eastern Grassfields, and their closely related fondoms— usually termed "Grassfields kingdoms"—in the British-dominated western Grassfields.

This complex colonial history left a legacy of official bilingualism, dual legal and educational systems, and religious heterogeneity. Under French and British mandate, education and health care for indigenous Grassfields populations were largely left to a variety of Christian missionary groups (Ngongo 1982). Indeed, provision of health care became a recruiting tool for new converts (Debarge 1934). Women and noninheriting men, seeking alternative contexts for self-realization, made up the majority of early converts (Basel Mission n.d.). They expressed their sense of belonging to their new religious communities through ritual practice (attending church), dress (wearing tailored cotton-print clothing), patterns of commensality and time discipline (e.g., men, women, and children eating together at set mealtimes around a table using European-style cutlery), and health care choices (attending mission clinics rather than visiting diviners and herbalists).

Colonial-era Grassfields peoples had to manage complex, overlapping belongings as religious converts and subjects simultaneously of a colony and a fondom. We see that the same person may have been recognized and accepted and have found comfort in multiple forms of connection. Their belonging may have been imposed, when census-takers forced Grassfields peoples to assemble at designated points on designated days so they could be listed within a particular jurisdiction (Egerton 1938, 177–79). They may have performed belonging through following protocol toward members of the royal family, or through donning the clothing of a "modern" Christian convert. These performances simultaneously reflected feelings of attachment or loyalty and enabled the person to enact rights, such as participating in feasts or being able to send one's child to a mission school.

Labor relations added an additional layer to the complexities of belonging in colonial Cameroon. Through forced labor (ending officially in the French territories only in 1946) and in response to an expanding need for cash, young men increasingly migrated to southern commercial centers such as Douala, Nkongsamba, Buea, and Yaoundé (Dongmo 1981). There they worked on colonial infrastructure projects, in tea, palm oil, and banana plantations, as truck and taxi drivers, and opened small businesses. They earned cash to participate in an increasingly monetized economy, thus paying taxes, buying consumer items, and paying money and gifts—bridewealth—to future parents-in-law.

Male labor migration left many rural Grassfields women as de facto heads of households, subtly altering women's relationships with their families of marriage vis-à-vis their families of origin. Visits from natal kin, and temporarily sending children to live with natal kin, were important ways that rural women managed their increasing repertoire of tasks (Feldman-Savelsberg 1999, 57). Moral support, exchange of foodstuffs, and circulation of children contributed to rural Grassfields women's affective circuits in the context of male labor migration. Because, during visits home, male labor migrants spread sexually transmitted infections to their wives and lovers in the Grassfields (Retel-Laurentin 1974), women depended on their affective circuits to seek therapies for these infections and the secondary infertility resulting from them.

Over time, rural-to-urban labor migration included ever more women, and Grassfields families began to settle and form diasporic communities in Cameroon's urban centers. In Yaoundé, for example, the first Bamiléké immigrants arrived in 1918 (Feldman-Savelsberg and Ndonko 2010, 375). In 1923, French colonial housing decrees forcibly removed Bamiléké settlers from Yaoundé's city center to (then) peripheral neighborhoods (Dongmo 1981, 87), encouraging the formation of "urban villages" (Gans 1962). These ethnic enclaves enabled frequent face-to-face interactions and became the basis for urban Bamiléké social reproduction. By 1957, three years before Cameroon achieved independence, Bamiléké migration to Yaoundé was no longer male-dominated; sex-ratios of Bamiléké migrants showed a slight preponderance of women (Dongmo 1981, 93).

Visits, circular migration, sending remittances, and fostering-in rural nieces and nephews kept urban dwellers connected to their rural kin. Attendance at weddings, funerals, and propitiatory rituals toward ancestors further cemented urban Grassfielders' ongoing sense of belonging to families, now stretched between their rural home places and urban outposts. In addition, many urban dwellers built houses in the land of their ancestors, simultaneously investments in a possible future retirement home and in a rural economy of social prestige (den Ouden 1987; Ndjio 2009). By forming hometown associations, members of Grassfields "domestic diasporas" (Mercer, Page, and Evans 2008, 12) maintained not only their feelings of belonging toward their hometowns, but also their rights and recognition as citizens of their chiefdoms of origin. In the early twenty-first century, hometown associations continue to maintain both affective and jural connections between urban diasporic populations and their Grassfields homelands.

These firm ties to an ethnic homeland complicate how others (mis)recognize Grassfielders' belonging as Cameroonians. Struggles over "primary patriotism" (Geschiere and Gugler 1998) have a history in Cameroon that goes beyond mere questions of split loyalties between "particularistic" ethnic identities and more "universal" identification as a citizen of a nation-state. Over a seventeen-year period (1956–1973) spanning Cameroon's transition from a dual trusteeship to independence (1960) and reunification (1961), a radical nationalist political party waged an armed battle with the colonial and immediate postcolonial government of Cameroon. Beginning as a trade labor movement, the Union des Populations du Cameroun (UPC) was outlawed in 1955 and transformed into an armed anticolonial struggle, accompanied by violent state reprisals. Although at its core political, this conflict took on an increasingly ethnic character over time. Popularly termed *"les troubles"* (the troubles), much of the violence between UPC militants (*maquisards*, or guerrillas) was concentrated in the Bamiléké highlands, and both government reports and some scholars labeled the insurgency as the "Bamiléké Rebellion (Joseph 1977; Terretta 2013).

Bamiléké women remember the trauma of an extended period of violence through their expressions of reproductive insecurity (Feldman-Savelsberg, Ndonko, and Song 2005) and through the ways they conceptualize "home" as a unit of belonging (Feldman-Savelsberg and Ndonko 2010, 382). Josiane, during an interview in Yaoundé in 2002, recalled a childhood memory:

> I was already eleven or twelve years old . . . It was the guerrillas who destroyed *chez nous [in our village]*, at Bazou. The guerrillas, they burned down the two-story building in our village. It was the palace [that burned], eh eh! My grandmother told me that if she hadn't fled with a particular uncle, they would have killed her.

On the one hand, this event was one expression of a rebellion of disenfranchised youth against local elites thought to have been coopted by colonial powers. On the other hand, in local political-religious thought, Bamiléké and other Grassfields fons spiritually control the fertility of their territory and its people. Thus, an attack on the palace was simultaneously an attack on women's ability to bear children and to grow the food that feeds them.

Josiane's friend Nanette related the violence of the 1950s and 1960s to Bamiléké experiences of exclusion at the turn to the twenty-first century: "When there's the slightest problem, they say 'let's chase away the Bami, let's chase the Bamiléké.' They chase us away to seize our goods . . . [The Bamiléké are] strangers everywhere." This feeling of painful marginalization, of being treated as strangers in one's own country, reached a new high when the 1990s brought dramatic political change to Cameroon. An economic recession and structural adjustment programs had been wreaking havoc on Cameroonian families' incomes since the mid-1980s. Countries of the "global north" cut their foreign aid following the end of the Cold War. In this historic context, Cameroonian politicians—and particularly youth—vociferously called for the establishment of a multiparty democracy. They organized the "ghost town" (*Villes Mortes*) movement, a general strike lasting more than a year. Participants' perseverance helped precipitate a national constitutional conference and a change of law in December 1990 (Kelodjoue, Libité, and Jazet 2012, 2). During the elections of 1991, multiple political parties were allowed for the first time in what had for decades been a one-party state.

The political and economic crisis of the 1990s sharpened attention to ethnic difference and to the distinction between first-comers or people "of the land" (autochthons) and more recent arrivals (*allogènes*). This "politics of belonging" (Geschiere and Gugler 1998; Goheen 1996; Nyamnjoh and Rowlands 1998) was expressed in doubts about loyalty, in denigrating comments, and in outright discrimination at the level of organized political parties and statecraft as well as in informal interactions among merchants and clients, among neighbors, and among real estate speculators (Socpa 2010). In the quarter century since the beginning of the Ghost Town movement, Cameroon's multiple political parties have become increasingly associated with specific ethnic groups and/or regions.

In this political context, individuals have become more self-consciously aware of lineage, ethnic, and regional identities. They sometimes literally wear their ethnic identity on their sleeve, fashioning clothing out of printed cloth combining an imitation of Grassfields blue and white royal display cloth (Feldman-Savelsberg 2005) with a double-bell motif depicting a musical instrument employed in nearly all Grassfields public festivals. In their verbal expressions, during the 1990s and early 2000s Cameroonians became more demonstrative about boundary maintenance. In Yaoundé in 2002, Georgine complained to me that Bamiléké women's mutual support activities were perceived as evidence of "tribalism" by competing ethnic groups:

> People meet according to their tribes. The Bamiléké go have their meetings . . .
> which makes things stay within the tribes, and like that, generally, the Bamiléké
> are always and always badly seen. You feel that perhaps 'This person is more
> Cameroonian than me.' To feel Bamiléké nowadays, they say that in Cameroon
> there are always those who are more integrated than others. [It's] a hierarchy
> among the tribes.

Cameroonian scholar Jacques Kago Lele states that Bamiléké ministers hesitate to be seen together, lest they be suspected of conspiracy against the regime (Kago Lele 1995, 87–88), simultaneously revealing painfully convoluted strategies of inclusion and the emotionally charged perspective of the excluded in the politics of belonging (Feldman-Savelsberg and Ndonko 2010, 384).

In sum, Cameroonian mothers—and indeed all Cameroonians—belong simultaneously to families, to communities, and, as citizens, to the state of the Republic of Cameroon. Each of these nested belongings has the potential to create a haven of secure connections to significant people and places, in other words, a feeling of home. Belonging to families, communities, and countries also brings practical and emotional predicaments. These predicaments of belonging are the historical and political roots of Cameroonian mothers' migration to Europe.

PREDICAMENTS OF REPRODUCTION: MOVEMENT, MARRIAGE, AND MATERNITY

Throughout the Grassfields, including both the French-speaking Bamiléké in the West Region and those from culturally related paramount chieftaincies in the English-speaking Northwest Region, women's reproduction is tightly intertwined with predicaments of belonging. Well into the beginning of the twenty-first century, many perceived that ethnic-political strife contributes to such physical reproductive challenges as infertility, miscarriage, and inadequate obstetric care. In this line of thought, conflict threatens reproduction through its weakening of the fon's spiritual authority and by creating jealousies; these jealousies are expressed through witchcraft attacks, direct physical attacks, and armed coercion. In addition, traditional rules regarding land tenure and inheritance create a class of noninheriting men, who must venture away to find new land for their wives to farm or new ways of making a living to make family life possible.

Local marital practices are the basis of regenerating life in a socially and spiritually acceptable manner; they serve as a centrifugal force, propelling young men and women outward, beyond the boundaries of their natal villages. In the past, men sought land to farm and bridewealth to enable them to get married and have rights over the children they hoped to sire. For many still living in rural areas, the groom builds a house and kitchen for his bride upon marriage, thus setting up the conditions to reproduce a family around the symbolic cooking-pot womb. In addition, weddings continue to be embedded within a process of ongoing exchanges. The transfer of bridewealth gifts, sharing of food, and pronouncement of blessings forge ties between the couple's families. All of this costs money, and the pursuit of money to enable socially acceptable procreation motivates male rural-to-urban migration.

Women, too, have long migrated between rural chiefdoms to bear children in ways that seem proper to them, following the customs of Bamiléké and other Grassfields peoples. Couples must marry people who belong neither to their patrilineage (the group of relatives related to them through their father and paternal grandfather) nor to their matrilineage. Anthropologists call this practice lineage exogamy. At least since the twentieth century, marriage in most rural Grassfields communities has been virilocal with patrilocal preference—meaning that a bride joins the groom where he has settled and built her a house (preferably near his father's and brothers' households). Thus, rural women almost always move from one village or chiefdom to another when they get married. Because women marry outside their lineage, they sometimes move quite far to reproduce in the "right" way. They may move from village to village, from one fondom to another; since the mid-twentieth century, women have been moving to urban areas as well. When joining their husband in a new place, women must often show fealty to a new fon and master a new language upon marriage.

The men and women who pursue the regeneration of life by participating in this internal migration must adjust to living as ethnic strangers in their own country. In addition to adapting to new climates, languages, and customs, they often face prejudice. Internal migrants soon learn that there is not one "Cameroonian way" to raise a family; they need to work hard and purposefully to rear their children to internalize Bamiléké and Grassfields values.

To understand the predicaments of reproduction, we begin with the context of Grassfields kinship systems and notions of the family within customary law—rules that still pertain for most rural dwellers and for many urbanites as well. Descent, forms of connection created by relation through the generations to a common ancestor, is the core of Grassfields kinship systems. While various Grassfields kingdoms may emphasize either patrilineality (Hurault 1962; Pradelles de Latour 1994), matrilineality (Nkwi 1976; Vubo 2005), or dual descent (Feldman-Savelsberg 1995), lineage remains the core concept governing social belonging, inheritance, obligations toward ancestors, and whom one is allowed to marry. In the Bamiléké kingdom of Bangangté, lineages are referred to as *ntun nda*, the foundation of the house (Feldman-Savelsberg 1999, 50). Bangangté invoke two lineage affiliations in different social settings, what anthropologists call dual descent. Patrilineal descent determines village membership and for male heirs the inheritance of traditional honorific titles, land, houses, and wives. Matrilineal descent determines the inheritance of moral and legal obligation to lineage members, and for female heiresses the inheritance of titles and movable property (e.g., blankets, metal pots, and other household goods). People descended from the same mother, called a *pam nto'* or uterine group (Brain 1972, 53–59), may stand in for one another in traditional jurisprudence, including the resolution of witchcraft accusations through divination and poison ordeals. Each lineage head chooses a single heir or heiress who then "becomes" the legal person of their ascendant, taking on their titles in customary associations, their rights and duties toward all dependents (i.e., noninheriting siblings and, for male heirs, the father's widows), and their custodianship of ancestral skulls.

Ancestors act on the fortunes of their descendants, "seizing" them with illness and infertility when angered, or protecting them from misfortune and blessing them with fertility when satisfied. To keep the ancestors in good spirits, descendants perform propitiary rites to the ancestral skull (*tu*, the head)—talking to them, feeding them sacrifices, and protecting them from the elements. Within a few years after burial, heirs and heiresses exhume the skulls of their ancestors and shelter them in clay pots and/or in specially built tombs. Nonheirs are dependent on their inheriting siblings to keep the ancestors happy, lest they suffer from illness and other misfortunes.

Such was the case at an exhumation that I witnessed in 1986. One of the fon's wives had designated a granddaughter as her heiress. A couple of years after the royal wife's death, multiple misfortunes had befallen the family. One person had a car accident, another failed the entrance exam for a civil service job, and yet another found herself unable to bear children. Because the dead woman's heiress was overseas pursuing her education, one of her matrilineal relatives—an older woman—temporarily took over her job as custodian of the dead queen's skull. First a diviner was called in to determine the exact location of the grave. Then the matrilineal relative of the heiress arrived with some helpers to dig a pit and search for the dead queen's skull. Once the skull was located, she carefully freed the skull from the surrounding red laterite soil. The woman spoke normally in a quiet voice, addressing the skull and explaining to it why she was coming in the heiress's place. She promised to shelter the skull from the cold rains and hot sun, and to feed it with offerings of the new harvest. She begged the skull to leave the family in peace and protect it from all future misfortunes. Finally, she placed the skull in a plastic shopping bag and left for home.

In Grassfields custom, taking good care of the ancestors is an essential part of the regeneration of life and families, because only with ancestral blessing can one bear children. Indeed, fertility is the greatest marker of fortune, and infertility a grave misfortune. In the late twentieth century, Bamiléké men and women explained sex, conception, and gestation through the imagery of cooking. Sex, they said, is hot, and like fire it contains enormous transformative power as well as potential danger. When a man impregnates a woman, he "cooks the woman" (Goldschmidt 1986, 58). Men "tend the fire" and "open the way" to ease childbirth when they have intercourse with their wife during her pregnancy (Nzikam Djomo 1977, 61; Feldman-Savelsberg 1999, 84). From a woman's perspective, cooking and sexual flirtation are closely intertwined. Rural women express love, the desire to have sex, and the hard work of marital duty when they cook a meal for a man (Njiké-Bergeret 1997, 14–45).

The Bangangté term for marriage, *nâ nda*, literally means "to cook inside." Tamveun, a wise and elderly man who tutored me in the Bangangté language, *Medumba*, during my rural fieldwork in 1986, explained the deeper meaning of this expression:

> Nâ nda *is marriage. An unmarried woman cooks on the road, in the open where just anyone can smell the delicious aromas from her cooking pot. A married woman cooks* inside, *cooks inside her kitchen. Only her husband tastes her food and sniffs the aroma from her cooking pot. Her husband builds her the kitchen. Then she does not have to cook on the road. Later her kitchen is full of children* (Feldman-Savelsberg 1995, 484).

The imagery embodied in the term for marriage reflects the experiences of brides moving from "outside" to "inside" their husbands' lineage and territory under rules of lineage exogamy. Since the twentieth century (and probably before), women learned that to forge belonging in this new conjugal setting, they needed to bear children within the marital kitchen their husbands had built.

In this marital kitchen, husband and wife "measure" to get the proper balance of male and female ingredients—the husband's water (semen) and blood mixed with the wife's water and blood. The sex act mixes these ingredients just as a good cook stirs the sauce thickening and taking form in her cooking pot (her womb), thus procreating or "measuring a person." Women explain their sensations of swelling or growing during pregnancy as analogous to maize meal expanding when a wife cooks the ubiquitous daily porridge (*foofoo*). While waiting for her prenatal checkup at the mission-run maternal-child clinic in Bangoua in 1986, Celeste, a mother in her twenties, described biomedical prenatal checks using this same culinary imagery: "Pamé, you can hear noises in your belly. It is like a bubbling pot, and the doctor hears it through his horn [stethoscope]" (Feldman-Savelsberg 1999, 86).

In Bangangté during the 1980s, the symbolism of hot sex, maternal hearths, cooking-pot wombs, and procreative ingredients figured prominently in women's explanations of infertility. Rippling out across several social fields, cooking metaphors give language to reproductive insecurities located in what Scheper-Hughes and Lock have labeled the "three bodies" (1987, 7). The lived experience of the "individual body-self" is evoked in women's metaphoric descriptions of the bodily sensations of pregnancy. At the analytic level of the "social body" (Scheper-Hughes and Lock 1987, 19), Bangangté women commented about the fon's physical suffering from liver cirrhosis and complained that his weak governance (that he was a "bad cook") diminished the fertility of the land and its people. In this way, they used the body as a natural symbol

(Douglas 1970) to express concerns about social reproduction (Scheper-Hughes and Lock 1987, 24). The disciplining aspect of the "body politic" (1987, 26) is evident in the ways that women protested strained marital relations in the gendered household economy by cooking tasteless food, thus enacting key culinary symbols such as salt and palm oil. In sum, women's complaints about infertility comment on their lives, pointing out areas of personal and social unease (Feldman-Savelsberg 1999, 100–101).

Birthing children and reproducing Bamiléké lifeways are no easy matter. Hard labor, poor nutrition, and disease all make women's fertility fragile. Mothers in rural Cameroon commonly clap and then open their hands, palms up, indicating "we have nothing"—not enough children, not enough food or material goods or the conditions to grow healthy families. They use culinary imagery to complain about husbands who do not provide the proper "ingredients," in other words, husbands who fail to sufficiently provide for their households and who spend long periods away, lessening their wives' opportunities to get pregnant. In addition to poverty, rural women fear witchcraft attacks resulting from competitive jealousies among cowives in polygynous households. Women speak of witchcraft once again using idioms of cooking and eating. Competitors use occult powers to "steal" ingredients, to make the fetus "stick to the sides of the pot," thus preventing its proper development (Feldman-Savelsberg 1999, 116–19). Witches devour the organs of their victims, selfishly destroying rather than regenerating life. Women's physical distance often weakens the protection and support emanating from their families of origin, rendering reproduction yet more insecure (Feldman-Savelsberg 2016).

Reproductive insecurity has historical roots in the Grassfields. We have already read that colonial-era labor migration contributed to the spread of sexually transmitted infections such as gonorrhea, resulting in secondary infertility in the Grassfields region (Farinaud 1944, 79). Draconian measures in the fight against sleeping sickness, led by colonial physician Eugène Jamot in the 1920s, as well as smallpox vaccination campaigns in 1945 (Farinaud 1945, 113) were interpreted by many Bamiléké at the time as simultaneous threats to self-determination and to fertility (Feldman-Savelsberg 1999, 146). At least through the beginning of the twenty-first century, memories of the "time of troubles," when the UPC engaged in an extended armed conflict with French colonial forces and later with the Cameroonian state, figured prominently in Bamiléké expressions of reproductive insecurity. Through petitions to the UN Trusteeship Council, the women's wing of the UPC—the Union Démocratique des Femmes Camerounaises (UDEFEC)—enumerated the multiple ways that the colonial powers attacked the fertility of their largely Bamiléké enemies.

Female petitioners complained about the lack of obstetric infrastructure on the one hand, as noted in the following petition:

> As soon as they built the Dibang dispensaries, they forbade us to have our babies anywhere in the village other than the dispensary. There were cases of still-births. A room of three square metres is used to accommodate ten new mothers. Look at the diseases our newborn babies catch.[1]

On the other hand, they deeply mistrusted the potentially genocidal aims of health care personnel (Feldman-Savelsberg, Ndonko, and Yang 2005, 13–14).

> Whites came to Cameroon for no other reason than to cheat blacks . . . The Doctor infects us with all sorts of sicknesses. For us dying is as common as shitting; this is what decreases the population so they can uproot our liberation movement.[2]

During a period of regime change, when President Ahmadou Ahidjo resigned in 1982 and Paul Biya established his presidential authority in the subsequent years, Bamiléké men and women complained bitterly about government policies that threatened their ability to thrive as Bamiléké. They felt that government control and cooptation of local healers left them vulnerable to witchcraft attack. Actively referring to the time of "the troubles" as a period when those with bad hearts got the taste for blood, Bamiléké women worried that an epidemic of witchcraft threatened their ability to bear children.

Through the imagery of a procreative kitchen plundered by absent husbands, jealous wives, an epidemic of witchcraft, and a predatory state, Bamiléké women tie reproductive insecurity to multiple layers of experience. Paulette's story illustrates how reproductive insecurity became implicated in one young woman's migration within Cameroon—from the city to an unhappy marriage in the countryside, and back to the city once again.

AN UNFORTUNATE WIFE: PAULETTE'S STORY

Paulette, an urban-raised descendant of the royal family, married the fon of Bangangté during a visit "home," *au village*, to the town and chiefdom of her ethnic origins. After months of not conceiving, visits to healers and diviners revealed that Paulette was descended from a king of Bangangté several generations back. Because the current fon was part of a direct line of heirs, in strict kinship rules he counted as Paulette's father. Paulette believed that this unintended classificatory incest had rendered her marriage to the king infertile and her life in the palace untenable. Her departure for Douala, Cameroon's major port city, generated heated discussion among the fon's wives and their female neighbors.

We know that Bamiléké women's reproductive careers commonly involve both spatial movement and genealogical examination. If the diviner's diagnosis of incest was correct, the failure to thoroughly check Paulette's lineages in Bangangté's dual-descent system must surely be symptomatic of the breakdown of traditional knowledge systems. Otherwise both Paulette's parents and the king's ritual specialists would have examined the betrothed's lineages several generations back. What a sad indicator, people tsk'ed, of contemporary ignorance and disrespect for the rules of kinship.

But, some asked, was Paulette's infertility instead caused by witchcraft? "Everyone knew" that during the time of the *maquis* (guerrilla fighters during the years immediately preceding and following independence), people with "bad hearts" (*ntʉ kəbwɔ*) got the "taste for blood." During a historical period when power hierarchies between chiefs and subjects and between seniors and youth were disrupted, many in Bangangté began to explain violence through a witchcraft idiom. They believed that evildoers emerging during the troubles continued their nefarious acts even after the insurgency and its violent repression had subsided, subjecting the vulnerable to increasingly rampant witchcraft attacks.

And if Paulette could adjust neither to rural life as a cultivator nor to the special duties of a fon's wife, this only shows how hard it is to reproduce a Bangangté way of life among a growing urban "exile" population. Gossip surrounding Paulette's departure referred to the complicated and uncomfortable incorporation of their fondom into the political and economic structures of the Cameroonian state. People spoke of the kingdom being "eaten" by the state, using a cannibalistic witchcraft idiom to describe political and economic exploitation. More and more young people sought their fortunes, or at least to make ends meet, by migrating to the cities and plantations of southern Cameroon in search of work or commerce. There they learned new orientations, became too "soft" to engage in rigorous agricultural labor, and neglected their duties toward their elders and ancestors. As many a grandmother bemoaned, young people like Paulette were "forgetting where their umbilical cord is buried."

These emic (insider's) explanations complemented my own etic (analytic, observer's) perspective that Paulette departed because most of her network ties in Bangangté were of shallow depth and carried considerable negative affect. Paulette's kin and acquaintances did not provide her with sufficient emotional support in her status as the fon's new wife.

Predicaments of Connection: Affective Circuits between Village and City

In the same year that Paulette left Bangangté, Hortense—the fon's niece—was also living in the palace grounds. Staying in a fostering arrangement with the royal wives enabled Hortense to attend school in the nearby town. Hortense had ambition and dreamed of achieving a more comfortable and fulfilling life than that of the impoverished and sickly mother who was unable to raise her. It was never clear to me how much Hortense understood her mother's perspective, that her mother had drawn upon her affective circuits, mobilizing her ties to her brother and his many wives to build for Hortense the very social connections necessary to create a better life.

Hortense's story introduces us to the predicaments of maintaining connections that emerge for Cameroonians whose relationships are stretched between the village and the city—and, as is the focus in what follows, beyond to international locales. How do mothers on the move manage the ties that bind them to scattered family members, to significant places, and to the memories that give them a sense of home and belonging?

A CIRCUITOUS PATH: HORTENSE'S STORY

A diligent lycée student when I first met her in 1986, Hortense subsequently sought the social status, material comfort, and intellectual stimulation of life at the École Normale Supérieure in Yaoundé. A decade later, Hortense had completed her studies and became a lycée teacher. Hortense had gotten married, and after trouble conceiving and repeated miscarriages, finally had a young child of her own. Hortense remained in touch with the cousins she had grown up with in Bangangté, who by now were scattered across Cameroon and Europe. Indeed, during several visits I made to Yaoundé in the late 1990s and early 2000s, and through e-mail exchanges over the ensuing years, Hortense was the one who most frequently kept me apprised of the whereabouts and fates of those I had known as young children. According to her own self-presentation and to the reports of her cousins and her onetime foster mother, Hortense seemed to be the one who had made it to a life combining maternity, career, and the relative ease of urban life.

But Hortense also faced whispered complaints from her colleagues about how she and other Bamiléké were taking over the civil service and buying up land from the capital's rightful owners, the autochthons. Currency devaluations and irregular disbursement of pay meant that Hortense and her small family were barely squeaking by financially, squeezed into a high-rise public housing project at Cité Verte in Yaoundé. At our last meeting in 2002, Hor-

FIGURE 2.2. Hortense as a lycée student, posing with one of the fon's wives on the palace grounds in Bangangté, 1986.
Credit: Pamela Feldman-Savelsberg

tense arrived with her face and arm bandaged. She had been mugged two days before in a Yaoundé taxi. This mugging deeply disturbed Hortense's sense of security. She began applying for teaching jobs overseas, even involving me in her quest to find private schools that would take on a native speaker of French and specialist in language pedagogy and the high school French literature curriculum. It seems that Hortense may have caught the bushfalling bug, an intense desire to seek an easier, more adventurous life overseas (Alpes 2011; Graw and Schielke 2012). Although she did not confide to me, Hortense may have already been searching for a European partner on international dating sites, strategizing to create new affective circuits that could lead to marriage migration and a more comfortable family life (Johnson-Hanks 2007).

As sometimes happens, the affective circuit between us—of memories and updates exchanged in letters and e-mail messages, of visits and phone calls, and of small gifts that expressed fondness—thinned over the years. After a six-year hiatus, I got back in touch with Hortense in 2011. I learned that twenty years after Paulette left the fon's palace hoping for a better future, in 2006 the once-dreamy schoolgirl Hortense left her husband and only child to marry a Frenchman and move to Europe. Hortense did not tell me many details about her own life or her long-distance parenting, only that she was living in Paris and that her daughter was already in a secondary school in

Yaoundé. As Hortense draws upon the repertoire of child fostering that she had herself experienced as a child, I can only imagine how hard she must work to support her daughter emotionally and financially across international borders.

Paulette and Hortense's stories illustrate that it is hard becoming and being a mother in the Grassfields Bamiléké fondoms and in Yaoundé. They hint at the predicaments of connection faced by women in the urban "domestic diaspora." We experience how Paulette and Hortense manage the difficulties of belonging and of reproductive insecurity through the social ties they maintain—and break—between their village "homes" and their urban places of residence. Hortense's story in particular reveals how biography and history intersect in the way one young woman creates and breaks social ties, reconnecting in new ways as her circumstances change.

When Hortense moved from Bangangté to Yaoundé, she joined a Bamiléké urban diaspora that was several generations deep. This internal or domestic (as opposed to international) diaspora maintained ties to their home places of origin. Their connections to a home place were based on a shared identity contingent on larger political, economic, and social contexts (Mitchell 1969; 1987; Schildkrout 1978; Shack and Skinner 1979; Trager 1998, 2001). Thus, they changed over time and exhibited marked variation by gender and social class (Feldman-Savelsberg and Ndonko 2010, 1). While urban male elites used hometown ties mainly as a resource to build a business or support a political career, at the turn to the twenty-first century, hometown identification also posed a liability for rural-to-urban migrants like Hortense. The whispered resentments Hortense faced at her workplace reveal a climate of "increasing obsession with autochthony" (Geschiere and Gugler 1998, 309). On the one hand, the emotional, practical, and even spiritual exchanges among kin between rural homelands and new rural residences were essential elements of both physical and social reproduction. How else could a woman become a mother and raise her children to belong to a family, a lineage, or a people? On the other hand, expressing this sense of belonging and obligation for mutual support through organizing into hometown associations underscored ethnic difference and provided fodder to the resentments other urban residents felt toward ethnic "strangers" from Cameroon's Grassfields region.

Among Bamiléké living in Cameroon's capital, Yaoundé, hometown associations are an essential part of urban social organization, supplementing kinship as an important basis for trust, mutual aid, and access to housing and employment (see also Barkan et al. 1991; Englund 2001; Little 1965; Woods 1994). Most Bamiléké hometown associations in Yaoundé are sex-segregated as well as differentiated by elite and nonelite designations. Between 1997 and 2002, Cameroonian anthropologist Flavien Ndonko and I undertook a study of the social networks formed among Bamiléké women in six hometown associations, investigating ways that mutual support, ideas about reproductive practices, and collective memories of ethnically-based violence flowed within these networks (Feldman-Savelsberg and Ndonko 2010). We found that Bamiléké reproduction, including cultural survival as well as aid at vital conjunctures (birth, death), is a major focus of women's hometown associations. While economically and educationally elite women frame their relation to the hometown differently than less privileged women,[3] social reproduction broadly conceived was the raison-d'être of formalizing common ties to a home place via the hometown association.

Bamiléké women's urban hometown associations build on a rich history— for men and for women, in the precolonial past to the present—of associational life originating in rural areas, including royal title associations, chiefdom-based youth associations, and work groups providing mutual aid in agricultural tasks (Tardits 1960; Hurault 1962; Njiké-Bergeret 2000). Perhaps most important in rural Bamiléké women's extra-kinship associational life is the tontine (*ncüa* in Bangangté), or rotating savings and credit association (ROSCA) (Ardener and Burman 1995; Niger-Thomas 1995; Rowlands 1995). As I learned through my membership in a rotating savings and credit association in Bangangté, rural Bamiléké women's tontines meet regularly; each week one tontine member receives the pot of weekly cash contributions. Women's household responsibilities usually obligate them to spend the pot on school fees, health care, food, and clothing rather than investing their savings in a small business venture, even though many yearn to use the pot as start-up capital (Rowlands 1995).

Once Bamiléké began arriving in Yaoundé, beginning in 1918 (Dongmo 1981, 87), they organized mutual aid associations based on the tontines of their hometowns. These hometown associations allowed them to bypass discriminatory practices of colonial banks, and personalized the savings and credit system; default was rare, because it was an offense against social relationships of trust among a network of women who regularly met face-to-face. Hometown associations provide a point of entry and welcome for visiting kin, trading partners, and colleagues in other parts of Cameroon. For many of the women we interviewed, hometown associations had played a helpful role for their parents fleeing the troubles during the 1950s and 1960s, and had facilitated their own education, courtship, and migrant itineraries toward Yaoundé (Feldman-Savelsberg and Ndonko 2010, 377). Thus, in addition to helping urban dwellers

to get by economically, Bamiléké hometown associations in Yaoundé reinforce
and even produce place-based identities. They are an important element in
urban women's efforts to seek and perform belonging, to provide themselves
and their children with anchors in a mobile world.

Thus, hometown associations help rural-to-urban migrant women from
the Grassfields create a malleable structure of ties that overlap with and supplement ties based on kinship. Ghislaine's story illustrates the way urban Bamiléké women, including new arrivals, draw upon their hometown associations for help in three main concerns: economic survival, reproductive health,
and funerals. Each of these three areas involves the circulation of ideas about
the proper way to comport oneself, the exchange of material goods, and emotions of mutual obligation, gratitude, and occasionally resentment. Through
Ghislaine's story we thus see the role hometown associations play in the construction and maintenance of affective circuits.

Hometown Support after Tragedy: Ghislaine's Story

Ghislaine grew up in the Bamiléké diaspora in the Moungo Valley, near the
city of Nkongsamba. Bamiléké first came to the Moungo valley a century ago,
through forced labor on infrastructure projects and as laborers and petty
merchants in search of cash to pay taxes and bridewealth. Originally migrating to the Moungo valley as plantation and railroad workers, Bamiléké
helped found Nkongsamba. Located at the end of the railway built between
the port city of Douala and the plantation-rich hinterland of the Littoral Region, Nkongsamba became an important commercial hub. Later, during the
political violence associated with decolonization and repression of the UPC,
many Bamiléké fled the troubles in their homeland, settling in the Moungo
valley to farm or start small businesses in and around Nkongsamba. Thus,
Ghislaine grew up in a Bamiléké-majority milieu, but outside the geographic
Bamiléké homeland. In this milieu, Ghislaine had learned that membership
in a hometown association was an expected part of being Bamiléké, and indeed of being a properly socially embedded person.

Ghislaine moved to Yaoundé as an eighteen-year-old schoolgirl. Following the pattern of urban dwellers fostering-in the children of their rural kin,
Ghislaine moved in with an older cousin so that she could attend secondary
school in the nation's capital. They lived in the Yaoundé neighborhood called
Mokolo, since 1923 a largely Bamiléké working-class enclave (Dongmo 1981,
87). There Ghislaine met her future husband; within a year she became pregnant. Not yet married, Ghislaine returned to her parents' home to give birth.

I returned home to my parents to give birth. [My husband] then came there to join me. We performed those customary things, a traditional marriage, and then [got married] at the registry office.

After remaining with her parents for a year, Ghislaine and her husband returned to Yaoundé. With their baby son, they settled in the same Bamiléké-dominated, economically impoverished Yaoundé neighborhood of Mokolo, where they had first met.

Ghislaine's move back to Yaoundé is a story of hopes dashed by reproductive tragedy, and of loneliness mitigated by the support of her hometown association. Upon her return to Yaoundé, Ghislaine joined the *Femmes Bangangté de Mokolo*, one of the hometown associations that Flavien Ndonko and I studied. Newly married and with no friends in the neighborhood, Ghislaine suffered two devastating losses. First, her delicate and sickly infant son died of malaria.

He regularly fell ill. Even before dying, he was not very, very suffering [seriously ill]. He had a light case of malaria, and then it was death [he died]. When I took him to the hospital, he was [already] dead.

Soon thereafter Ghislaine miscarried her next pregnancy. Remembering these events a decade later, Ghislaine recounted the support she received from her neighborhood hometown association members.

At this time, being new in the neighborhood, I did not yet have any friends. When you arrive in a neighborhood, you are new, you don't have friends. In any case, the neighborhood meeting [association] helped me morally and even financially. Among us, when a member loses her child, the association stays with her throughout the evening. Only when the corpse departs for the village [to be buried], do they [the association members] return home.

Ghislaine's emotional pain, evident in her telling of the double tragedy ten years later, was all the more difficult because she lived geographically distant from her closest relatives. Her pain was partially mitigated by the support of new ties she had built through her hometown association. In addition, her husband, brother-in-law, and mother-in-law rallied around her when Ghislaine suffered her miscarriage, forming a spontaneous therapy-management group (Janzen 1987). Ghislaine described discovering spotting on her panties one afternoon and frantically running to her husband's workplace to tell him. Her husband then took Ghislaine to the nearby urban hospital, where she was put on bed rest. But his mother and older brother were concerned about repeated misfortunes, and wanted her to be treated in a trusted mission hospital near their home in the Bamiléké city of Bafoussam. There, she would not only be cared for in a renowned mission hospital, but would also be near diviners who could investigate possible spiritual causes of her repeated misfortune.

> At the hospital, they prescribed bed rest. In the meantime, my brother-in-law from Bafoussam left [the West Region] with my mother-in-law. They came to find me [in Yaoundé, to take me with them]. Thus, I don't know if it was the long distance there that made it that this child [was miscarried], I don't know. Since bed rest means really laying down resting, because with that long journey, yeah, the bumpy ride in the car . . . When I arrived in the West [Region] . . . the next day, I went to the hospital, in the morning with my sister-in-law . . . Well, there, they weren't able to do anything . . . It [the fetus] had already left.

Ghislaine's story shows how fragile fertility can be, part of the pathology of poverty and of power (Farmer 2003). Because the combination of colonial labor regimes and a brutal anti-colonial insurgency pushed families like Ghislaine's out of their home areas, many Bamiléké found themselves creating diasporic ethnic enclaves in others parts of Cameroon. Long-standing mistrust of the Bamiléké combined with a patronage system that sent resources to the home areas of powerful government actors meant that young people like Ghislaine had to travel to larger cities to attend secondary school. This type of internal migration fostered affective circuits among kin scattered across multiple Cameroonian locales, but it also made immediate physical support in times of medical emergency impossible. Networks of nonkin, such as hometown association members, could provide limited moral and financial support, but not the level of care provided by close family members. In quest of healing reproductive problems in a manner combining biomedical and local modalities of diagnosis and treatment, women like Ghislaine and the kin caring for them traveled under dangerous conditions over poorly paved roads. Such conditions increased the likelihood of medically and emotionally tragic outcomes.

Ghislaine's husband's family took care of her as best they could, fulfilling through great effort their sense of obligation toward vulnerable kin. Reproductive mishaps such as neonatal deaths and repeated miscarriages often involve protracted searches for the cause of misfortune. The deaths of newborns and the not-yet-born constitute an "unnatural and horrifying event" in Cameroon (Njikam Savage 1996, 95). In the village, miscarriage, stillbirth, and neonatal death thus create great unease among a woman's extended kin. They consult diviners to diagnose the source of these reproductive disruptions and implore the ancestors to bless and protect the rest of the family. Families may also subject the unfortunate mother to purification rites, and consult healers to "shield" her from future spiritual attacks through rubbing herbal concoctions into scratches made on her arms, wrist, and by her temples (Feldman-Savelsberg, Ndonko, and Yang 2006, 21).

Because reproductive difficulties are stigmatized, and because diagnosis and treatment for repeated reproductive mishaps are so protracted, not all women I met in Yaoundé sought out their relatives' help. While there is no explicit prohibition against talking about miscarriage, stillbirth, or neonatal death, many Bamiléké women at the turn to the twenty-first century feared being seen as possible victims of witchcraft, the focus of ancestral wrath for their own or another's wrongdoing, or even as witches themselves for "eating" their babies. These fears contributed to many women's wish to keep their loss to themselves. Furthermore, many urban women preferred to rely exclusively on biomedical treatment, stating that "rather than the herbs of the past, we now need the hospital" (Feldman-Savelsberg, Ndonko, and Yang 2006, 22). They thus avoided telling relatives—or at least *certain* relatives—about their reproductive tragedies. Urban Bamiléké women I spoke with expressed being caught between contradictory emotions—a wish for privacy regarding their reproductive mishaps, combined with intense feelings of loneliness and abandonment (Feldman-Savelsberg, Ndonko, and Yang 2006, 22). The emotional force of their responses underscores that this is more than an illustration of the stop-and-start nature of affective circuits. Rather, cases such as Ghislaine's remind us that Bamiléké and other Grassfields women in urban diasporas within Cameroon face predicaments regarding which social connections they wish to foster, when, and how.

Predicaments of Movement: Migrant Pathways within Cameroon and Beyond

Cameroonian women's predicaments of belonging, reproduction, and connection occur in a context of migration. We have seen that multiple histories of movement have created the conditions for current-day predicaments of belonging facing Cameroonians from the greater Grassfields area. Precolonial movements of peoples and colonial-era labor migration have contributed to complex and temporally unstable ethnic formations. Postcolonial struggles for livelihoods and power have charged both group and individual ethnic and place-based belongings with political and emotional force (M. Rosaldo 1980; R. Rosaldo 1989).

Emotion and politics also infuse histories of movement related to marriage and social regeneration—actors' efforts to "reproduce, contest, and transform their social relations and cultural norms" (Cole and Groes 2016, 7; Cole and Durham 2007, 17). Grassfields women move from one local political unit (e.g., a village or chiefdom) to another, not only to join their male spouses, but also to forge alliances among families. Women's marriage migration within the Cameroon Grassfields combines gender politics with diplomacy among lineages, villages, subchiefdoms, and kingdoms. These women move again, away from local Grassfields kingdoms to the cities and industrialized plantation areas of southern Cameroon. There they forge connections with other rural-to-urban migrants by organizing hometown associations, prominent loci in which women reproduce a sense of belonging. With the help of these associations, Grassfields women access specifically urban conditions in which they can bear and rear children safely, prosper, and achieve valued markers of modern personhood.

Being "someone" among the Bamiléké and other Grassfields peoples is linked to a long tradition of "dynamism" and achievement orientation, often linked to movement (e.g., Dongmo 1981; Wakam 1994). Historically expressed through the pursuit of traditional titles and advancement in title societies (Notué and Perrois 1984), in the twentieth century Bamiléké achievement orientation became increasingly evident in the accumulation of wealth (Tardits 1960). One way Bamiléké men pursued wealth was to practice *ta nkap* marriage, whereby instead of receiving bridewealth for his daughter, a patriarch would retain rights over the marriage and patrilineal identity of his daughter's daughters. In becoming his granddaughters' *ta nkap*—literally, "father by money"—the patriarch could later capitalize on these matrimonial rights, controlling marriages and receiving bridewealth for large numbers of granddaughters. Although the practice was outlawed by the French in 1927 and 1928, throughout the colonial period it continued to stoke colonial concerns about concentration of wealth among the colonized (Rolland 1951; Tardits 1960, 22). Through ta nkap marriage, one form of Bamiléké achievement orientation was closely tied to senior men's control over younger women's movement, marriage, and reproduction.

For the majority of Bamiléké, especially noninheriting young men (and later women), the pursuit of economic achievement meant migrating south in search of wage labor. Migration in search of economic well-being began in the early twentieth century, parallel to more coercive forms of movement (Argenti 2007). By midcentury, once French colonial agricultural policy loosened, men began planting coffee and, to a lesser extent, cocoa. Women expanded their food crop production to provision growing urban centers (Guyer 1987). The search for agricultural land for these new forms of wealth accumulation pushed many to migrate to the Moungo valley, near the end of the railroad line in Nkongsamba, as was the case for Ghislaine's kin. And the search for the accumulation of wealth via commerce, transportation, and salaried employment engendered migration to commercial and administrative centers in the southern part of Cameroon. Urban living allowed Bamiléké and other Grassfielders to acquire consumer items. These commodities not only made daily living more comfortable; they also became forms of symbolic capital (Bourdieu 1983), signaling success and modernity through what Rowlands (1996) has described as a shiny, luminous aesthetic.

Increasingly, being a successful, modern person entails seeking the skills and credentials of higher education. Much more than a means to wealth and the symbolic display of a "modern" aesthetic, technical skill and intellectual prowess are sources of pride. During my fieldwork in Yaoundé, Bamiléké characterized themselves as intelligent, hard-working, and eager for education. They complained bitterly about how their access to higher education in Cameroon is limited by an ethnic quota system. Most Cameroonian universities are public institutions, controlled by the central government. The ethnic quota system in public university admissions has the purported aim of ensuring that representatives of all ethnic groups have access to university admission, part of a national policy of "regional balance" (Nkwi and Nyamnjoh 2011). But, because it is formulated without regard to Cameroon's demographic structure, the ethnic quota system serves to limit university access for Bamiléké students as well as for English-speaking students (Kom 2011; Zambo Belinga 2011). The regional balance or ethnic quota system contributes to the loss of transitional pathways and paucity of future perspectives plaguing Anglophone and Bamiléké youth (Jua 2003). Foreign education thus gains allure not only for its symbolic prestige but also because it seems to offer a solution to the problem of feeling "blocked" in Cameroon.

The pursuit of higher education looms large in Cameroonians' migration rationales. In the late 1990s and early 2000s, young people in Yaoundé told me that personal ties to powerful actors had become more important than merit in securing admission to coveted courses of study, such as medicine, within the Cameroonian university system. A decade later, Cameroonians in Berlin described this situation as a central motive for migrating to Europe. Bamiléké migrants use migration as a means to avoid Cameroon's discriminatory quotas for university admission. Similarly, many Anglophones migrate because of the paucity of options for higher education in English in a country that is officially bilingual but whose institutions are dominated by the French-speaking majority.

Since the mid-1980s, targeted scholarships have led Cameroonian university students to both the Federal Republic of Germany (West Germany) and the German Democratic Republic (East Germany) (GTZ 2007, 7). When they returned to Cameroon from preunification Germany, beginning in the late 1980s and early 1990s, these educational migrants brought the possibility of migration onto the horizon—the imagined possible future—of ever more young people (Johnson-Hanks 2006). Return migrants also established practical networks for later chain migration to expanded opportunities in postunification Germany. With its nearly-free university education, and the distant colonial connection that created an early, if thin, migratory path, Germany has become a particularly popular destination among Cameroon's emerging middle class (Fleischer 2012).

Like many African migrants, Cameroonians also seek economic opportunity in Europe's economic powerhouse. Through conversations, news reports, and some return visitors' exaggerated displays of good fortune, Cameroonian youth develop expectations for readily available work and an easier life in Europe (Graw and Schielke 2012). The combination of educational, economic, and refugee movement out of Cameroon results in Cameroon's net migration rate of -0.5 (per thousand population), compared to Germany's 1.3 and the United States' 3.1 net migration rate (United Nations 2012). Because German immigration law makes legal labor migration nearly impossible, Cameroonians use multiple, largely class- and status-based strategies in their search for economic opportunity. A select few of the highly educated with saleable skills manage to get work permits. Others are "bushfallers," adventurers who seek their luck in the distant, mysterious European "bush," often falling in and out of regularized immigration status (Alpes 2011; Fleischer 2012; Nyamnjoh 2011).

Bushfallers draw upon knowledge circulated among their acquaintances to gain access to migration brokers—*doki men*—in Cameroon (Alpes 2011) to aid their quest to migrate. Once arriving, they also mobilize what social connections they have to learn about how to get along and secure their residency in a new place (Fleischer 2012). As we shall see below, less advantaged Cameroonian migrants' legal and social vulnerability plays out in struggles to found and raise families—in new reproductive insecurities engendered by the conditions of migration.

Family reunification and educational migration remain the most frequent forms of legal migration from Cameroon to Germany. Of approximately two thousand Cameroonians who migrated to Germany in 2012, 1,044 arrived with temporary residence permits following the new residency law.[4] Of these, 636 came as students, 250 via family reunification, 219 as asylum seekers, and only 53 with work permits. Over six thousand Cameroonian students were registered in Germany in 2012, representing 27.2 percent of all students from sub-Saharan Africa (Rühl 2014). Consistent with these figures, many Cameroonian migrant mothers arrive as students or come to join a student spouse.

Indeed, periods of transnational educational migration loomed large in reproductive life histories and stories of family formation among Bamiléké women living in Yaoundé at the turn to the twenty-first century. Among the emerging educated elite, mothers described preparing for their overseas studies by taking language courses at the Goethe Institut and the British Council. They used the Internet to become familiar with courses of study open to foreign students. And French-speaking mothers increasingly sent their children to English-speaking schools, cultivating skills to make their children "emigratable."

Migration was also a conjugal strategy among the emerging educated elite. Couples' coordination of various life-course events—including pursuing an education, starting a career, getting married, and bearing children—was complicated by spouses taking turns seeking education and professional experience abroad (Johnson-Hanks 2006). This coordination work became evident in an initially surprising manner, through a comparison of elite and nonelite women's abortion practices in Yaoundé's Bamiléké diaspora.

Although elite women of the urban Grassfields diaspora have more means and greater knowledge of new contraceptive technologies, they make frequent use of abortion. Urban elite women are able to seek abortions in medically safe conditions and have less to fear from the consequences of abortion (Feldman-Savelsberg and Schuster n.d., 20). Elite women have immediate access to professional abortion services because their immediate social networks include gynecologists and other medical specialists. Abortions performed in well-equipped private clinics, run by physicians whom the women consider trustworthy because of their Grassfields origin, afford elite women both medical safety and protection from socially and legally risky public exposure.

Elite women distinguished themselves from less economically advantaged women in Yaoundé, however, because they made their abortion decisions as part of a conjugal strategy coordinating family formation, education, and work. In contrast, nonelite women decided for abortion covertly, most frequently at the beginning and end of their reproductive careers, to avoid teen pregnancy or to "retire" from childbearing.[5] Both childbearing and abortion were part of elite couples' planning toward educational and career advancement, fulfilling their vision of the ideal modern family. Because they were scrutinized by mothers-in-law and other kin and acquaintances, elite couples established marital legitimacy by having two or three children; they could then pursue advanced training abroad and complete desired family size after reuniting in Cameroon. But what if a woman became pregnant when her husband was abroad? Consistently, elite women who participated in our study of Bamiléké social networks and reproductive health, when faced with an unwanted pregnancy, turned to abortion during the gap before the fourth child. For example, one mother of three became pregnant just before her husband left for higher education overseas, after she herself had recently secured admission to Yaoundé's renowned École Normale Supérieure. Her husband encouraged her to seek an abortion, drawing upon the advice and discretion of physicians within their friendship circle. The couple then conceived their fourth child after completing their degrees and reuniting in Yaoundé. They thus achieved what most elite women considered the "perfect modern family."

Increasingly, though, Cameroonian migrants are choosing to stay and settle in Germany, founding and raising their families in a new, European setting. Because so many women enter Germany with student visas or through family reunification regulations, the Cameroonian migrant population in Germany is young, relatively well educated, and of childbearing age. Many arrive with spouses, and occasionally with young children. Others start new relationships, finding spouses within the growing Cameroonian diaspora. These young couples welcome new babies into their midst. The nearly nine thousand births registered in Germany by Cameroonian mothers between 2005 and 2012 are one indicator of Cameroonian family formation in the diaspora (Rühl 2014). In this new setting, mothers care for their infants, engaging with German health care providers and state bureaucracies. Busy with their educational pursuits and various forms of employment, they place their children in state-subsidized day care. Eager to provide the best opportunities possible, mothers inform themselves about a variety of neighborhood, bilingual, international, and gifted/talented schools in Berlin. And worried about the loss of cultural identification, mothers also bring their children along to Cameroonian community events. The following chapters detail the variety of ways that Cameroonian mothers manage the predicaments of belonging, reproduction, and connection once they have settled in Germany.

3

Starting Cameroonian Families in Berlin

> In Africa, the family is important—more important than elsewhere I'd say.
>
> L I L Y , Berlin, 2011

Lily had a rare moment of quiet, permitting us time to sit together on her sofa, looking at her family photo album of wedding portraits and baby snapshots. Lily's three children were all either at school or day care (what Lily called Kita, short for Kindertagesstätte), her own classes at trade school were over for the day, and it was not yet time to cook. This was my fourth visit to Lily's home, after Magni had introduced us at the day care center the previous autumn. I had since helped Lily to carry her heavy shopping bags, visited her church, and advised her on polishing résumés for internships. Early on, Lily had told me about the important wisdom of *"les mamans"*—experienced female kin who, in Cameroon, were always available to help a woman through pregnancy, birth, and those precious, overwhelming early weeks of infant care. On this gray afternoon, just before spring returned to Berlin, gazing at Lily's album brought our conversation back to family ties.

Lily came from a large Bamiléké family, most of whose members migrated from the Cameroonian port city Douala to the outskirts of Paris when Lily was in her late adolescence. She moved to Berlin after meeting her husband at a Bamiléké event in France. At the time, her husband was both a university student and a deacon in his Pentecostal church. Their church underscored an ideational transformation already underway among most Cameroonian migrants to Berlin—an increasing focus on the nuclear family in which parents raise their biological children. Lily discussed with me the lived tension between the needs of the nuclear family versus migrant spouses' emotional and material obligations toward their families of origin and extended kin.

Sometimes one confuses things a little, frequently putting family in front of one's proper family—that's to say one's husband and one's children. Sometimes one

*pays too much attention to one's mother or father, before [looking after] one's
husband and kids. And vice-versa. The husband will look after his mother too
much in relation to his wife and children*

    *. . . But nonetheless, I think that family is very important, especially when
one's relations with them are very close—when you have good relations, as is the
case in my family. I have great relations with my mother, my sisters, my brothers.
And that—that's important, eh.*

For Lily and other women whose stories are told here, kin-based affective
circuits between Cameroonian places of origin and European destinations are
much more than obligations in tension with transformations toward nuclear
family ideals. Affective circuits among scattered relatives are a critical part of
getting along as migrants. Migrant mothers draw upon these affective circuits
when facing both pragmatic and emotional challenges to reproduction and
achieving a sense of belonging in a new place. We have seen that through mobility, women from both the French- and English-speaking Grassfields seek
to overcome the reproductive insecurity they face in their rural homelands
and in their urban residences within Cameroon. By migrating, however, they
generate new forms of reproductive insecurity and new problems of belonging. These challenges vary over the mothering career, generating changes
over the life-course in mothers' attempts to resolve them. Each step in the
life-course creates new needs, new moral imperatives, and new ways of connecting to others.

This chapter addresses kin-based affective circuits that are formed and
transformed when Cameroonian migrant women found families. It focuses
on how these circuits of emotional and material exchange with kin become
involved in the challenges of reproduction that women face at the earlier
stages of family formation. These include finding and keeping sexual and romantic partners, and often formalizing partnerships through marriage. Early
family formation also involves negotiating family planning and adjusting fertility goals to the realities of migrant life. Some couples are able to conceive
easily, while other migrants must make greater efforts to seek conception in
an unfamiliar medical system. This burden most often falls on women. Additional challenges emerge with the experience of pregnancy and prenatal care,
childbirth, and caring for newborns.

So much is new, full of potential, when one enters into a relationship, bears
a child, or starts a family. Both potentiality and newness involve facing the
unknown, the demands of choice, and the partially hidden power dynamics
that shape what choices are available and acceptable (Taussig, Hoeyer, and
Helmreich 2013, S4, S6). Facing the unknown can be disconcerting; coupling
the new potentialities of family formation with the uncertainties of migration

can be downright overwhelming. Migration adds new and exceptional layers to what would otherwise be relatively routine, individual-level reproductive insecurities. Thus, these early stages of family formation lend themselves particularly well to investigating the solutions Cameroonian migrants find to the challenges of making families and raising children within a mobile diaspora.

In Cameroon, this is a period of life when women mobilize and are enveloped by their kin-based social networks in a particularly intense fashion. When describing the ways that "it's hard being a mother" in Berlin, Cameroonian mothers contrast Cameroonian expectations with Berlin realities; they lament the difficulties of being "all alone" with the challenges of newborn care.

Being physically distant from home and family may also contribute to difficulties between migrant mothers and their communities and families "back home." The very affective circuits that provide support also create complications. Kinship ties occasionally short-circuit under the weight of family disputes or the shame of unmet migration goals. Women forge transnational affective circuits with family members and with fellow migrants to manage the difficulties of reproduction and belonging that they face, but they also learn to avoid, to dissimulate, and to act independently when these connections become too burdensome.

What do Cameroonian migrants' statements indicate about the affective circuits young mothers establish with kin across national and continental boundaries? How do women, through their reproductive activities, build up circuits with scattered family members? What kinds of advice, goods, money, support, and demands flow along these circuits? Do they flow in one direction only, or do they constitute an exchange? How do the types, symmetry, intensity, and emotional charge of these exchanges respond to the physical distance of transnational family relations? Most importantly, how do migrant mothers experience these kin-based affective circuits when struggling to manage the challenges of reproduction on the move?

We now turn to the relationships Cameroonian women enter into with the future fathers of their children. Becoming involved with a man is tied up with Cameroonian women's migration trajectories as well as their reproductive futures. These dyadic relationships are simultaneously embedded in and productive of a wider network of family belonging.

"Madame ou Mademoiselle" in Deutschland: Marital and Family Ties

Anthropologists have long written about ways that marriage creates relationships between families. Marriage can form alliances between kinship groups

(Lévi-Strauss 1969). In chapter two we saw that among Bamiléké and other Grassfields peoples in Cameroon, marriage has long been a basis for strengthening alliances and demonstrating fealty among royal lineages, lower-ranked nobility, and commoners. Above all, marriage sets off a cascade of exchanges that tie kin together—legally, structurally, and emotionally. Affective circuits form when the families of bride and groom meet. They transfer material goods to the bride's family, transfer rights in the bride's labor and children to the groom's family, and exchange pronouncements regarding solidarity, obligations, care, and morality. The affective circuits launched when a couple comes together continue beyond the wedding and period of marriage prestations.[1] Married sisters and daughters travel home for visits and, ideally, to give birth to their first-born child. Children visit their grandparents, aunts, and uncles, and sometimes are foster-raised by them. Later, affines cry, mourn, and dance at funerals and commemorative death celebrations.

Marriage also transforms relationships within kinship groups. Bride and groom have made a step on the journey toward adulthood. Their status changes vis-à-vis their parents, siblings, and other kin. Once a couple is married, ever-wider circles of kin take an interest in their reproductive lives, expecting children to "make people" that expand the network and reach of the family (Smith 2001).

We have seen how marriage promotes migration within Cameroon. The physical movement of kin for visits and ceremonies brings new sets of people into contact, weaving connections that let people belong in new ways. For example, in urban Cameroonian contexts, bride and groom may return *au village*[2] for traditional ceremonies, to stage a "white wedding" at a church, and/or perform a civil marriage in front of a judge. Witnesses and guests travel, bring gifts, and party before the young couple forms a new (neolocal) household.

In this chapter we witness how finding partners and getting married are adapted to the international migration context, as women seek a variety of ways to coordinate their migration goals with finding partners and the work of reproduction. In the Cameroonian context, marriage establishes a common household for husband and wife, and ideally precedes childbearing. Contradictory expectations and structural conditions make it difficult for couples to coordinate romance, family obligations, work, education, and childbearing to realize an idealized timeline (Johnson-Hanks 2006). This coordination work is even more challenging when Cameroonians move abroad, and family members may become temporarily or permanently scattered across international borders. Those with middle-class ambitions are most emotionally committed to an idealized, "modern" order of things in founding a family. Their ideal model is to initiate courtship based on romance and "rational" assessment of future fidelity and material responsibility, be well established in educational and career pathways before marrying, marry under conditions of parental approval, and bear children only after marriage. Ironically, Cameroonian women with middle-class ambitions are also most likely to migrate, adding layers of complication to finding and keeping partners, growing families, and being mothers on the move.

COMPLEXITIES OF ROMANCE, MARRIAGE, AND BELONGING: FIVE LOVE STORIES

The question "Madame ou Mademoiselle?" (Mrs. or Miss?) as a prelude to flirting and romance takes on a particular quality for Cameroonians in Berlin. The love stories of Maria, Jucal, So'nju, Mrs. Black, and Fanny illustrate a variety of ways that Cameroonian migrant mothers combine romance, migration, and starting families. Their stories of finding partners and staging weddings reveal how their marriages transformed ties to parents, siblings, and in-laws that would later shape their experiences of becoming mothers. Maria's story of rediscovering a long-lost love presents the contours of managing several types of marriage along with childbearing and other migration goals. The stories of Jucal, Mrs. Black, Fanny, and So'nju show variations in the circumstances of marriage and their effects on sustaining kinship-based circuits of belonging.

Maria Mar's Love Story

Maria Mar is a warm and jovial 29-year-old mother of three who has lived in Berlin for nearly eight years. Maria has a German degree in business and finance; when we met in 2010, Maria was on maternity leave from her position with an industrial firm. Maria's apartment displayed a portrait of herself, her husband Paul, her two daughters, and—she joked—her baby son hidden in her protruding belly. As became apparent in Maria's self-presentation, her photo was visual evidence of the importance of companionate marriage and the nuclear family in an emerging middle class (Hirsch and Wardlow 2006).

Maria's love story illustrates that stepwise migration patterns contribute to couples' work coordinating education, occupational attainment, and reproductive activities. Maria and Paul's class status allowed them to eventually enact three possible modes of marriage: traditional, civil, and church or "white" weddings. In chapter six, we will examine in greater detail how Cameroonian migrants like Maria Mar and Paul meet the costs and bureaucratic hurdles of international travel with innovations in fulfilling marital rites. Here we note that these innovations tie family members to the young couple in fresh ways, creating pathways for future advice and exchange. In Maria's story, we observe how chance meetings intersect with the structural conditions that frame how love grows in a globally mobile world (cf. Cole and Thomas 2009). And we note that these structural conditions impose complex coordination work for migrant families to realize their ambitions.

Maria Mar and Paul grew up in the same neighborhood of Bamenda, the provincial capital of the English-speaking half of the highland Grassfields region. Maria described that they grew up in the same "village," by which she meant that they were from the same fondom of Mankon, now located within Bamenda city boundaries. Paul's family lived near the church that Maria Mar's family attended, which gave them frequent opportunities for mutual observation and conversation.

> We really knew each other, but like youth . . . we were really close to each other, we even used to go out together but just like normal friends. I think we had feelings for each other because I liked him, he liked me, but we never, you know . . . officiated anything.

Then Paul had been in Yaoundé, the capital, in the stepwise migration pattern common among Cameroonian transnationals—migrating from rural or provincial towns to major cities before finally going overseas. For many years, Maria and Paul lost touch with one another.

In the meantime, Maria had migrated to Berlin on a student visa, having been fascinated with German colonial history since hearing the story of the German colonial explorer Eugen Zintgraff[3] as a schoolgirl. Later deciding that business and finance held more career promise than history, Maria was two years into her university studies when, by chance, she met Paul again, this time in Berlin. "Then love started growing here . . . it was a wonderful surprise, I can't explain. Sometimes I feel it is the will of God that it is just working that way."

Like many migrant couples, Maria and Paul's relationship grew while they were simultaneously juggling language learning, coursework, part-time jobs, and continuing obligations to kin and to community organizations. And like many, managing reproductive events—a tragic pregnancy loss, a joyful birth—was part of Maria and Paul's coordination work that shaped the timing of their marriage. Over a period of five years, Maria and Paul performed traditional rites, a civil marriage, and a church wedding, albeit with a twist of adaptation to the financial and legal constraints of migrancy.

Weddings are occasions that publicly embed the union of husband and wife in a larger network of family ties. As in other fondoms throughout the Grassfields, and in many sub-Saharan African societies, in Maria's home place of Mankon, bridewealth transfers productive and reproductive rights and duties between kin groups (cf. Comaroff 1980). Only when the groom's family has given a previously negotiated combination of money, material, and (possibly) labor to the bride's family is the marriage considered legally binding. It was important to Maria and Paul to perform the exchange of material goods and vows among their kinship groups before the civil and white weddings. However, Maria and Paul's financial situation as students, combined with the visa complications involved in moving across borders, kept both Maria and Paul from traveling to Cameroon. So they innovated, performing a marriage-by-proxy, in which relatives stood in for the bride and groom during the traditional ceremony. Soon thereafter, Maria and Paul held a legally binding civil wedding in Germany. Only several years later, when both Maria and Paul were employed in Germany, did they travel to Cameroon to complete the traditional rites in person and to stage a white wedding.

Like all rites of passage, weddings are moments when transformations of social status are made publicly visible (Piot 1999) and social relationships are documented (Ferraris 2013, 286). Maria and Paul's kin documented the couple's marriage-by-proxy ceremony by producing a video. The video not only served as proof of the validity of the legal relationship established by marriage, it demonstrated—in vivid technicolor—the loving care of the relatives who stood in for the absent couple. This involvement in the wedding, as well as actions surrounding the wedding, such as helping with expenses, created ongoing ties of indebtedness and obligation for mutual aid. Enjoying a wedding party together also creates collective effervescence (Durkheim 1915; Collins 2005), an emotional energy that carries positive sentiments forward into the future. Like other Cameroonian couples, Maria and Paul played and replayed their wedding videos, taking part in that emotional energy. Along with friends who dropped by to watch, the couple relived and reperformed both the wedding's protocol and the caring involvement of kin. In this way, their wedding video became an ongoing demonstration of webs of relatedness, of enduring family belonging. Maria and Paul's wedding video chronicles emotional and material exchanges that launched long-standing affective circuits between and among the new couple and their kin.

These affective circuits were the pathways along which the families' interest in Maria and Paul's childbearing, and advice regarding health care and child rearing, later flowed. In my experience at traditional weddings in Bangangté during the 1980s, anointing the bride with palm oil and camwood powder— both "red like the blood of childbirth"—was accompanied with blessings for fertility. Consistent with her later presentation of self as making reproductive decisions on her own, with some input from her husband but free of "family

FIGURE 3.1. A still shot from a marriage-by-proxy video sent to a couple by relatives in Cameroon. Such videos document traditional marriage ceremonies performed in the bride's and/or groom's absence. Credit: Anonymous

pressure," Maria downplayed the centrality of fertility blessings in traditional wedding ceremonies. Maria instead describes transformations in Grassfields traditional wedding rituals. The blessings at the follow-up rites, performed once she and Paul could travel to Cameroon, emphasized protection over fertility, and the rite had been "modernized," becoming "just a symbol."

> *The family of my father and that of my mother, they have to put their blessings together, so they both brought their oils, from both sides . . . They use palm oil and camwood and they bless it . . . And they only do that after the dowry [bridewealth] has been paid [by the groom's family] . . . And you know everything has been modernized, because at first . . . it was a must that they will pour the oil on you . . . But everything it is just a symbol, they didn't find it necessary to be doing all the [details, with palm oil and camwood] . . . from your head to toes. And thereafter you have to run around and share the blessing, you catch people and rub them with the oil and it is a nice gesture but that oil [laughing, with a disgusted face] . . . It is like protection, you know? They say if you kick a stone let the stone . . . break instead of your leg.*

These blessings for protection emanate from both sides of the bride's family, her patrilineage as well as her matrilineage. The groom's family demonstrated that they value, even love, Maria through the amount and kind of bridewealth they have transferred. Nonetheless, the daughter needs protection as she ventures into life among her husband's kin. Perhaps Maria needed especially strong protection because she had risked international migration, with all its stressful unknowns.

It took the couple several years to finish their educations, find permanent employment in Germany, and secure their new visa status before returning to Cameroon. Maria and Paul needed to save up to meet the costs of their white wedding in Cameroon. As returning migrants, they were expected to bring gifts to family members. They paid for food and drink and for the church hall at the Roman Catholic church in their part of Bamenda-town. And no white wedding would be complete without Maria's white bridal gown, Paul's tuxedo, and pretty dresses for the two little daughters who had been born between the first and the last of these many marriage rites.

From Maria Mar's story we learn that childhood ties and a sense of belonging to a place can serve as the basis of a later love story. While Maria emphasizes individual choice and companionate marriage in her self-presentation, she also indicates the many ways that family members became involved in her marriage to Paul. Maria and Paul adapted the form, timing, and coordination of multiple wedding ceremonies to their situation as young African migrants to Europe. The ties among family members established through these weddings were potential pathways; some grew into kinship-based affective circuits of belonging that supported Maria later in her mothering career and when she faced reproductive crises. As we will see in the next chapter, other mothers also benefit from the positive affect produced during weddings, and even simple visits home, when they need to find fostering arrangements in Cameroon for one or more of their children.

Maria's story also illustrates the way class background enhances the likelihood of successfully coordinating educational, occupational, and reproductive activities as a migrant. Through visits, rituals performed with and without their presence, and the exchange of phone calls and snapshots, Maria and Paul shared the milestones of marriage, birth, and their children's development with their family members in Cameroon. Raising their children bilingually (to speak English as well as German) further enhanced the ease of intergenerational communication and sense of belonging. Not all migrants share their happy fate, despite their best hopes and plans. Some with high educational credentials and legal pathways to migration, like Jucal, nonetheless experience severe status decline that affects their reproductive lives. Others, like So'nju and Fanny, arrive with fewer credentials and less secure residency rights. In these conditions, romance and reproduction can become instrumentalized—and horribly complicated. Both women faced initial struggle and isolation. After these experiences, So'nju continues to be mistrustful of migrant community gossip, while Fanny is making a concerted effort to repair short-circuited ties between her fiancé and his parents in Cameroon.

Jucal's Love Story

Jucal's family history has taught her about being uprooted and making a home in a new and unfamiliar place within Cameroon. Jucal's marriage intensified her belonging in this new Cameroonian locale while, ironically, bringing her to a foreign land and new insecurities concerning belonging, status, and reproduction.

Jucal is a 36-year-old Bamiléké woman whose family has lived for two generations in the English-speaking region of Cameroon. They originally left their village near the chiefdom of Bangangté in the 1950s, when an anticolonial insurgency and its brutal repression rocked the entire Bamiléké plateau. Jucal's family found safety from the troubles, and employment in the industrialized palm oil plantation area of the Southwest Region. They became what are known in Pidgin as "come no goes," migrant workers who settle rather than returning to their homeland. Demonstrating that problems of belonging are variable, Jucal feels a stronger sense of emotional identification to the small town where she grew up than to her village of origin. In contrast to many of her fellow Bamiléké in the Francophone capital of Yaoundé, Jucal perceived no discrimination from locals that would have reinforced her Bamiléké ethnic identification. Her marriage and social relationships support other findings that marriage and friendships can occur across ethnic lines in Cameroon (Pelican 2012), despite increasing politicization of ethnic difference over the past twenty-five years. For Jucal, the combination of common language (and the commonality of being a linguistic minority in Cameroon), affinities in custom between Bamiléké and English-speaking Grassfielders, and an adolescent friendship established in school provided the basis for her relationship with Francis, who was to become her husband.

Like Maria, Jucal rediscovered an old flame in adulthood. Unlike Maria, Jucal was not yet a migrant. Instead, she rejuvenated her relationship with Francis, a migrant to Berlin from the English-speaking Grassfields, when he visited his alma mater, the University of Buea, on a vacation home.

My husband is my first boyfriend. I knew him back in Cameroon. We went to school together, then he first of all migrated to Deutschland. Then, later on, he came back and [we] made a traditional marriage. By then I was at the university

in Buea [at the time the only English-speaking university in Cameroon]. Then,
later on, after my bachelor's [degree], I [migrated via] family reunification . . . So
I came here to Germany.

That Francis was a bushfaller with papers may have made him even more attractive. In her novel *Snare* (2013), set in the Berlin Cameroonian diaspora, Priscillia Manjoh describes a cast of characters who first romanticize going abroad, and then instrumentalize their romantic relationships to improve their chances to get and stay there. Jucal did not describe her courtship and marriage in these strategic terms. She was studying sociology at the University of Buea when Francis visited Cameroon after being away for eight years. Jucal had been close to Francis from their early school days. But then, after a misunderstanding, the two of them lost touch when Francis traveled to Germany as a student in 1996. There he met, married, and had a child with "the German lady," as Jucal describes her. During this time, Francis changed career directions to have more immediate job chances in Germany. As in other European and North American countries, a nursing shortage combined with an aging population in Germany creates a high demand for geriatric nurses and nurses' aides. Requiring relatively low levels of training and German language skills, these are common positions for immigrants. For Cameroonian immigrants who enter German university programs or even arrive with bachelor's degrees, retooling as a geriatric nurse's aide (*Altenpfleger*) means taking a drop in status to secure a job. Francis withdrew from his agronomy program to complete a two-year training in geriatric nursing. In the meantime, after three years of marriage to his German wife, Francis was able to obtain German citizenship. A few years later, his German wife fell sick and died.

When Francis visited Cameroon after her death, he returned as a widower, single father, and German citizen, who needed a visitor's visa to his birthplace. During this visit, Jucal and Francis reignited their relationship. They made plans for a future together, speaking to their families in the Southwest and Northwest Regions. Before Francis returned to Germany, they performed a traditional wedding ceremony, complete with presentation of the bridal package (bridewealth) and exchange of vows toward each other, toward their parents, and toward their extended families.

By the time Jucal graduated with her BA in sociology, Francis had arranged the paperwork for Jucal to join him in Berlin via the family reunification immigration process. To put Jucal's migration via family reunification rules into perspective, in 2012, 31 percent of Cameroonian new arrivals receiving temporary residence permits in Germany did so through family reunification rules; for Berlin in particular, the figure was 40 percent.[4] Other pathways to migration—such as for education, or work, or on humanitarian grounds—may be de facto for family reunification purposes.

Binational Marriage: Love Stories of Mrs. Black and Fanny

Nearly all of the migrant mothers I came to know were in intimate relationships with other Cameroonians. Quite a few, though—or, more commonly, their current partners—had previously been in relationships with ethnic Germans. Many had strong opinions about such relationships. Certainly, some loving and lasting relationships between Cameroonian migrants and ethnic German partners endure. Just as certainly, German-German and Cameroonian-Cameroonian marriages are entered into for more reasons than romantic love (Fleischer 2012). Nonetheless, the Cameroonian migrant mothers I spoke with characterize binational marriages between Cameroonians and Germans as fraught with tension over issues of caring for extended families and founding families of their own.[5]

Mrs. Black, a 33-year-old production assistant, came to Germany on a tourist visa after an earlier, difficult migration experience in another European country. She met Klaus, a German, and traveled with him to Cameroon to get married. After seven years of marriage, Mrs. Black describes Klaus as her *"best friend,"* and yet, *"you know my husband is a German—I am a Cameroonian. And we have these cultural differences and there are some things that . . . my husband would never understand."* Mrs. Black chose her pseudonym explicitly as a wry commentary on ways that, in Germany, her skin color became a master status-determining trait (Hughes 1945, 357). She felt this master status particularly during periods of conflict when Klaus complained about the affective circuits she maintained with kin.

> Sometimes I would like to send money to Cameroon to help my family or so, but my husband . . . you know, he doesn't see it like it is very important. He will ask me, "Why are you doing that? It is not really your money you have to [give away]" . . . He cannot understand, because I know the situation . . . I have my mother [who] is still living. I have three, like two brothers and a sister, there in Cameroon that I have to take care of them. And I have aunties and uncles, cousins, all those, you know. We Africans, we have really big family . . . When you are here in Europe they all look at you, you know . . . "you don't have to help all of them," but you know you cannot hear [about] problems and just sit without helping.

Contemporary German ideas of relative independence clash with Cameroonian norms regarding family solidarity, evidenced particularly in sending remittances to Cameroonian kin. Mrs. Black interpreted her German in-laws' similar complaints as discouragement from maintaining ties with Cameroonian kin.

While Mrs. Black overcame differences with Klaus, Fanny's marriage with a German husband proved disastrous. Fanny had been a bilingual (English and French) secretary working in Yaoundé for an international firm, and was a reluctant migrant. Only under pressure from the German husband whom she had met at work did she leave her beloved stepmother and siblings to migrate to a southern German metropolis. When her husband turned emotionally and physically abusive, Fanny was too ashamed to return without having accomplished anything abroad. Fanny also could not return to her prior job, the same firm that employed her abusive former husband, whom she had divorced.

> While this was going on, time was also running out, I was like getting used to the system. It was difficult going back and starting things all over again . . . My family was there for me, but I had to think about my life too . . . When I looked [at] the both sides—back in Cameroon and here—I saw that I could make it easier and faster here than going back home at that moment.

By staying in Germany, Fanny experienced status decline; when we met she cleaned offices and lived in a tiny apartment. But Fanny is cheerful, happily engaged to Cedric, another Cameroonian immigrant.

In a roundabout manner, family-based affective circuits provided the basis of Fanny and Cedric's chance encounter and long romance. Throughout her troubles with her abusive German husband, Fanny had remained in close telephone contact with her stepmother in Yaoundé. She also spent quite a bit of time helping her sister—also a migrant in Berlin—with child care. Fanny picked her niece up from the day care center and brought her nephew to the pediatrician when her sister was busy. These family ties meant that Fanny remained linked to networks of kin—siblings and cousins—who acted as couriers carrying goods, presents, and news between Cameroon and Germany. Fanny met Cedric when she traveled to western Germany to meet a cousin, who had brought "*some stuff from Cameroon*" and had promised to bring some Tylenol back to her stepmother. Fanny described her courtship with Cedric as long, beginning cautiously with phone calls, because both felt vulnerable after previous disappointments. As Fanny explained, "*I have trusted people and they have disappointed me.*" Eventually, Cedric started visiting Fanny on weekends, his gifts of a handbag and shoes expressing mutuality in a symbolic language of the materiality of care.[6] Fanny was concerned about her sister's approval of her visitor, but when her sister encouraged her to use the handbag, Fanny knew that she had her sister's blessing.

Fanny and Cedric's romance provided an occasion to renew kin-based ties of belonging that had been short-circuited. Cedric had been estranged from his middle-class, ambitious family. Originally in Germany on a student visa, Cedric was able to complete his studies but had a hard time finding employment in his field. He met and married a German woman, but "*things weren't the way he thought. It was tough with him, too. But he had been with his wife for four years together before they separated. And he had no contact with his family because it [keeping up relations with relatives in Cameroon] was like a problem for his wife. So he just like isolated himself, no friends, nothing.*" Suffering from depression, and having been bullied by his German wife to cut ties with his family, Cedric still finds communication with his kin in Cameroon awkward. Fanny purposefully works to bring them closer together. "*Even 'til now his family goes through me to talk to him. They never had that access of getting to him, talking to him and stuff like that. Even the [his] mother was very, very happy.*"

So'nju's Love Story

Like Cedric, So'nju's husband Nya spent several years married to a German woman. But he and So'nju were already a couple with children, creating a complex situation with lasting emotional and social conequences for So'nju. Her story illustrates the difficult, complicated nature of establishing a family for "irregular" migrants.

So'nju is an English-speaking Bamiléké woman in her mid-30s who has lived in Berlin for several years. So'nju's ancestors were originally from Bahouoc, near the site of my first Cameroonian research in the Bamiléké fondom of Bangangté. In the first decade of the twentieth century, they had fled the intertribal wars accompanying the early German colonial period to the newly established refugee fondom at Bali-Bawock.[7] Proud of her family's history, So'nju maintained a strong Bamiléké identity, using a praise-name meaning "princess of Bangangté." Unlike Jucal and Maria, So'nju migrated to Germany without a college degree, pregnant, and leaving behind a child to be foster-raised by her mother. She arrived on a tourist visa, arranged by Nya, the father of her children who, at the time, was married to a German woman.

Back in Cameroon, So'nju had been a high school student and then an office worker when she first became romantically involved with Nya. She achieved O-levels (one year short of the highest high school degree) and completed an additional year-long computer software course before finding a job as a secretary. She lived in Bamenda with her mother and the young child she had borne with Nya. In the meantime, Nya had migrated to Germany on the invitation of a friend, stayed, and later regularized his status by marrying a German woman. After one of his visits home, Nya and So'nju's family collaborated financially to enable her migration to Germany. Nya obtained travel documents for So'nju, bought her an airline ticket, and rented a tiny apartment for her. Nya wanted to remain married to his German wife until he had obtained a more permanent residency status. So'nju's presence could have endangered those plans. Thus, Nya encouraged So'nju to avoid contact with other people and to mistrust other Cameroonians' advice. During this time of isolation So'nju became pregnant with their second child, and a year later with their third child.

> My husband told me not to ask, because when you go and ask, people will tell you one idea [i.e., give bad advice] . . . because he suffered the same thing when he came . . . Because at that time he was with a German woman, so I was just indoors, it was not easy. I didn't go out. Or I just go out to do shopping and come back. I did not visit anybody during that time . . . He rent a flat for me and I was there . . . [I was afraid to] have contact with people and then have problems. So I decided to stay alone with my pregnancy.

For several years after migrating, So'nju's community contacts in Berlin and her ties to her family back home were short-circuited. Although her relatives had helped Nya finance her trip to Germany, and although So'nju's widowed mother was raising her first daughter, So'nju was reluctant to let them know what life was really like in the distant European "bush." Avoiding her family was particularly painful during her pregnancies.

> But even if I am pregnant I don't always say until I deliver . . . because when you tell they will ask every time you make a call . . . Until I deliver after two days I call and tell. Yes, my mother is always angry about that . . . she is always angry when I am pregnant when I don't tell. "I am your mother, I am not your aunt or your stepmother, I am your mother, you could have told me."

A mixture of avoidance, concern, and anger flowed along So'nju's kinship ties, and some information did not flow at all. Exemplifying the stop-and-start nature of affective circuits, So'nju reestablished a more trusting, freer flow of communication with her mother and siblings once her life in Berlin became more stable.

Nearly five years after So'nju arrived in Berlin, Nya was able to divorce his German wife without losing his residency. He and So'nju travelled back to Cameroon for a traditional wedding, conducted in the home of the bride's family. This occasion allowed So'nju to demonstrate her devotion to her family and her respectability as a married mother. Five months later, So'nju and Nya performed a civil marriage at the Cameroonian embassy in Berlin. With the "papers" from her civil wedding and Nya's permanent residency, So'nju and her two German-born children were finally able to change to a more secure and permanent immigration status. When I met So'nju two years later, she and Nya had sponsored So'nju's younger sister's migration to Berlin, allowing So'nju's "*darling junior sister*" to help care for their fourth baby. So'nju had also completed a six-month state-subsidized course in geriatric nursing and had placed her two older German-born children in day care. At this point, So'nju had one child being raised by her mother back in Cameroon, two children in day care, and one newborn baby. She was searching, with some frustration, for a bilingual German-English school that would admit her five-year-old for the following school year. In her living room, So'nju displayed photos of the oldest child still living with her mother, in traditional Bamiléké-Grassfields attire. She described her affective and material exchanges with them as more relaxed once her own marital and immigration situation had stabilized. But as we shall see in the following chapter, So'nju's early experience of isolation makes itself felt in continuing mistrust of community organizations. Despite their tenuousness, it was family-based affective circuits, rather than a community of fellow migrants from Bahouc or Bali, that afforded So'nju a sense of emotional belonging to "home."

These five love stories illustrate diverse paths through which Cameroonian migrants form couples and get married. When migrant couples face the work of coordinating vital events such as marriage and birth, they face a multitude of choices. They must decide how, when, and where to get married—and indeed, whether to get married at all.

In ways that would have been nearly unheard-of in Cameroon a generation ago, in Berlin quite a few of my interlocutors lived together in *unmarried* long-term commitments, with several children together. Perhaps the public nature and long-distance family commitments of marriage were too complicated, or too financially, logistically, and emotionally burdensome for them. Or perhaps they believed (for reasons of legal consciousness that will be explored in chapter six) that single parents have greater access to social services in Germany. Single mothers, such as Iris and Eveline, cited gender conflicts rather than public entitlements in their decisions to raise their children without men. Iris explained that having a partner can be good, because it leaves one less alone with the emotional and pragmatic tasks of life. But sometimes, she related, it is better to be alone than to have the problems a man can bring. Eveline concurred:

If you have a husband who bothers you all the time, who only causes you prob-
lems, it's better if you are single. But some men are understanding, [and others]
have a hard character. If you have a man with a hard character, it's better to be
single. But if you have an understanding husband, that's the best.

While not all Cameroonian migrant couples with children get, or stay, married, marriage remains an idealized path toward respectable and secure family foundation.[8] Cameroonian migrants' weddings forge new affective circuits and transform established ones. Childhood loves, family reunions, and meeting migrant husbands during carefully staged visits home from the European "bush" are all part of the picture. So are situations of heartache, including leaving children behind in Cameroon, or keeping Cameroonian partnerships and even entire households with children secret while one partner "searches for papers."

This heartache sometimes leads to static in the affective circuits that migrants maintain with their family members in Cameroon (and, often, scattered in multiple locations abroad). Migrants wondered how much they should communicate or keep secret. Out of consideration for loved ones, not wanting them to worry, the tension between "truth and distance" (Baldassar 2007, 399) was a constant underlying concern in maintaining affective circuits and network ties to those at home. Other static in the circuits occurred when migrants became estranged from their families, depressed or disappointed about reaching their migration goals, or discouraged by their German partners from communicating with relatives. The Cameroonians I met characterized binational marriages as unstable, offering not only adventurous possibility but also risk.

Family-making, for most women, was a matter of partnerships with fellow Cameroonians who shared similar visions of familial obligations, childbearing, and child rearing. Although they are infrequent, reports of (white) German husbands' discouragement of fertility carry heavy symbolic weight in conversations about difference and belonging. Women like Mrs. Black shake their heads in disbelief that not everyone seeks to cultivate ties through children.

Bearing a Child in Germany

If marriage strengthens young women's existing affective circuits of belonging with kin and expands the family by establishing new circuits with affines,[9] bearing a child does so even more. The birth of a child—whether in Bangangté, in Yaoundé, or in Berlin—renders a Cameroonian woman fully adult in the eyes of her family and community. As in many other settings, the birth of a child completes a marriage, something "the ceremony itself merely gestures to" (Leinaweaver 2013, 76). It is part of "making people" for the lineage (Smith 2001), widening and rejuvenating family networks while creating dependents and "wealth in people" (Guyer and Eno Belinga 1995). Becoming pregnant and bearing a child satisfies the wishes expressed by the bride's parents and in-laws through fertility-laden wedding oratory and symbols. Bearing a child awakens interest among family members, energizing the care flowing along affective circuits.

Cameroonian mothers recognize that physical distance from informal familial control combines with the multiple stresses of migration to put migrants' marital stability at risk. Consciously or not, mothers can deploy their children to counteract this risk. KemKarine, a hotel worker and mother of two preschool children, points out that couples physically separated by challenging employment situations, and even by emotional strife, remain connected through their mutual obligations toward children.

PFS: *Did your relationship to your partner change after having children?*

KK: *It has not changed, we still love ourselves [each other]. It is just the distance [that is difficult], because he is not in the Nähe [nearby]. [Her partner could only find work in his field in another EU country.]*

PFS: *Do you think that having children makes the relationship last longer?*

KK: *With children, the relationship would be until the end of life, because even if you are not living under the same roof in the same house, but because of the children, [even] if he is angry with me he has to call the children and talk to me.*

Echoing KemKarine's sentiments, other migrant mothers stated that childbearing helped keep their husbands' eyes from "wandering."

While pregnancy and childbearing strengthen the obligations between husband and wife and through them to wider circuits of family belonging, they also bring challenges specific to this life stage. Cameroonian mothers naturalize their child wish as part of being a woman, being an African, or being Bamiléké (sometimes in contrast to what they perceive as the German way of being a woman). They find that their family dreams are hard to realize in Germany, and they change their fertility goals in response. Because extended family members are not physically present to pressure them, husbands and wives make their family-planning decisions largely as couples. Mothers I spoke to viewed this with relief. But, in the absence of extended family members' local knowledge and availability to provide escort and immediate support, facing difficult pregnancies and finding prenatal and obstetric care leaves mothers feeling "all alone."

I met Tessy, a thirty-year-old "not yet employed" computer programmer, at the offices of a German-language African magazine. Tessy grew up in Douala, Cameroon's largest port city, in a Bamiléké-majority neighborhood. She has lived in Germany for over a decade—first as a student, then as a wife, and finally as the mother of two preschool children. Switching back and forth between German and French, Tessy speaks passionately about the values she internalized as a youngster and that have stayed with her despite the radically different context she finds in Germany: *"Because I live in Germany, [what people do here] doesn't have anything to do with these principles. [Despite the environment] they will always stay within me."* Tessy articulates Bamiléké values from the perspective of motherhood. From fertility goals to terms of address to forms of care, parenting—and, particularly, motherhood—offers her a model for social solidarity. Like many of my interlocutors, Tessy naturalizes her wish to become a parent.

> *I've known that since I was a child. When I was six I didn't have a doll, it's true, but I cut branches of plants and I said, "This is my daughter, this is my son." So, already when I was a kid I had this idea in my head: you will [must] grow up, you will have children, you will . . . I don't know. I never asked myself if I would have children . . . it was always my idea: I grow, I have my children, I have my husband, I have my children and family.*

Like Tessy, Ariane migrated to Berlin for university studies. As a Bamiléké facing ethnic quotas in Cameroon, and as a woman in the male-dominated field of engineering, Ariane could not easily pursue her educational dreams in Cameroon. Once in Berlin, she balanced her time between organizing study groups at the Technical University, being an officer at monthly meetings of her hometown association, earning some money with a part-time student job, and caring for her boyfriend and toddler son. And like Tessy, Ariane speaks about childhood dreams of establishing a family, linked to Bamiléké pronatalist values favoring large families. But she also has learned how hard it is to realize these dreams in Germany.

> *So, for me it's true that I had a dream to lead a family life with a husband and children. But in Europe it's not easy. In Germany it's already not easy because you have to—well, with us, especially in the Bamiléké tradition, you have lots of children, three, four, five, for example. But then, in Europe, I mean here in*

Germany . . . I begin to notice that it isn't easy. Because kids here, to raise kids here takes a lot of money, a lot of time, truly.

Ariane continues, expressing the oft-heard distress of Cameroonian migrant mothers at being "all alone"—with their pregnancies, with infant care in the immediate postpartum period, and with the complicated challenges of raising young children while making a life for oneself in a new place. The absence of family contributes to the interwoven challenges of reproducing and belonging *"in der Fremde,"* in a strange or foreign place.

In Cameroon one doesn't have any cares, because your family is always there. But here, already when you give birth the child is your business only. You have to go to the doctor, you have to go to the day care center, all that is your business alone, or perhaps the papa's, your husband's, and yours. That's already a first handicap for not having lots of children. In other words, the dream already starts to die, because . . . when I arrived in Germany, I told myself, ah, I'll have . . . at least four children. But the more time passes, the more I tell myself, hey, maybe even two would be too many, because it's not easy. One child occupies all your time, eats up all your time. You don't have any more life, because you have to care for your child. So now, studies, job, kid.

Family dreams are hard to realize in Germany, and young women like Ariane change their fertility goals in response.[10] They do so not only as individuals, but by sharing experiences with one another, forming collectively held ideas about what is desirable and about what is possible.

I know girls who have studied, even medicine, they were students and they had kids. First they told me over and over, Ariane, you can't easily mix the two. If you want to have children, you'll do so, but know that you'll be very slow at the U. If, that is, you want to continue your studies. At the worst, you'll quit. Because if you have to go to school, with kids, go leave them at day care, pick them up, do your errands, come home and cook, sometimes go to your job, then you have to rest, not counting perhaps the times when one of the kids is sick, or . . . lots of stress, they told me. Really, it's not easy. So, imagine if you have a course of study that lasts five years, you plan to finish in seven or eight years and you go at your own pace because you'll have other burdens. You can't act like a student who has nothing but her studies and a job. Already it's impossible, even if you don't have a kid, the moment you have a man [husband, boyfriend], it's already different. You have to cook for him, you must [do this], you must [do that].

As Ariane indicates, Cameroonian migrant women circulate stories about the difficulties of combining matrimony and childbearing—in short, of founding a family—with the demands of study and earning a living. Turns of phrase such as "they frequently told me" reveal ways that recent migrants learn from their more experienced peers. Tales of the challenges of coordinating family foundation with other life projects pass through migrant networks and crystallize into shared orientations toward childbearing.[11]

Women's coordination work at the vital conjuncture of merely considering pregnancy (Johnson-Hanks 2006) is further complicated by the legal and social experiences of living as a migrant. Keeping one's immigration status—for Tessy and Ariane, as students—is necessary to maintain access to health insurance. Women without regularized immigration status are dependent on charity care for their reproductive health needs. Furthermore, although gender roles among Cameroonian migrant couples are slowly changing, the gendered division of household labor is still largely reproduced through migrant couples' gender-stereotyped expectations and practices. In Ariane's experience, women care for men's needs, especially regarding shopping, cooking, and cleaning. Some migrant men take on limited household tasks. Still, affective circuits with distant family cannot substitute for the daily help that only copresence of female kin provides.

Migration transforms the ways extended kin do or do not become involved in childbearing decisions. Whether in the small towns and villages of the Grassfields or in the Bamiléké urban diaspora in Yaoundé, in Cameroon newly married women experience considerable familial pressure toward high fertility. Migrants in Berlin can more easily ignore family members' wishes because these kin live far away. Sometimes family members develop new wishes for and expectations of their migrant daughters. Iris, a thirty-something Bamiléké single mother and freelance filmmaker in Berlin, was filming a reality show on diasporic life. She described to me that some families pressure migrants to *not* bear children, to maximize remittances that could be sent home to waiting relatives. "*I have a case where the family had to warn a friend of mine, don't give birth to children anymore, two is okay. We are dying here, you need to work. All those children you are having is for what?*" Iris related that those migrants who had not learned to be "strong and independent," who had not slowed down or halted their emotion-laden exchanges with kin, might shape their reproductive decisions under pressure from family demands. Iris described this as a major stress factor on conjugal relationships in the diaspora.

It has to bring a problem in their marriage. Because the man said it is impossible—the man overheard the telephone discussion [between his wife and her parents], because the girl was like . . . the man wanted children and the girl said, "No, for what? We just met here in Europe, I cannot go on with my life like that, having children. This two is okay. I have not helped my family since I came here.

*Two for me is okay." And the man said, "Hello, you are married and I am the
man, we are a couple, we need to decide our life, not your family telling you what
to do"... So it automatically brings a problem in the relationship.*

For migrants like Ariane and Iris, the absence of immediate family support is a disincentive to maintaining the fertility goals of the "ideal Cameroonian modern family" of four children. It is difficult for these women to realize
their dreams of family formation because their kin-based affective circuits
are thin. The density of ties and the density of emotionally charged exchanges
flowing along them may diminish with distance and with the public secrets
of migration—the difficulties that migrants tacitly agree not to tell. Furthermore, these affective circuits are thin because certain kinds of care, especially
for young mothers, require copresence. Traveling to Europe for long visits
to support new mothers is nearly impossible for female kin, because of both
pragmatic and legal constraints. Whether lamenting the missed comforts of
loving care, or pressured to send remittances, migrant mothers experience
the disadvantage of this thinning of ties and of exchanges with kin.

On the other hand, the thinning of family-based affective circuits creates
an advantage for couples who stress values of independent, conjugal decision making in family planning. These couples tend to have higher levels of
formal education and the greatest aspirations for middle-class achievement
and lifestyle. They emphasize companionate marriage, joint decision making
between husband and wife, and the positive aspects of parents raising their
own children in largely nuclear families. Even when the contingencies of real
lives do not reach this ideal, the migrant mothers I interacted with valued
independence from familial influence in family-planning decisions. They indicated that they alone could really understand the conditions under which
they lived as migrants, and thus were in the best position to make reproductive decisions.

Hannah, an environmental scientist running a small family business with
her Bamiléké husband, expanded on commonly held explanations for changing reproductive goals after migration to Europe. In addition to the challenges
of doing everything on one's own and "*getting tired*," Hannah related that in
Germany "*there are more intense expectations for parenting, and these expectations fall just on the parents' shoulders.*" After one miscarriage and two difficult and dangerous deliveries, Hannah and her husband "*decided together*"
to be content with only two children. In reproduction, child rearing, and
even religious ideologies (such as when she and her husband became born-
again Christians), Hannah presented conjugal decision making in the frame
of independence from extended family concerns. Although her stepmother

and her father's two sisters advise her to *"give many children,"* Hannah said that encouragement toward childbearing transmitted through long-distance phone calls *"is just talk, different from pressure."* From their position in provincial Cameroonian towns, these relatives cannot shoulder the day-to-day burdens of child rearing. Instead, responsibility falls almost entirely on the nuclear family. Like Hannah, most women deemphasized any pressure toward childbearing that they may have received from parents, mothers-in-law, and stepmothers. They described their distant relatives' "talk" as gentle reminders that life entails more than meeting educational and financial goals.

"ALL ALONE": WHO CARES FOR MOTHER AND BABY?

Cameroonian migrant mothers scale back their family dreams because they know that being pregnant and caring for infants in Germany "all alone" is hard. When women talk about caring for infants in Germany, they emphasize the practical and emotional difficulties of needing to do everything oneself in a foreign land without the supportive (though sometimes meddling) presence of extended kin.

In Cameroon, women grow up expecting their female kin to help out following childbirth. Whether living in the Bamiléké and English-speaking Grassfields or among the domestic diaspora of internal migrants to the major cities, mothers' affective circuits to kin remain strong. Not only words but also goods and people flow freely; mothers, sisters, and aunts can easily travel to and care for a new mother and her infant. They bring along lovingly handknitted caps and booties and favorite foods from the family farm. They let the new mother rest and spoil her with baths and fresh food to promote successful lactation, simultaneously enhancing maternal and infant health. As we will see in chapter four, Cameroonian mothers learn that when visitors bathe, hold, and play with the infant, they foster the child's physical and social development, helping her to grow a strong torso and to meet the world with a hospitable gaze (DeLoache and Gottlieb 2000; Gottlieb 2004; Keller, Voelker, and Yovsi 2005). Visits of kin contribute to cycles of reciprocal physical and affective care that build and maintain affective circuits for mother and child; they are simultaneously practices that constitute kinship as mutuality of being and as symbolic notions of belonging (Sahlins 2013).

Such expectations of copresence make distance from natal families all the more devastating for lonely new mothers. Whether it is searching for help to conceive or to make it through a pregnancy, Cameroonian migrant mothers in Berlin cannot count on their family-based affective circuits to provide the range of care that they would if they were physically present and in a familiar environment. Mothers,' sisters,' and aunties' visits to provide postpartum and infant care—with all its attendant socialization and love—are constrained by both costs and bureaucracies. Distant family members can provide only limited advice through phone calls or letters; they have neither the necessary local knowledge of Berlin nor the social networks to mobilize for medical referrals for their migrant daughters. Because of the expense and the frequent package thefts in Cameroonian post offices, sending timely gifts to the new mother and baby depends largely on the happenstance of trustworthy couriers traveling between Cameroon and Germany. Thus mothers like Eveline laugh with delight at the thought of the small packages their mothers send to German-born babies, but blink away tears when repeating the refrain of motherhood being difficult because as a migrant in Germany one is all alone.

Women transform their interior state of loneliness into the shared knowledge that "it's hard being a mother here" by telling each other stories about their experiences. For example, Christine, a Bamiléké political refugee, contrasts her experience as a teen mother in Yaoundé with that of bearing her second child after her migration to Germany.

> *In Cameroon you are surrounded, you have your family and here you are alone, alone, alone. In Cameroon, for example, when I had my first son . . . I was with my mother, I still lived at home with my parents. It was my mother who took me to the hospital, I gave birth, she was at the hospital with me, and afterwards she brought me back to the house. . . . At the house, they cooked—it was a party. Every evening we drank, we ate, there were visitors . . . lots of people. [They] held the baby. . . . For a month there were always lots of people, visitors, like that. And they helped me wash the baby's laundry. Me, I just lay down. When I got up in the morning they came to wash me, I came and they fed me. Afterwards I just rested, and they took care of the baby. But here . . . alone."*

Through sharing such stories, migrant women create a common orientation and vocabulary—a discourse—that organizes their experiences into the two ideal-typical spheres of a highly social and supportive Cameroon versus an overwhelmingly complex and solitary Germany.

The laments that young mothers circulate also remark on the loss of popular health knowledge and intergenerational transmission of knowledge. When Lily delineates the overwhelming tasks a new mother must accomplish all alone in Berlin, she yearns for the lessons she could gain from older female kin.

> *Here, no matter what your immigration status as a pregnant woman, the state will take care of you, all the medical care that you need, up to the birth. But after the birth, they don't give you a lot to live on. You need to fight to get all your*

papers in order so that they'll take care of you . . . You need to know the right people, to inform yourself. It's not written anywhere, there's not a place where you can go, you need to chase around and look before finding the right informa- tion . . . As for advice, in Cameroon, les mamans are there, they have their expe- riences, and that helps a lot. But even us here in Europe, we need the experience of our African mamas, who can tell us if we need to do this, do that . . . Here, your church [members] might come for a formal visit, but they don't come sleep at your place, like my mother would do. You can never replace a mother! . . . There's also the social security [welfare] system here, [but] it's not the [same as] family.

Older women's knowledge is embodied in physical practices of care, ges- tures and habits that are more easily demonstrated than explained. When grandma washes baby, holds him and looks up with unspoken emphasis into her daughter's eyes, she simultaneously provides physical, emotional, and didactic care. The wisdom of "les mamans," sadly, is not easily transmitted across continents. Because grandmothers and other female kin find it dif- ficult to visit, the care flowing through migrant mothers' kin-based affective circuits is limited to words of concern and advice, to nagging, and to limited exchange of medicinal therapies.

Migrant mothers make extra efforts to stay in touch, mitigating their physical distance from female kin by engaging in material and communica- tive exchanges and traveling to be with family during important life-cycle events. When migrant mothers face pregnancy, childbirth, and the rou- tine needs of infant care, health care products flow along circuits with their Cameroonian kin. Working with Ghanaian immigrants in London, Kristine Krause reminds us that sickness "can activate intensive exchange [of solace, information, materia medica, and money] between friends and family" in transnational therapy networks (2008, 236). Medicines and other material ex- pressions of care get exchanged when friends or relatives, acting as couriers, visit between Cameroon and Germany. For example, Fanny met her fiancé during a rendezvous with a cousin to get some "stuff" he had brought to her from Cameroon; she reciprocated by sending Tylenol back to her relatives in Cameroon. And when her baby "*is disturbing,*" So'nju chews the dried, sweet seeds from *ndzim ndzim* pods and sprays the saliva onto his fontanel or belly to quiet him. A staple in Bamiléké self-care apothecaries to calm anxiety and prevent seizure illnesses, *ndzim ndzim* pods travel the circuit from So'nju's relatives, to her husband during his visits home, and on to So'nju in Germany. "*They always give him, because for all the Bamiléké that must be in the house. When you are sleeping and have bad dreams, you [place it under your pillow].*"

Friends traveling back and forth serve as couriers not only for medicines but also for small gifts that express familial love and support mental health.

FIGURE 3.2. A *ndzim-ndzim* pod, which So'nju places under her baby's pillow to keep him "from disturbing," sent from Cameroon along affective circuits. Many Bamiléké believe that *ndzim-ndzim* pods prevent "bird," a seizure disorder afflicting newborns. In addition, pregnant women chew the sweet, anise-flavored seeds of the dried pods to alleviate their nausea.
Credit: Lindsey Walters

When conversing about medical products sold at African groceries, Ariane told me that she asks her parents to send her hair products, particularly hair extenders that are hard to find at a good price in Berlin.

> "*When it comes to health issues, I don't buy a lot. Otherwise, it's hair extenders [that I buy at the Afro Shop], to do my hair. But even there, it's a bit expensive, so I prefer to ask people in Cameroon, maybe my parents, my family, that they send them to me. When I have friends who go back and forth.*"

Eveline has had a more challenging time giving and receiving gifts from her parents and siblings. When Eveline first arrived in Germany, she lived in a camp for asylum seekers. There, her family contacts were temporarily cut off. In the metaphoric language of affective circuits, Eveline's situation created a short circuit. Once Eveline was awarded asylum, she moved to Berlin, where she currently is waiting for her baby to start day care so she can begin a German language and integration class. Eveline has now picked up the dropped connection to her family. She describes her mother sending small packages, material gifts that express love and connection to her tiny grandson: "*Yeah,*

she often sends small packages to her grandson, especially when she sees some-
one who is coming [to Germany], she'll put together a little package [laugh].
And me, I send . . . I don't send her much, because I'm not working yet, it's a
little hard." At this stage, the mother-infant pair received more than they sent,
but Eveline looked forward to having the means to reciprocate. She wanted to
express her appreciation and devotion to her mother through little gifts sent
through travelers returning to Cameroon. Invoking an emic understanding
of intergenerational wealth flows (Caldwell 2005) that emphasizes morality
over economic calculation, Eveline knew that her kin in Cameroon expect
that over time the direction of flow in these affective circuits will reverse,
sending remittances, goods, and care back to elders in Cameroon.

Nonmaterial exchanges between young mothers and families "back home"
can be just as important as gifts. Phone calls allow families to talk, to hear an
infant's coos, and to provide moral support to new mothers. When describing
how she deals with loneliness, Eveline explained: "*Yes, I'm content being here,*
except that I miss my family from time to time. [PFS: And what do you do when
you miss your family?] I call them. I look for a phonecard, I call them, we chat,
I listen to them and then it [the loneliness] goes away."

Mrs. Black phones her mother frequently, complaining about how hard
it is to convince her German husband of the seriousness of her wish to have
a child. "*He has three sisters, you know, and just one of them has children . . .*
The other ones . . . they don't see any reason why they have to have children. So,
like, where I grew up in Cameroon . . . to be a woman, you have to have a child.
That is our culture. You are supposed to have a child . . . I think it is [laugh] like
my right to have a child." A patient at the Berlin Fertility Center, Mrs. Black is
grateful that her mother does not pressure her to have a child. "*No, no, Gott*
sei Dank [thank God], I don't have [pressure]. My mother she is really . . . well
in the beginning, she was asking me, like, 'What is happening?' Well, I told her
what was going on in the house, you know. And [pause] she just said . . . she has
already about three grandchildren . . . She is just praying that the thing will hap-
pen." In fact, through their phone calls, her mother provides moral support at
a distance, all the more important because Mrs. Black had to struggle for her
emotional "*right to have [or even wish for] a child*" in her binational marriage.

Bih also sought moral support when facing her first birth; rather than
phoning, she traveled to be with female kin during this important time. Bih
became pregnant while both she and her Cameroonian husband were enrolled in graduate programs in Berlin. Bih strongly wanted to follow the tradition of returning home to spend the perinatal period with her mother, but
both her parents had died young, and her female siblings were spread across
five nations on three continents. How would she coordinate her wish to spend

her first birth under the tutelage of a female elder with her drive to complete her education—in addition to her legal requirement to maintain her student status and thus her residence permit in Germany? Such coordination of multiple life-course imperatives at the vital conjunctures of pregnancy and birth is a common feature of the transition to social motherhood in Cameroon (Johnson-Hanks 2006). Bih's heroic juggling act reflects her efforts to maintain several types of belonging simultaneously—to her distant kin and their notions of the proper way to be part of a family, and to the institutions and actors surrounding university life in Germany.

With her due date during the break between semesters, Bih studied ahead and arranged to take her final exams early. At seven months pregnant, Bih traveled to the United States to stay with her husband's mother and sister. Moving temporarily from Germany to North America meant disrupting her medical care. Bih's treatment at an American public hospital was harsh, characterized by delays in making appointments for necessary tests. At this delicate time of first birth, Bih also endured a three-month separation from her husband James, with whom she had a close, companionate marriage; on his end, to fund Bih's travels and save for their new family, James worked three jobs while maintaining the laboratory research for his dissertation.

Although in an unfamiliar environment, lacking the traditional visits of multiple female kin and friends, Bih placed herself in the company of two female affines who guided her through pregnancy, birth, and early infant care. Bih returned with her one-month-old baby to her husband and her studies in Berlin just in time for the start of the next semester. With the help of Bih's small maternity stipend from a student organization, Bih and James managed to get by financially. Ties to other Cameroonians through a Grassfields hometown association and through a student housing project kept Bih from feeling "all alone" after her return to Berlin. These "Cameroonian sisters" substituted for kin, sharing information and child care, permitting each other to survive motherhood in a strange land.

Bih is like many women who, in the absence of local family support, turned to friends or neighbors. Maria, whose love story appeared above, was dissatisfied with her obstetrician after undergoing a medically indicated abortion. When wracked with self-doubt, Maria received moral support from her family's phone calls, but at that distance she could not hope to get advice from them about medical personnel. She sought referrals from several Cameroonian friends in Berlin for ob-gyns with a reputation for friendly treatment of African patients, and she has been content with her care since. Friends also help with cooking, housework, and babysitting. Justine, who has developed friendship ties "like family" with her Cameroonian friend, Barbara, received help from overlapping networks when coordinating her first pregnancy with the end of her studies in computer science.

> *I think, like, my first son, I had him when I was still studying, that was a bit difficult, coordinating house, children, and then studies, and I had to work too. But as time went on . . . I was able to plan it effectively so that I could use the time effectively . . . The Kita helped and support was . . . from friends. I had also financial support from my family, and then the friends that were there and could . . . when I had to work I had to . . . [I could also] call for a friend or to come and take care [of the children].*

Not all migrant mothers were as lucky as Justine, with a strong friendship network and family financial support. Circumstances of migration sometimes temporarily cut women off from their families while simultaneously limiting development of new friendships. For example, Christine, the political refugee whom we met earlier, became pregnant and gave birth while living in an isolated asylum camp, waiting for years for her petition to be processed in immigration court. Christine had few options in choosing a gynecologist, needing to seek permission to leave the camp for each doctor visit.

> *Oh, no, you don't have a choice . . . to go to the hospital, to the gynecologist, for example. You have to take a Krankenschein [health voucher]. You have to go to social services, take the Krankenschein, and go to the gynecologist with it. And then when you go to the gynecologist, if he says, for example, that you have to come back in two weeks or a month, before that date you have to go get that voucher or Krankenschein, before you can go back to him.*

When she went into labor, happenstance gave Christine a modicum of social support from another Cameroonian asylum seeker.

> *When I delivered here there was this Cameroonian boy at the Heim [asylum camp], who helped us. But, for example, when I started contractions, it was this guy who went to tell the people at social [services] downstairs that they needed to call the ambulance. The ambulance came to get me. At the hospital, when I gave birth, I was there a week—no, I was there for eight days, because I delivered by Caesarian section . . . And during those eight days, how many visitors did I have? Only two visits! Yes. Because during this time the guy at the Heim also fell sick, so he couldn't—imagine the distance as well—leave the Heim to come to the hospital. It was far away, a great distance.*

Most asylum camps or "homes" near Berlin are in small towns in the surrounding state of Brandenburg, a part of former East Germany, whose residents often feel resentment toward the asylum seekers. Public transportation to and from these rural towns is complicated and expensive, as is access to

FIGURE 3.3. An asylum-seekers' camp in Belzig, a small town in the state of Brandenburg outside of
Berlin, 2011, similar to the camps where Christine and Eveline each spent over a year. Run by the Federal
Office for Migration and Refugees, such camps (also termed "homes" or "hostels") provide housing and
social services to asylum seekers awaiting decisions on their asylum claims.
Credit: Pamela Feldman-Savelsberg

telephones with the ability to call home; the rule of *Residenzpflicht* (residence
obligation/restriction) requires written permission from state authorities each
time an asylum seeker travels outside the county (*Landkreis*) of her asylum
camp.

Both the circumstances that initiate refugee movement and conditions at
camps for asylum seekers may generate mistrust, attenuating potential lines
of social support. Eveline speaks to the vulnerability she felt as an asylum
seeker, which made it difficult to accept help during her pregnancy. First,
she remained traumatized by the political violence during Cameroon's Ghost
Town movement that motivated her migration: "*I came here to Germany because there were already too many problems at home in Africa . . . political
problems, people who attacked each other and all that. People who lost their
lives due to politics and all . . . That's why I came here.*"

Second, she was aware that very few Cameroonian asylum seekers are actually awarded asylum in Germany.[12] Third, given the years of waiting, the
opaque procedures (at least from the perspective of refugees), and the strain
of living in tight quarters with strangers, Eveline learned not to trust people.

She mourned her loss of trust; new mothers, Eveline recounted, need the trustworthy advice of friends, even if this may later backfire: "*In any case, at the beginning one needs a lot of help, one always needs information. That's to say, the first time you go to the doctor, you need someone to guide you . . . [But] even a trusted friend can betray you; you always have to take risks in life.*"

The hardships encountered by asylum seekers and undocumented migrants foster caution with "friends" and circumspection in communication with parents remaining in Cameroon. Women do not want their parents to worry or to realize how difficult it is to meet one's migration goals. So'nju, incurring her mother's anger by not informing her of her pregnancies until after her children were born, is perhaps an extreme case in a general tendency of self-control and circumspection.[13]

Distance from kin can occasionally be advantageous to migrant mothers, allowing them to ignore infant-care practices with which they disagree and quietly neglect using products that flow through their affective circuits. For example, after receiving unwelcome advice regarding her baby's colic, Ariane delayed buying the recommended remedy at a local African grocery (Afro Shop) until, finally, her son outgrew the condition. "*OK, yeah, for the child, when he was still a tiny baby, with those tummy pains, the pains the baby has during the first three months . . . yeah, colic, that's it . . . they told me to take a product there at the Afro Shop. But I didn't even look for it. I kept stalling and then the three months passed by quickly.*"

Most often, though, distance from family contributes to other stresses of starting families in a foreign land. Echoing Bamiléké ideas relating emotional disquiet to infertility, Jucal attributes her difficulties conceiving to the stress she experienced as a migrant and as a newlywed. Jucal worked multiple odd jobs well below her qualifications to supplement her husband's meager nursing salary. She struggled with learning German so as to enter a master of social work program at a private Catholic *Hochschule* (a university specializing in a narrow range of fields, often with an applied bent). After a year of marriage, she still had not conceived. She and Francis visited the Fertility Center, where Jucal received hormone therapy and eventually conceived a baby boy.

Jucal's long-sought pregnancy, however, did not put an end to her stress. Both she and her husband, unwittingly, had traded the distancing of family ties and a paradoxical drop in social and occupational status for admiration back home and the hope of future opportunity (Nieswand 2011). During her pregnancy, Jucal felt too stressed to continue working and had to drop out of her privately funded social work program. Francis's occupation as a geriatric nurse allowed him to support his family (minimally), but not enough to support his wife's private tuition. Happily, he was present at the birth of their son, speaking *"nice words"* to her throughout labor. And he congratulated Jucal when she cradled their chubby baby with his big shock of hair.

Jucal is not the only woman I met who had to drop out of university as a result of the stresses of being pregnant far from familial support. When diagnosed with gestational diabetes, Sophie was unable to continue her studies at a technical university in the nearby state of Brandenburg. After becoming pregnant, Marthe left her master's program in another European country to join Alain in Berlin. She faced a difficult pregnancy, and—despite Alain's unusual level of household help—extreme loneliness during the long wakeful nights with their colicky baby. She summed up the situation: *"One doesn't come here to make babies."* And although she was able to remain in her university program, Hannah suffered with her first pregnancy, which ended in a miscarriage. Hannah describes that her entire *"system"* was *"depressed."* She felt stressed from her studies, from her financial needs, and from worrying what her family would think of her pregnancy, as she was not yet married at the time. She felt lonely and uncertain, informing only her sister about the pregnancy and miscarriage. Her doctor referred her to a psychologist to talk about alleviating stress. *"This was some sort of therapy,"* Hannah stated, remembering how at the time the bland taste of university cafeteria food became the focus of her homesickness.

The commonness of Cameroonian women's lament that they are "all alone" in Germany at this delicate time of birth and infancy underscores the emotional cost they suffer when the exchanges that flow through family-based affective circuits are limited to moral support from a distance. These limits to affective circuits affect mothers differently than fathers, as So'nju points out:

SO'NJU: *A mother in Cameroon, it [she] is not really a mother because people will be always there to help you. But here you must do everything alone . . . [In Cameroon] they will always take the child and I relax . . . Here it is not easy.*
MAGNI: *Why is it not easy? You have your husband.*
SO'NJU: *A husband, wow. [All three—So'nju, Magni, and I—laugh.] Not easy.*
PFS: *So your husband doesn't take care of the children too much?*
SO'NJU: *He takes care of them not so much. So for me, I don't even care if he takes care or not, because my [widowed] mother brought us up without our father.*

The relative persistence of a patriarchal gendered division of labor and weak transnational therapy networks combine to give migrant mothers sole responsibility for infant care in Germany. Like many mothers, So'nju expresses this in terms of the hard work of self-care and infant care, and feeling sadly "alone."

Conclusion

Cameroonian migrant women in Berlin face multiple challenges to reproduction and belonging. Mothers juggle demands stemming from their personal aspirations and from their families, their diasporic communities, and the state. This chapter has focused on the intersection of women's personal aspirations, their shifting reproductive goals, and broader family needs and demands. To give form to this complex story, this and the next chapter follow the different kinds of ties and demands that mothers face at varying points in their mothering careers—from finding a partner to getting pregnant, giving birth, and raising infants, children, and teens. As any parent knows, these stages often blur into each other. Rearing children is always full of surprises, just when one thinks one has mastered or learned to cope with a particular developmental stage. But both child development and the medical, educational, and religious institutions that parents and children interact with create some clear demarcations and a sense of stages.

The early stages of family formation lend themselves particularly well to investigating ways that women manage the challenges of biological reproduction through mobilizing kin-based social networks. Simultaneously, women's reproductive practices—the vital events of partnering, marrying, and giving birth—shape their ties with kin. When Maria, Jucal, So'nju, and Fanny got married or engaged, they forged new relationships. When Tessy, Ariane, Hannah and Bih became pregnant and gave birth, their relationships with their extended kin were transformed. These relationships endured over time and across national and even continental borders. Distance, however, dramatically shaped the quality of these relationships and the exchanges they engendered surrounding these important reproductive events.

When migrant women face the everyday and sometimes extraordinary challenges of family formation, advice, material items, and moral support flow along kin-based affective circuits. Not only support, but also intrusive questions and annoying demands sometimes travel along these circuits. Despite financial and legal barriers, people travel as well—when couples reunite, when children are sent to Grandma for care, and when family members visit. The types and intensity of exchanges flowing along kin-based affective circuits vary over time—and, specific to the migration context, they differ from the same types of circuits for situations in which all family members live in

Cameroon. Like an uneven radio or Internet signal, kin-based affective circuits thicken and thin, experience flurries of activity (for example, surrounding a wedding or a birth) as well as signals that are slowed, dropped, and often picked up again.

The newness of entering into a relationship and starting a family is simultaneously exciting and overwhelming; it is even more overwhelming for migrant women in a new, strange, and sometimes hostile environment. Ironically, just when migrant women are most in need of familial warmth and support, their kin-based affective circuits slow and thin out. Differences in everyday lifeworlds in Cameroon and Germany can lead to misunderstandings. Most importantly, though, even the closest of ties cannot overcome physical distance. Women find they must manage without the copresence of kin to provide pragmatic everyday support. This challenge finds its expression in two oft-repeated phrases: "It's hard being a mother here" and "Here I am all alone."

Despite the thinning of affective circuits in transnational families, as Lily told us, family ties remain pragmatically and especially emotionally important. In a study of relations between grandparents and grandchildren in a rural Ghanaian town, anthropologist Sjaak van der Geest reminds us that "kinship and relatedness need to be demonstrated in public even when their 'content' has dwindled" (2004, 47). Ironically, when Cameroonian migrant women share stories bemoaning the difficulties of becoming and being a mother in Germany, they demonstrate the continuing significance of kin. Their laments about the anguish of loneliness are one way of performing kinship and belonging.

This chapter on founding Cameroonian families in Berlin has revealed ways that migrant women forge affective circuits *through* marriage and childbearing. Of course, kin-based affective circuits are important not only for migrant women bearing children; they remain crucial for migrant women rearing children. In the following chapter, this investigation of women forging family connections for themselves continues with a focus on migrant mothers' socially reproductive work to construct affective circuits for their growing children. When they parent their preschoolers, schoolchildren, and teens, mothers seek to anchor their children via emotional identification with their Cameroonian roots. This is the work of belonging—but belonging to what? What "culture" do Cameroonian parents aim to transmit? In what ways is this social reproduction in tension with social mobility? And what roles do affective circuits with family members in Cameroon play in mothers' attempts to create belonging for their children?

4

Raising Cameroonian Families in Berlin

[I don't feel] strange or foreign, [I don't get] weird looks from others, [there's] no system that's really new for me. It's at home, after all, with the family, with all that familial warmth and all that goes along with it.

ARIANE, Berlin, 2011

Musing on what it means to belong, Ariane evokes the warmth of family ties. For this young mother and international student in Berlin, memories of family life involve memories of home. Home, for Ariane, is simultaneously a place and a feeling.[1] In fact, it is at least two places—her parents' apartment and neighborhood in the Cameroonian port city of Douala and her grandparents' land and ancestral shrines in the Bamiléké chiefdom of Bangangté. Home also elicits emotions associated with warmth and protection, loyalty, familiarity, a place of effortless belonging. Ariane contrasts her feeling of being at home—*chez moi*—with the foreignness she experiences in Berlin, the strange looks she receives, the sense of being different, and the continual effort of navigating in an unfamiliar social and bureaucratic environment. Ariane's framing of belonging in terms of familial warmth may be a reference to specifically Bamiléké symbols of the warm hearth and cooking pot-as-womb. The hearth upon which the cooking pot rests is conceived as a site of the shared substance, sustenance, and storytelling that constitute kinship (Feldman-Savelsberg 1999). Alternatively, Ariane's invocation of familial warmth may merely be a readily available turn of phrase, a clichéd reference to how families ought to be.

At the very least, Ariane's words remind us that most of us, including Cameroonian migrant mothers, achieve the many layers of belonging through being part of families. Above, we have seen that by bearing children, young migrant mothers such as Ariane enhance their sense of belonging *to* their families by taking on new roles and contributing to lineage continuity. Here the focus is on mothers' tasks of creating that sense of belonging *for* their growing children. How will Ariane and other mothers from Cameroon, now living in Berlin, give their children a sense of home? What will that home be? Are Ariane and her fellow Cameroonian mothers raising Cameroonian children in Berlin, or are they Cameroonians rearing culturally German children?

Through their child-rearing practices and their cultivation of social networks, migrant mothers attempt to provide their children with guidance and stability in a world of global mobility. They seek to instill in their children a sense of having roots and traditions, of pride and acceptance of one's identity—rather than shame. At the same time, mothers work hard to develop attributes in their children that will permit or even facilitate global mobility. These include emotional dispositions and specific life skills. Mothers also work to ensure their children have legal rights. Mothers train their children, for example, to be adaptable and to speak several languages; and they maneuver to grant their children citizenship rights in a European or North American country. Mothers hope to enhance such attributes as well as their children's Cameroonian belonging through establishing ties between their children and wider circles of kin. These ties create circuits that carry exchanges of goods, advice, visits, and care, supporting mothers in the work of social reproduction.

Child rearing is socially reproductive labor, as we know from a variety of studies on the creation of kinship (e.g., Gottlieb 2004; Howell 2006; Stack 1974). However, within the context of African migration to Europe, it is not always clear what is being socially reproduced, and how. The lack of clarity that Cameroonian migrant parents face resonates with recent insights about culture and ethnic bases of belonging, as explored by anthropologists elsewhere. In the last few decades, anthropologists have increasingly come to view culture and belonging as "inherently unfinished" (Hutchinson 1996, 28), resistant to typification (Abu-Lughod 2008), and mediated by a combination of political maneuverings (Asad 1973; Geschiere 2009) and personal agency (Barth 1969; Cohen and Bledsoe 2002). If culture and belonging are up for grabs, it becomes clear that the social reproduction involved in migrant child rearing entails adaptation, adjustments, compromise, and the creation of new understandings.

In a brilliant study of Ghanaian transnational families, Coe demonstrates that parts of cultural child rearing repertoires[2] that otherwise would be too taken-for-granted to articulate come into greater consciousness and awareness when confronted with the newness of the migrant experience. African migrants' sense of their competence as parents "feels fragile and hard-won" in Europe and the United States (Coe 2013, 151). Parents' reputations are monitored by gossip within the immigrant community, parents fear that their children may lack ambition and squander opportunities, and parents' disciplinary responses might be sanctioned by the state. "In this state of unease, parents become self-conscious about their [parenting] repertoire" (Coe 2013, 152).

Likewise, as their children grow up in Berlin, Cameroonian parents confront a variety of situations in which they become more or less self-conscious about their parenting repertoires. New situations emerge as children grow from infancy through school entry to adolescence, and concurrently, as mothers move through their mothering careers. At each stage, through their children, mothers interact with various groups of kin as well as with German medical, social service, and educational institutions. Examining these situations permits us to discern the emergence of new ideas and practices concerning social reproduction and belonging in a mobile population.

When Eveline, for example, compares her German-born baby's situation to that of an older son whom she left with her mother in Cameroon, she becomes aware of what good parenting means to her, and how hard it is to achieve in her current conditions. Because Eveline has not yet mastered reading and writing in German, worries about language become her way to express her many-faceted uncertainties about parenting in a strange place.

> Here, you are alone. Raising a child alone is not easy at all. In Africa, we have our mamas, our brothers, our sisters, our friends—you can leave your kid with your friend and go out. But that's not the case here . . . Well yeah, I want to say that raising a child is much harder here . . . because already the language gets in the way . . . At school he will speak German. And imagine, suppose that in the future, if he's already at a school . . . when he returns home you need to help him with his homework, but there . . . you can't show him what you have to do like that . . . With the one who is in Africa, you . . . understand everything that he does at school. You can help him better than the one who is here. To help the one who is here, you really need to integrate yourself. It's difficult. Every day we think about the life of our children. You have children and you watch them grow, it's nice to watch them grow, but education . . . We ask ourselves, I ask myself every day how will it be with his education.

Eveline's lament reveals several themes: being alone, lack of a common language, unfamiliarity with the German school system, and concerned hopes for her German-born child's future. Above, Eveline and others explained that the physical distance from extended families—particularly from female kin— leaves new brides and birthing mothers on their own to adjust to their new life stage and their new setting. Here Eveline indicates that the overwhelming feeling of being alone with the multiple tasks of child rearing haunts migrants throughout the mothering career.

Mothers of preschoolers, primary school children, and teens face three major challenges raising their children in Berlin. First, they must adapt child rearing practices to a new environment, somehow transmitting to their children what they view as the most important elements of their culture. Second, parents must consciously decide what to pass on from "back home," because distance renders the Cameroonian physical and social environment an imagined landscape of belonging.[3] Third, mothers need to keep their efforts to forge Cameroonian belonging for their children in fine balance with their attempts to help children adapt to and integrate into German society.

Cameroonian mothers approach this balance by raising their children for academic success and resilience to hardship. Mothers hope that Cameroonian-coded dispositions such as respect, discipline, and identification with familial and cultural roots will provide their children the strength they need, as black Africans, to move through the German day care and school system despite racialized stereotypes about immigrant children's academic aptitude and achievement (Eggers 2006). Cameroonian mothers forcefully express their resentment of German stereotypes that African migrants are poor, disadvantaged, and illegal, instead invoking their educational achievements. Arriving with the belief that their educational achievement orientation sets Cameroonians apart from other Africans, and even sets Bamiléké and Anglophone Cameroonians apart from other Cameroonians, Cameroonian migrant mothers practice intensive parenting to cultivate their children's human capital.[4] From preschool to later grades, mothers seek to equip their children for academic success in the face of perceived or anticipated discrimination. To achieve this tricky task, mothers draw simultaneously on Cameroonian forms of belonging as well as perceptions about how to work the German system to best guide their children.

In presenting mothers' everyday child-rearing practices, this chapter raises an underlying question: Is social reproduction in tension with social mobility? If so, how do mothers navigate between these two endeavors? Because the practices and moral imperatives of rearing children change across the life course, I trace the interweaving of social reproduction, belonging, and mobility for mothers of children in different developmental stages.

Rearing Preschoolers and Ambiguities of Belonging

Cameroonian parents interact with their newborns and young children in ways that foster culture-specific dispositions. Through games, language choice, and bodily practices, they help their children internalize what they refer to as "Cameroonian-ness."[5] But because migrant mothers (and fathers) need to work, they spend many hours of the day separated from their young children. In almost all cases, this means that, rather than being among kin or other members of a cultural community, young children are cared for in publicly organized or subsidized day care centers. There, children largely interact with German playmates and caregivers. Children not only learn the German language and German interaction etiquette; they also begin to identify with a German habitus, to find it normal and unmarked. Yet, after day care hours, parents expect children to act according to Cameroonian expectations. Thus, from an early age, children of Cameroonian migrants face the ambiguities of simultaneous belonging in multiple cultures.

In the following, I begin with ways that parents foster their babies' and toddlers' embodiment of belonging. I then examine the child care center as a site where mothers struggle with the contrast between raising Cameroonian children in Germany versus Cameroonians raising culturally German children. I end with mothers' varied efforts to keep their children Cameroonian.

EARLY EMBODIMENT

Cameroonian—or, in increasing specificity, Grassfields, Bamiléké, or Bangangté—modes of infant and toddler care help these young people embody a culturally specific habitus (Bourdieu 1977; Csordas 1994; Strathern 1996). Such practices connect the child to its parents, their kin and kin-like friends, and to a home-place. As has been documented elsewhere in Africa, both mothers and fathers readily pass their babies to visitors to hold, encouraging comfort with multiple caregivers and discouraging stranger anxiety (Gottlieb 2004). They speak French or English to their babies—the preferred languages of migrants who themselves mostly hail from multiethnic urban centers in Cameroon. Even if they do not master the language of their home village, parents create local-language nicknames and may address their children with their *ndap*, a praise-name indicating the mother's or father's village origin. Fathers and, particularly, mothers, remember "give-and-take" games in local language, a favorite pastime that introduces infants and toddlers to simple practices of reciprocity. The first time I visited Marthe and Alain in their home, they laughed enthusiastically when I looked squarely at their toddler daughter—sitting on Marthe's lap—and, saying "*kò*" (take) in Medᵾmba,[6] initiated the give-and-take game. While I repeatedly offered and then held out my hand for little Yvonne to return my pen, Marthe chimed in with the words "give" and "take."

But even these simple practices have their limits among the Cameroonian diaspora in Berlin. First of all, as has been discussed, few family members come to visit. For those few relatives and friends who have also migrated to Europe and happen to live in the same country or city, distances are long, tram fares expensive, and time is short. This reduces daily interaction to a small group—members of the same household, usually a nuclear family. Other common body techniques (Mauss 1938) that emphasize motor stimulation and the early achievement of motor competence (Keller, Voelker, and Yovsi 2005, 160), such as carrying babies on one's back in a cloth wrapper, are impractical in the cold, wintry climate when mothers and babies alike must wear overcoats. Furthermore, bodily practices, such as the circumcision of young boys, are anything but self-understood in Germany. As Jucal told me, male circumcision *"is not a tradition, it's not a culture here in Germany, they don't do circumcision."* In contrast, throughout the Cameroonian Grassfields, male circumcision is a way to make your son look like all other boys; some might say that male circumcision literally carves Cameroonian belonging on the body. Chapter six details the dilemmas this form of early embodiment of belonging poses for Cameroonian parents living in Berlin—dilemmas involving health insurance, state and religion, and the ambiguous reach of law.

THE KITA: BUILDING AFFECTIVE CIRCUITS IN A ROUTINE ORGANIZATION

Like many Cameroonian mothers I met, KemKarine clapped her hands and exclaimed, *"Thank God for the* Kita!" Kita has made its way into migrants' everyday language, German slang that peppers their conversations in Cameroonian-inflected French or English. Kitas are publically subsidized day care centers. Without their ready availability in Berlin, mothers of young children would be unable to work, enroll in language or integration courses, or attend university. KemKarine, for example, cleans rooms in a large hotel. Working as a chambermaid,[7] she tells me, is poorly paid, low-status, backbreaking labor—an undesired but common entry-level job for African immigrants in Berlin. When KemKarine is at work, her two young sons, both preschoolers, attend the Kita near her apartment in former East Berlin. There, the rents are low, and a nearby student hostel lodges a small concentration of African immigrant mothers sending their children to the same Kita.

KemKarine tries to work as many hours as possible, because she is saving up for a visit to Cameroon with her two children. Her closet is filled with cases of Nutella, paper diapers, and other gifts that she plans to distribute among friends and relatives in Cameroon. This will be KemKarine's first visit home after escaping from a Cameroonian prison, following participation in a political protest against government abuses nearly a decade before. Since then, KemKarine endured several lonely years in an asylum camp, was granted political asylum, and established herself in Berlin. As she says, *"Things are very OK for me now . . . At least I can be able to pay my bills, I can be able to take my children out for a weekend . . . like, for a change, to eat something in McDonald's."*

As a low-level employee, KemKarine is not able to negotiate ideal working conditions in the hotel. She is always "on call," making her work hours both irregular and unpredictable. KemKarine often works weekends. Because the Kita is open only during daytime hours on weekdays, KemKarine's work schedule necessitates finding alternative forms of child care. The children's father, a Cameroonian man with German citizenship, now works in another European Union country; his monthly visits to KemKarine and their two little boys do not permit him to fill in the child care gaps. KemKarine describes her anguish at needing to beg favors from friends: *"Yes, when I have to work during the weekend, like Saturday and Sunday when the Kita is closed, I find it at times very difficult. I have to start making calls [to find a babysitter] from Wednesday . . . , 'Please, I have to work on Saturday; I have to start [my] job at 8 o'clock. Can you please help me, can I bring my kids to your place?'"*

Mothers, particularly single mothers like KemKarine, cultivate connections with other Cameroonians to help them manage working conditions that are out of sync with public child care provision. Illustrating the interweaving of kin-based and community-based networks, these other Cameroonians include both relatives and friends. Familial terms of address indicate that, in the migrant context, nongenealogical relationships involving reciprocal exchange of child care can become like kin. *"So, at times my own Cameroonian sister, we do cooperate, we love ourselves, but if not, I wouldn't have been working for two years . . . If we don't cooperate, single mothers like us, we find it very difficult. There are times that Kita is also closed during holidays, [but] you have to work. So you look. We have to cooperate. You have to call friends and relatives."* The sisterhood of shared migrant experience, mutual need, and mutual aid may be particularly pronounced for single mothers in low-level employment, such as KemKarine. By forging affective circuits for their children's care, migrant mothers create pseudo kin connections through their children that aid mothers' financial survival.[8]

Preschool children help their mothers create informal social-support networks with a particular social and institutional geography. For mothers who are students—the majority of regular Cameroonian migrants[9]—the Kita overlaps with other settings of routine interaction. Like many other students, Bih and Barbara started their years in Berlin by residing in a student hostel. Students are likely to live near other students, giving them opportunities for spontaneous meetings, mutual observation, help-seeking, and the development of trust in the student hostel and its immediate neighborhood as well as at the Kita. Nonstudent migrant mothers are more dependent on the Kita to meet other mothers in a situation of daily interaction. For both sets of mothers, children serve as glue in what sociologist Mario Small terms "routine organizations" (Small 2009, 108, 115).

Bih and Barbara met each other at the Kita located next to their student hostel. They helped each other out—picking each other's kids up from day care and swapping babysitting to attend night classes and work at the grocery clerk jobs that kept them afloat as students. When Barbara gave birth, Bih was there to cook, clean, and support Barbara, her husband, and their older children. Bih became, echoing KemKarine's words, Barbara's *"Cameroonian sister."* Their mutual aid complemented the caregiving practices of those few genealogical kin who had migrated to Berlin and its immediate surroundings. Now, both women are pursuing their doctorates. The trust they built crossing paths in two routine organizations—the student residence and the child care center—enabled the two young mothers to meet their migration goals while raising families, for, as Barbara told me, *"All reproduction in the diaspora is a reproductive challenge."*

This trust is a crucial element of women's child-rearing strategies, as women seek out positive environments for their children. For KemKarine, the best care possible for her children means reliability when she has to work nights and weekends. Bih, in contrast, is more particular about her child's care environment. Only a few people, including Barbara, reach her standards in child care. Bih's energy in pursuing, as she put it, *"the best interest of her child"* was evident when she travelled to the United States to give birth under the tutelage of her internationally scattered relatives. *"Actually,"* says Bih, *"it matters a lot to me, the person whom I leave my child with. I have two people, [Barbara] and another friend. Even if someone offers to, I do not feel [like] keeping my child everywhere. I have people that I trust. When I don't know you well it will be difficult for me to leave my child. It is a child, you understand, it's not a [piece of] luggage."* Bih chooses caregivers who enforce her strict expectations regarding respect toward adults, settings that foster intellectual development, and situations where her child feels comfortable.

When Bih's child was an infant, Bih took some time to learn to trust the publicly subsidized Kita in her neighborhood.

Actually, the thing is, here we are lucky, here in Berlin, to have a very good system, when it comes to Kindergarten or Kita, with students. Because just directly behind our home there is a Kindergarten there that [serves children] . . . especially from students . . . So, actually, my baby got an admission there when she was two months old. But I never wanted to, because she was still very young, so

I was scared. So I [stayed] at home with her for two more months . . . But then I realized I could not do anything [neither work nor study], so I had to give her to the Kita when she was four months old . . . So I was paying to keep the space, but I stayed at home with her because I was scared.

Subsidies for students made the Kita very affordable for Bih and James, at a mere 54 € ($74) per month. Once James graduated and found a job in his field, the cost rose to 200 € ($275); this was a considerable strain on the young couple's budget, but many times less than what parents would pay for comparable care in the United States. Luckily for Bih and James, their daughter celebrated her third birthday soon after James began full-time work. This allowed them to take advantage of an important benefit. In Berlin, Kita attendance is free as of the child's third birthday.[10]

Without safe and affordable care, many Cameroonian migrants likely would place very young children under the care of relatives living in Cameroon. Such fostering patterns are common among West African migrants living in countries with less developed social services (such as the United States) (Coe 2013).[11] The ready availability of affordable child care in Berlin enables working mothers to keep their children with them, raising them in Germany. Daily interactions when dropping children off or picking children up from the Kita help mothers make connections to others. Ties thus built to other Cameroonians create networks of mutual aid, beginning with filling in gaps in off-hours child care provision, and contribute to building a diasporic community. Ties to other parents—of Asian, East European, Turkish, or ethnic German origin—and to majority German caregivers provide occasions for observation and discussion of parenting styles. Cameroonian women's participation in group parent-teacher meetings as well as in individual conferences is an important aspect of their social integration in the destination society. Not only mothers, but even more so their children, become integrated into German social and cultural norms through their attendance at Kita; parents view this ambivalently.

"I HAVE A GERMAN CHILD":
BETWEEN PRIDE AND EXASPERATION

In my conversations with women such as Bih, Barbara, and KemKarine, I recurrently heard variations on the statement, "I have a German child." In some instances, mothers referred to their children's German citizenship. In most cases, they described a set of preferences and behaviors that marked their children as culturally German. Most children preferred speaking German rather

than the English or French of their parents' home setting, and most played
with their siblings in German. At Kita, children learned to be relaxed about
generational boundaries, addressing adult caregivers by their first names, talking back and even questioning authority. Children developed new tastes in
food, preferring spaghetti dinners and ice cream to the sharply spiced Cameroonian *pepe soup*.

Parents observed their children's German socialization with a mixture of
pride, exasperation, and fear. Their little ones were somehow "making it" culturally in Berlin, gaining a cultural fluency that would ease their future life
course in Germany or elsewhere in Europe. But parents experienced their
children's food and consumer preferences as mildly alienating. More importantly, most parents were horrified at what they saw as German children's
serious lack of respect toward elders. Parents feared that lack of respect could
later translate into unruly behavior. Parents worried that their children might
later become unmotivated or unwilling to take advantage of the opportunities
available in Europe. Mothers projected into the future, concerned that their
children would feel foreign when visiting their Cameroonian homeland, and
as adults would feel uncomfortable spending time with aging parents who
might retire to Cameroon. Some migrant parents felt "caught" in Germany
by their children's needs, debating vigorously how long a child could remain
in Germany before he or she reached a point of no return, unable to adjust
to Cameroonian consumption patterns, or to forms of interaction with elders
(respect), with peers (sharing, playing), and with school authorities.

Between the mid-2000s when I first considered following Cameroonian
migrants to their European locales, and the rolling ethnography I have been
conducting since my 2010–11 fieldwork in Berlin, migrants' orientations toward their European destinations seem to have shifted. Earlier migrants came
temporarily, to get an education or make money, and later returned with enhanced status to Cameroon. Increasingly, newer migrants are establishing
themselves in Berlin—completing degrees, gaining employment, starting businesses, and founding a variety of associations addressing cultural, religious,
and development goals. Starting and raising Cameroonian families in Germany is an important aspect of a gradual shift toward more permanent settlement.[12] Most mothers I spoke with placed themselves somewhere between
the two poles of temporary migration and settlement. Many intended to return eventually, but had no definite plans as to when they might do so.[13] This
living in the subjunctive, in a world of maybe-could-should-would return
or stay, affected their child-rearing strategies and the type of belonging they
hoped to instill in their children.

KemKarine is one of the many mothers who have vague plans to return to Cameroon once her children have become grown and independent. In Cameroon, she says, she would feel "free," "relaxed," and "at home." But for KemKarine, Cameroon was also a site of political violence, from which she had fled. In the meantime, she is raising her children to get along as well as possible in Berlin, assuming that Germany is where they will stay. When I asked her about Cameroonian versus German child-rearing styles, KemKarine responded, "*I raise them in both, particularly in the German way, because they stay here. They just have to know [a] little about Cameroon, because I am the one going to settle back home. They are going to remain here. So they need to know much about their system.*" To KemKarine, language use was a key indicator of her sons' ability to be successful in what she termed "*the German system,*" as well as to communicate with her and her relatives. "*They speak German in kindergarten; they speak English in the house. Mostly English in the house. At times they want to speak German, but I don't want them to speak German in the house.*"

Raising children in a different language and culture from that of the child's peers and everyday environment is both cognitively and emotionally trying. KemKarine expresses her distress in terms of contrasting identities and her continuing responsibility toward her children's best interests.

> *This is really difficult because, first, my children are German and I am a Cameroonian. So at times, like when you have stress, I wish I could go back home. Then, in turn, when you look at your children, they are still very young and they are Germans. At times you even cry. But for me, I know that I am a Cameroonian. Because I am here [in Berlin], I want to raise my children, I want to give them the best. When they are big—twenty years, eighteen years—I [will] go back. That's why I keep in touch with my people at home.*

KemKarine gives her children "*the best*" by raising them "*in the German way*" and taking out life insurance policies to secure their future financial well-being. She combines this with familiarizing her sons with "the Cameroonian way" through phone calls and visits with kin in Cameroon. Realizing that she and her children do not share a common *primary* cultural allegiance tears at KemKarine's heart.

Other parents share KemKarine's distress. Jucal describes her baby as "*German by citizenship, Cameroonian by culture.*" Alain, Marthe's husband and the father of toddler Yvonne, strongly criticizes Cameroonian parents who do not "bother to tell their children about Africa." For him, gaining German citizenship is understandable as a pragmatic step to improve one's chances in the labor market; identification with one's culture and place of origin, however, is a moral imperative. Although Alain and Marthe's child was about to begin attending a local German-speaking Kita (rather than one of the few French-German bilingual child care centers), Alain was convinced that parents could achieve the moral imperative of crafting their children's belonging through language use in the home, ongoing connections to kin, and participation in community festivals.

Bih and her friend Barbara were more concerned with what their children were learning at Kita while they were becoming "German children." They worried about the formal curriculum—regarding cognitive development and school readiness—as well as the co-curriculum—what their children were learning about their place in German society as people of color. Bih and Barbara often expressed their astonishment, and even exasperation, at the preschool curriculum. "*Why,*" Bih asked, "*do they spend so much time at the Kita drawing pictures rather than learning letters and numbers?*" Barbara regaled us with stories of discrimination and perceived slights in her Kita, while Bih nodded vigorously in affirmation. Barbara had observed an African child being offered the last crumbs when others in the class got the first pick of holiday cookies. She complained that teachers encouraged her son to drum rather than fostering his verbal skills. Barbara and Bih interpreted the latter incident in terms of stereotypes about Africans being "only good for" sports and entertainment. Like many other mothers, Barbara and Bih worried that their children would internalize slights and stereotypes as normal, diminishing their self-confidence.

Narratives about conflicts at the Kita revealed that mothers' self-confidence was vulnerable to attack as well. Several of Barbara's children attended the same Kita, most of them doing quite well. But one daughter seemed to be learning aggressive behaviors in a particular playgroup. When Barbara discussed her concerns with the leader of the playgroup, the teacher retorted that Barbara was unable to give her daughter sufficient attention because her family was "so large." Barbara not only perceived that her competence as a mother was insulted. She also felt that her larger-than-average family had come to symbolize the "demographic threat" of high-fertility foreigners in low-fertility Germany (Castañeda 2008). Repeatedly, I observed that children became a vehicle for mothers to express their anguish about not-belonging. With the ferociousness of a protective mother, Barbara remarked, "*I may be a foreigner, but my children are not—why should they be excluded?*" This protectiveness carries the sting of mothers' own exclusion and the alienation they may feel from their own children, socialized in a foreign language and context.

KEEPING CHILDREN CAMEROONIAN

How, then, do mothers counteract their creeping sense of alienation from their German-socialized children? How do they keep their children Cameroonian in a German context? Keeping children Cameroonian requires much forethought in parenting. Because Cameroonian migrant mothers are still primarily responsible for child rearing, the bulk of this socially reproductive labor falls on mothers' shoulders. To instill Cameroonian mores and identification with Cameroonian roots, mothers employ daily strategies of discipline, bilingual parenting, naming, and acknowledging gifts from hometown associations. The exceptional situations of visits home, often requiring years of preparation, are high points in connecting children to Cameroonian tastes, sounds, and relatives.

Consider Bih, who aims to take the best from German opportunities and Cameroonian values to raise her child as a flexible but grounded cosmopolitan. Bih understands cultural adaptability as a tool to cope with the challenges of a transnationally mobile life. "*At times I try to take my child to some programs that are attended predominantly by foreigners or Germans too, so that she can integrate. We are in Germany . . . so I must introduce her so that she can be able to cope. She is living here, she is growing here. I am living here and I can't cope here if I don't know much about the people, too.*"

Bih (who later sent her daughter to an English-German bilingual international school) also appreciates the German school system. "*I always want my child to have the Cameroonian identity . . . As a mother you always want the best for your child. I want her to have the best values from Cameroon and the best values from here, too . . . The schools, the formal education here is more advanced than that in Cameroon—talking about books and everything, it's better.*"

Nonetheless, Bih sees clear limitations to a German upbringing and strong reasons to raise her child "in the Cameroonian way."

Bih's biggest concern is with comportment. She is shocked by German children's disrespectful behavior toward adults.

> *When we talk about the character of the children growing here, that is my personal opinion, I don't really like it because I find a lot of children here disrespectful . . . We have that kind of strict boundary that children are not having boyfriends when you are very young . . . It is almost like an unwritten law to stand up and let an elderly person sit. It's like you don't talk back to your parents when they are talking to you.*

Bih realizes that Cameroonian children absorb sassy behavior from their German peers and from the lax attitudes of day care providers.[14] Like other

Cameroonian mothers, Bih expects her child to switch behavioral codes from setting to setting. Bih describes (and I have observed) that Cameroonian mothers police each other's children's behavior, helping them to maintain an idea of boundaries that should not be crossed. "*She would never do things that she does with her friends with me or elderly people. [When] she is with [Barbara] she can never answer her back . . . She would never do that because I try to be very strict and she knows she is not right.*"

German-born Cameroonian children police each other's behavior as well. Bih relates a story about her and Barbara's daughters confronting other children at the Kita.

I was at day care two days ago and I had to pick up her and [Barbara's] daughter. And there was one German child there that was just shouting to the mother, 'Du blöde Mama!' [You stupid mama!] Then my child and [Barbara's] child were saying, 'Du darfst das nicht sagen. Es gibt keine blöde Mamas, es gibt nur blöde Kinder!' [You mustn't say that. There are no stupid mamas, only stupid kids!] [laughing] It was very funny. I was so shocked. I told them after that, 'Yes, es gibt auch keine blöde Kinder.' [Yes, there are also no stupid children.] But it's because they [Cameroonian children] have known that with parents there is a very strict boundary. You can say something when you play with your friends, but not to your mother . . . The [German] mother was just standing there and saying nothing. And that is what I really find amazing with the German culture. They say it is not good to be so strict with the child, but I believe to some certain level [it is].

Bih described her reaction to her daughter's hitting or throwing sand.

You hold [her hands] down and you very seriously talk to her. Not like "nein, man darf das nicht machen" ["no, you may not do that" (with a soft voice)], like the Germans do. . . . When it comes to respect I am very strict on her with that. Because I realize it is something else here. I interjected, "*Do you worry about her being more like German children?*" Bih responded, "*Yeah. I worry about that so much, ja so much and that's what I think makes me be a bit harder on her, because of those worries . . . I wouldn't be that very strict if I was in Cameroon because I knew she would grow up adopting to those values there. But I try to be a bit harder, because I know that she has only me to learn from. But in Cameroon she would have me and the society.*"

Bih regards respect toward elders as a Cameroonian trait and discipline as an Anglophone characteristic influenced by British colonial styles. In contrast, Tessy (the unemployed engineering graduate) views respect in ethnically specific terms, as a particularly Bamiléké characteristic, reflecting the unique minority status and politicized ethnicity of Bamiléké in Cameroon.

Nonetheless, Tessy and Bih outline as "Cameroonian" or "Bamiléké" a similar combination of childhood obedience toward elders and adults' shared responsibility in caring for children's moral education. Tessy describes her own upbringing in a Bamiléké milieu in urban Cameroon in the following terms: *"We had these, how do you say, guidelines, that said you have to do this in this way, do them so so so, and then you just have to simply do them without posing questions, because that's how it is with us Bamiléké."*

Tessy continues that respect is a recognizable Bamiléké characteristic that she is determined to transmit to her daughter and baby son to counter the influences of what she perceives as German permissiveness.

> *To be Bamiléké is for me merely respect . . . That means, I cannot insult someone, because we just can't do that, whether as a child, as a mother, or as a grandmother, for us such behavior is forbidden. And I try to teach this to my children, which means they should be friendly, show respect . . . And when a Bamiléké speaks, you feel it. Because there [with the Bamiléké] at least one will say "Good day, sir," and the other will say "Good day." Thus to be Bamiléké, already, that means respect, and whatever the case, you can see it.*

Tessy explains that Cameroonians, and especially Bamiléké, have mutual responsibility to teach children respect through discipline. She describes this as a value of "motherliness" that adult women must practice and children must learn to recognize.

> *Among us Bamiléké, being "motherly" means . . . all children are my children . . . When I meet a child from Cameroon, I don't need to know who your mama is, when you do something wrong I can . . . tell you exactly that that's not allowed, you can't do something like that, even though I don't know your mother. For me it doesn't matter—because it's a child, I am also a mother. This means, the mother of this child could also say something like that to my daughter. For me, for example, one doesn't say, "my mama," that's forbidden. One says "mama" . . . This is what I also try to teach my children, because I am a Bamiléké and this is how it is with us . . . That means, the mama is the mama of all children, it's the mama who cooks, it's all of that. Thus for me this is what it means to be Bamiléké.*

German early childhood education makes it difficult to transmit these Bamiléké values to children. Tessy shares Bih's concerns with teaching her children respect in an environment of laissez-faire, antiauthoritarian child-rearing practices. Both mothers realize that their children receive contradictory messages at home and at day care or school, *"because that which one tells the child at home, she comes home with something else from school. I mean the German mentality at school, and I don't mean to say that the German mentality is bad, but it doesn't fit with what we are familiar with.*" Tessy expects a lot of her five-year-old daughter—for example, that she speak three languages (French and German fluently, and some Fe'e Fe'e-Bamiléké). Tessy also expects her daughter to know when to apply a Cameroonian behavioral code and when to apply a German behavioral code. A common situation is that of knowing when to apply certain terms of address. When Tessy's little girl started at Kita, the other children made fun of her. "*Why do you say Madame Ines? It's just Ines.*" Even the teacher was bothered, not understanding that the child was applying a code of respect toward adults. "*Because in fact she knows that when you see an adult, you say, 'madame, madame' . . . because it's an adult, it's not someone of your own age, you need to give [them] respect.*" Sympathetic with her daughter's complaint that "*everyone will make fun of me,*" Tessy now encourages her daughter to switch codes according to the situation. Tessy also strives to give her daughter the vocabulary with which to respond to other children's taunts, comebacks that stress her own pride and self-confidence in her Cameroonian roots.

Tessy's examples reveal the huge forethought in parenting required to raise children into a situation of dual belonging and biculturalism in forms of social interaction. Tessy dreams of an Afrocentric school for her children.

> *If there were an African school, but there isn't one. Thus . . . she tries to dif-ferentiate between school and home, between the context of her friends and the context of her family, that's all. And with this effect [in mind] we try to see a little if every year perhaps we can send them [our children] to Cameroon, so that they have [experienced] at least this African mentality, or one could say Bamiléké or Cameroonian. And they would know to make the difference [between Cameroon and Germany], that's all.*

In the absence of a dreamed-for Afrocentric school, Tessy and others employ additional strategies for keeping their children Cameroonian. Both Barbara and Bih, for example, give their children "African" names (see also D'Alisera 1998). Barbara explained to me that her parents were influenced by colonial-era schooling and church teachings to give their children European-origin names derived from literary figures and Christian saints. In contrast, Barbara wanted her children "to know where they are from, every time they sign their name." Maria takes every opportunity possible to remind her children about the gifts they received as babies from relatives and from ceremonies held at her hometown association meeting. Reminders of gift-receiving helped her tie her children to a Cameroonian imagined community (Anderson 2006).

When reflecting on ways to produce or maintain their children's identifi-cation with Cameroon, Tessy, KemKarine, Solange, and Justine all described trips back to Cameroon. Solange, a student active in her Bamiléké home-town association, presented her new baby to her family during her semester break. KemKarine spent years preparing for her grand vacation home, saving up to pay expensive airfares and buy gifts to distribute. Shortly before her son started first grade in Berlin, Justine travelled to Cameroon and enrolled him in a Cameroonian preschool for two months. She wanted him to expe-rience not only family, but also the organization of daily life in a Cameroo-nian context. Upon their return to Berlin, Justine was concerned about the image of Africa that her child absorbed from television broadcasts focusing on wild animals: *"One day I was telling him that Cameroon is part of Africa. He told me, 'No, Cameroon is not part of Africa. Cameroon cannot be part of Africa because in Africa there are just animals there, and Cameroon is differ-ent. The people in Africa are very poor, they don't have anything, they cannot wear clothes, but Cameroon . . . .'"* In Cameroon he had observed that children wear freshly ironed school uniforms, that banks are air conditioned, and that tall buildings have elevators. During the visit to Cameroon, he had seen no large game, not even a small monkey. Justine contends that her son remains unconvinced that Cameroon is part of Africa. Despite her upset at public images of her continent, Justine is relieved that her son has developed an independent image of Cameroon.

Trips "home" are rare and punctuate ways that Cameroonian mothers con-nect their children to family members and hometowns in Cameroon. These visits offer intense experiences of the emotions, sights, tastes, and smells that serve as the sensuous underpinnings of belonging. They complement more sustained, everyday forms of child rearing through which mothers foster their children's emotional connections to Cameroon.

Cameroonian mothers recognize that their German-born children feel al-legiance to two—Cameroonian and German—geocultural points of identity. Mothers worry about the emotional challenges their children face manag-ing these simultaneous belongings. Mothers also worry about maintaining their children's identification with their Cameroonian roots in the face of the predominantly German social and institutional environment in which their children grow. Through phone calls with distantly located kin, playdates with Cameroonian friends, and special occasions featuring the exchange of gifts and food, mothers work to create and maintain their children's networks of relationships with other Cameroonian migrants. These affective circuits pro-vide opportunities for children to *feel* and *act* Cameroonian.

In sharing stories about child rearing (with me as well as with fellow mi-grants), Cameroonian mothers reveal that social connectedness is but one aspect supporting their children's growth into moral, successful adults. To develop their children's character—and to ensure that their children express their character through good Cameroonian behavior—mothers enforce strict rules regarding respect for intergenerational boundaries. Cultivating this respect is meant to lay the groundwork for self-discipline and resilience to hardship that mothers find essential for their children's later success in school and in life. Once their children enter school, Cameroonian mothers continue the strategies described by Bih and Tessy and reflect the experiences of Kem-Karine, Barbara, and others. They develop additional ways of keeping their children Cameroonian, as they and their children move through new developmental stages and interact with new institutions.

Thus far, I have focused on preschool children, because when I conducted the bulk of my fieldwork in 2010–11, most of my interlocutors' children were in that age range. As the Cameroonian population in Berlin ages and becomes more settled (Beloe n.d.), more and more children of Cameroonians enter school. The tensions mothers experience between socializing their children as Cameroonians and encouraging their adaptation to German society intensify as their children move through the local school system. Barbara reported her distress over the discrimination and stereotyping of young African-immigrant children in day care centers; mothers of schoolchildren are similarly concerned with exclusions their children may face. The next section addresses ways that mothers aim to protect their school-aged children from anticipated discrimination, by cultivating their children's human capital (skills and knowledge) and teaching them resilience through belonging.

Rearing Schoolchildren: Success and Belonging . . . to What?

Mothers want their children to be at the top of their class at school. Cameroonian mothers hope that academic excellence will buffer the hardships that their children will face as immigrants and as blacks at the bottom of an implicit racial hierarchy (Campt 2004; Oguntoye, Ayim/Opitz, and Schultz 2006; Partridge 2012). Mothers seek to give their children tools for academic success, including multilingualism, cognitive development, respect toward authorities, and discipline. Although the particular shape these traits take is relatively new, mothers nonetheless identify them as specifically "Cameroonian" or even as "Bamiléké." By constructing skills and comportment as identity markers, mothers believe they are simultaneously reproducing Cameroonian lifeways and fostering social mobility in a global context. In practice, mothers must constantly make compromises between their Cameroonian ideals and the demands of child rearing in Berlin. The following scene of a school-starting party illustrates such compromises in the context of a recently invented ritual.[15]

THE *EINSCHULUNGSPARTY* (SCHOOL-STARTING PARTY)

In contemporary German society, a child's entry into school is marked by rituals that link home life with school life. Beginning in the nineteenth century, German first-graders have brought *Schultüten or Zuckertüten* (literally "sugar bags"),[16] large cardboard cones filled with sweets, to the first day of school. Originally, godparents prepared Zuckertüten for their godchildren to sweeten their entry into the world of learning, a task gradually taken over by parents. Over time, Zuckertüten have become ever more elaborate and commercialized, decorated with the latest children's film motifs, and filled with school supplies and small toys as well as candy. Class status and even a family's political orientation are evident in the size and style of a child's Zuckertüte; some eco-friendly families create personalized, 100 percent organic Zuckertüten for their little ones. A more recently introduced ritual is the private Einschulungsparty, or school-starting party. Durand (2004) refers to the Einschulungsparty as one of several German rituals of individuation. Of varying size and elaboration, the Einschulungsparty is generally arranged by the child's parents and has the character of a special birthday party. The following vignette describes how one Cameroonian family turned this German invented tradition into a Cameroonian festival.[17]

Barbara wanted her daughter Happi to start school with enthusiasm. What better way to do so than to make her feel special? Barbara had heard about school-starting parties from other parents at the Kita and at an orientation session organized at her daughter's school. She convinced her husband Kelvin to set a weekend date, shortly before the start of the school year, to throw a party. Barbara, her friends, and her young daughter all referred to the event with its German name, die Einschulungsparty. Barbara's close Cameroonian friends Bih, Anne, and Justine devoted days helping her to prepare food for the big festival.

I arrived at Barbara and Kelvin's apartment on the designated late-August afternoon, a cool nip in the air hinting that autumn was just around the corner. Happi was nowhere to be seen, buried in a knot of children playing board games in one of the bedrooms. Instead, the living room was full of adults. In Cameroonian fashion, chairs lined all four walls, creating one large square rather than small clusters. Adult guests—some forty of them—conversed with their neighbors, milled around getting food, keeping toddlers entertained, and occasionally leaving to change a child's diaper. I could hear various groups

FIGURE 4.1. Happi's best friend poses with her Zuckertüte and two of her mother's friends outside the school building on her first day of school.
Credit: Elizabeth Beloe

of people recounting stories from everyday life, discussing local Berlin news items as well as Cameroonian politics. The din of conversation was punctuated by loud laughter from a group across the room that must have been regaling each other with hilarious tales. Most of the guests were black African, although neighbors of ethnic German and Latin American heritage had also joined in the festivities. The conversational buzz switched easily from English to German and back again.

Meanwhile Barbara and her women friends were busy replenishing the lavish buffet set up on the entryway table. Plantains, beans in tomato sauce, chopped bitterleaf with ground pumpkin seeds, and boiled fufu (porridge) made from packages of *Gries* (grits) created a colorful display. The tastes and smells of Grassfields cuisine reminded the guests of home. Tablecloths of printed Cameroonian fabric contributed to a décor flaunting Cameroonian identity.

Several hours into the celebration, Barbara clapped her hands for attention and brought out a large frosted sheet cake. Young children between the ages of four and seven streamed out of the bedroom to join their parents and younger, baby siblings. Happi stood with formal stiffness, and twitches of anticipation, to receive the first piece of cake. The arrival of the cake dissolved the earlier spatial boundary between adults and children. Several adults wished Happi well for the start of school. Six-year-old Happi brought me a piece of cake at my seat beside the bookshelf. She took the occasion to show off her school supplies—a pink schoolbag decorated with Princess Lilifee motifs, a matching pencil-holder, and a shoebox full of art supplies. I would learn later that Princess Lilifee—a Tinkerbell-like cartoon fairy—is a sought-after character whenever Cameroonian girls need to dress up in costume. Encouraged by my interest, Happi then brought out a stack of workbooks she had completed for school preparation, and proudly showed me how she could write her name, read aloud in German and in English, and do simple sums. Kittens were her favorite animals, and pink and purple her favorite colors.

The arrangement of chairs around the living room, the relative spatial segregation of adults' and children's activities, and the choice of foods all reminded me of parties I had attended in urban Cameroon—including children's birthday parties among the urban middle class. Although Happi was the girl of honor, the living room, kitchen, and hallway were all adult-oriented and adult-dominated. I was not certain if Cameroonian identity was being publicly performed primarily to create a sense of togetherness among the assembled guests, or to instill a sense of belonging in Happi at this crucial moment.

With the appearance of the frosted cake and Lilifee-decorated school supplies, the enactment of identity became a lesson in compromise. The German institution of the school-starting party became a melding of a Cameroonian party and a display of German consumer desires. It would be wrong to assume that these consumer products—marketed to young children and their parents—merely helped a Cameroonian child fit in with her German peers. Instead, this young child of Cameroonians had internalized German consumer desires as part of a larger package of becoming a "German child." Happi's seriousness, her ability to switch back and forth between German and Cameroonian behavioral codes, and her embeddedness in groups of Cameroonian and German youngsters marked this six-year-old's ambiguous, simultaneous, and multiple belonging. Happi was (and remains) both Cameroonian and German—and ready for school.

EARLY STARTS: CIRCULATING ADVICE, CULTIVATING ACHIEVEMENT

Recalling events such as the Einschulungsparty, Cameroonian parents expressed a certain sense of disconnection from their "German children," shaking their heads at their children's love of Princess Lilifee school supplies and sweet kittens.[18] Looming much larger than these superficial signs of a cultural gap between parents and children, though, was mothers' fear that their children might be excluded from avenues toward success. On the edges of interviews, Magni (my Cameroonian research assistant) and other mothers swapped information about Kitas, school readiness, waiting lists, and special bilingual and accelerated programs. Because Magni had lived in Berlin slightly longer than most interviewees, and had children who were already in school, my interlocutors were eager to learn from her.

Magni stressed the importance of school readiness, and her advice fell on fertile ground. Mothers like Barbara and Bih wanted their children to learn letters and numbers in day care. Barbara's daughter Happi was proud to show off her budding academic achievements, even before starting school; Happi's stack of workbooks demonstrates the care that Barbara had put into preparing Happi for school. Barbara's effort focused on fostering cognitive development, very much in line with the counsel Magni dispensed when chatting with mothers before and after our interviews.

Magni advised her fellow mothers to prepare their five- and six-year-olds for the mandated developmental exams that test for school readiness by teaching their children numbers, letters, colors, similarities and differences, and manipulation of puzzle shapes. Magni explained to me that Cameroonian parents, building upon their experiences in Cameroon, assumed that preschool prepared their children to enter school. Relatively new Cameroonian immigrants did not realize that educated, middle-class German parents supplemented the preschool curriculum with numerous enrichment activities. At the Kita, Cameroonian mothers were exposed to German parents' definition of preschool as a precious period of freedom and self-expression (Durand 2004). Observing German parents' efforts to "protect" their little ones from the constraints of school, it was hard for Cameroonian parents to imagine German parents making efforts to prepare their children to read, write, and count. Magni tried to set them straight, urging parents to teach concrete skills to their five-year-olds. Magni was worried that "foreign," and especially black, children would be judged differently and even funneled into special education programs if they did not excel academically from the beginning.

Magni also advised interviewees about optimizing school placement. Savvy mothers like Magni—professionals, university students who had been in the country for several years, and their friends—strategized by registering their children for early school admission (what Germans call being a *Kann-Kind*—a "can" child—rather than a *Muss-Kind*—a "must" child)[19] and hedging one's bets by applying for the child's placement in a variety of types of schools (public and private, German-language neighborhood schools, bilingual schools, and international schools). Doing so requires a good understanding of the German school system and of the landscape of schools throughout Berlin. Interviewees sought this information from Magni.

The mothers I met were suspicious of their neighborhood schools, worrying about their children's safety in what were often relatively impoverished neighborhoods. Many sought to place their children in bilingual schools. Such schools, they reasoned, would teach the children to read and write in the French or English of their Cameroonian relatives, and would later open up pathways to international opportunities beyond Germany. Barbara's daughter Happi entered a bilingual German-English school, where she participated in a variety of after-school enrichment activities from music to karate. In the years immediately following my fieldwork in Berlin, Bih kept me posted on her quest for the perfect school for her child. Should it be a bilingual school, like the publicly subsidized one that Happi attends? Should it be a school catering to Germans who seek bilingual enrichment for their children, or one with a more international orientation? Or should she take advantage of her daughter's American passport to get her into the John F. Kennedy American School for an English-language curriculum? Bih spent hours visiting schools, speaking with administrators, and observing classrooms and after-school programs.

Highly educated Cameroonian parents intensely cultivated their children's academic skills. Several—such as Barbara, Bih, and Tessy—had children who were identified by their teachers as academically gifted. This helped these women place their children in coveted bilingual schools. Some mothers with less formal education and fewer means, such as Lily, were still able to find bilingual schools, even if not the most prestigious ones. Lily's eldest child, at age nine, transferred subway lines (on her own) every day to attend a bilingual German-French school in the working-class neighborhood of Neukölln. Other mothers were less lucky, reflecting social inequalities among Cameroonian immigrants in Berlin.

So'nju was particularly frustrated in her search for the optimal school placement for her five-year-old son. When asked about her plans for her children's education, she stated that "*going back home would be best.*" So'nju had no concrete plans of return or of sending her child back to Cameroon to attend school under the watchful eyes of kin. Nonetheless, she expressed many of the same misgivings about host-country conditions for child rearing that are documented in research on migrant children returning to fostering arrangements in West Africa (Bledsoe and Sow 2011b; Coe 2013; Mazzucato and Schans 2011; Whitehouse 2012). *"For me, I don't see good education here. Just when I see the children in the* Straße *[street], I don't [want to] see my child grow up like that."* So'nju was worried about bad influences in her impoverished, working-class neighborhood, where she had developed very few relationships of trusting support. *"Just like now my child this year will be going to primary school. But we cannot find a good school for him. Everywhere we are going it is full, it is full. And now he even has to go by August [only four months after the interview], he is going to start primary school then."*

The schools in which So'nju was seeking admission were all bilingual or English- language schools, because *"English school is good, like for example, when the child is schooling in Cameroon and going to English school, then there will not be too much problem."* So'nju wanted to prepare her child for an eventual return to Cameroon, thinking that if her son already was schooled in English he would fit in more easily. She and her husband were slowly building a house in Bamenda, not far from her husband's kin. Whether they would permanently return to Cameroon was uncertain. More certain was that So'nju's class status—as an economically impoverished immigrant with a high school education—and her son's lack of school-readiness enrichment activities made him a less attractive candidate for selective bilingual schools than the children of graduate students like Barbara and Bih. So'nju shared these women's aspirations for children's schooling, but she lacked their ability to create optimal conditions for success.

Cameroonian mothers' social position affected their ability and their motivation to cultivate their children's academic readiness—a form of early-childhood human capital (Bourdieu 1983)—with sufficient intensity to give them a head start. These differences in turn affected mothers' ability to foster two types of belonging for their children. First, viewing academic success as a Bamiléké (Kamga 2013; Kamga and Tillard 2013), an Anglophone, or a Cameroonian characteristic means that intensive cultivation of children's academic skills helps Cameroonian children belong to a group distinct from other African or European migrants. Second, mothers hope that their children's academic success will help them gain acceptance within their children's German social milieu.

"WHERE DO YOU COME FROM?" TEACHING
RESILIENCE THROUGH BELONGING

Whether or not Cameroonian children are academically prepared to excel in school, their teachers and classmates sometimes make them feel as if they do not belong. Their skin color makes Cameroonian children conspicuously different from the majority of their classmates, who are mainly of European, Turkish, or Middle Eastern descent. Their dark skin tone prompts perhaps well-intended curiosity about "multicultural" (i.e., non-German) origins, but nonetheless unwelcome questions from children's classmates and in chance encounters in public settings. Mothers told me of their German-born, Berlin-raised children's confusion in deciding how to answer the perpetual "Where do you come from?" question. Their concerns were reflected most pointedly in a theatrical performance, "*Heimat—Bittersüsse Heimat*" (Home—Bittersweet Home), performed by the troupe Label Noir at the Ballhaus Naunystrasse theater in Berlin in April 2011. This play about the Black German experience opened with a young Afro-German woman's encounters while sitting on a park bench, in which apparently ethnic Germans ask intrusively, "Where are you from?" and are amazed at the young black woman speaking "such good German, when it's such a hard language."

The bitterness inherent in questions such as "where do you come from?" grows from the context of German racial politics, a theme too vast to address fully here.[20] "Where" might indicate an understanding of belonging rooted in place, represented in German painting and literature of the Romantic era (Saul 2009). But in Germany, both citizenship and dominant notions of belonging draw upon ethno-national notions of descent (Brubaker 1992, 114ff.). Germanness as being part of a bloodline was codified in Germany's first citizenship law in 1913, toward the end of the Wilhelmine imperial era (Eley and Palmowski 2008, 6). Scholars have debated continuities and discontinuities underlying criteria for German citizenship law (e.g., Brubaker 1992; Eley and Palmowski 2008; Sammartino 2008), its biopolitical undertones (Grosse 2008), and related anxieties regarding cosmopolitan difference (Mandel 2008). The cultural context of citizenship finds its expression in inchoate notions of belonging. Expressions such as "but you don't look German" translate ideas about bloodline into visual cues (Yue 2000, 178, 181). At at a podium discussion on "the racism trap" at the Workshop of Cultures that I attended in Berlin, speakers stated that German public discourse values *Unauffälligkeit* or inconspicuousness.[21] Taking jus sanguinis citizenship principles and generalized public discomfort with visual difference as the sole indicators of German racial politics risks recreating essentialized notions of German national character, indeed a distorted caricature. And yet, these indicators contextualize Cameroonian mothers' resentment when their German-born children face racially toned questions. Some mothers are well aware of Germany's troubled history; their sentiments are echoed in the painful recollections of women's everyday experience of blackness in Berlin gathered in *Plantation Memories* (Kilomba 2008) and *Deutschland Schwarz Weiss* (*Germany Black & White*) (Sow 2008), both given to me as a gift by one of my interlocutors.

Cameroonian mothers reported similar encounters that they and their children had experienced, as well as their struggles to articulate an appropriate rejoinder. The ever-thoughtful Tessy wished to give her children the vocabulary to respond when people ask them, "Where are you from?" In kindergarten, Tessy's daughter had answered that she was born in Berlin, to which her classmates countered, "But you are from Africa." Embedding her narrative of her daughter's experiences within her own story of immigration, Tessy remembered the sting of insults she herself had faced when she had recently arrived in Germany, and her feeling of helplessness at not being able to answer back in a new language.[22] She did not want her daughter to suffer in this way. Particularly concerned with her daughter's upcoming transition from kindergarten to school—which in the German system means a change from a nursery-school setting to a new school building—Tessy worked hard to instill her daughter with pride about her African roots and Bamiléké culture, believing such rootedness would make her resilient in the face of other children's racialized microaggressions. At the same time, Tessy coached her daughter how to respond firmly about her dual belonging—to the Berlin of her upbringing and her African roots.

"*I don't want her to insult anyone—no, [that's] far from my intention—but I want her to try [to respond] also because if she doesn't say anything in fact it's she who will suffer . . . Because when you don't respond, you go home angry.*"

Iris, the filmmaker introduced above, likewise equips her daughter to withstand slights by teaching her about her roots. Iris talks with her seven-year-old daughter about her grandfather's home in the Bamiléké fondom of Bangangté, as well as her own childhood in English-speaking Buea. Iris brings her daughter along to hometown association meetings and, occasionally, for visits to family in Cameroon. She responds frankly to her daughter's observations that "*African people are always too loud. They are always like quarreling. And . . . they are always laughing.*" Iris also views Nigerian movies with her daughter, feeds her spicy Cameroonian dishes, and teaches her to speak English, French, and Pidgin.

> When she was small she would ask me why is it that she is black. And I would tell her, "Yes, you are black because you are from Africa. Africa is a continent like this," and [I] take the map and show her . . . "It is not that [because] you are black you are not beautiful" . . . And sometimes if I see that she is, like, asking me some question that is a little bit painful and embarrassing, . . . like—what I can

say—racism . . . I will cover it up with religion. If she says, "Mama you know I was playing today; the other child said you should not play with her because she is brown." . . . I really feel the pain, you know . . . But she is still young for me to tell her. So I will just put it religiously. I will say, . . . "It is just children, I don't think they really believe in God, because then God said you should not hate this person."

Iris's child-rearing toolkit includes teaching about Africa and communicating a "black is beautiful" message. She supplements her resilience-through-belonging strategy by cushioning racial discrimination with religious explanation.

As is the case for many Cameroonian mothers and their German-born children, Iris recognizes the everyday negotiations her daughter makes between her Cameroonian roots and German identity.

She will say, "My mama is from Cameroon, I have an auntie from Nigeria." And the little children say, "and you?" She said, "I am Deutsch [German]." You know. For her, identity is Deutsch [German]. But I make her to know, "You were born in Deutschland [Germany]. Yes you are Deutsche [German]. But I am Cameroonian and Bamiléké Cameroonian, that is where my parents were born, that is my Opa [Grandpa] and everything." I tell her. So her identity, she has decided her own identity, her own community."

Iris simultaneously acknowledges her daughter's agency in forming an identity vis-à-vis her schoolmates, and her own responsibility as a mother to anchor her with "roots and culture." The roots Iris transmits range from the attitudes toward respect and discipline that we saw were also important to mothers of preschoolers, to the folkloric and the linguistic.

But what I . . . emphasize mostly is just her roots and culture . . . She used to be naughty sometimes and I always told her, in my culture it is like this . . . [It] helps me a lot if I can hand . . . this cultural heritage to my daughter. She dances, I teach her to dance my traditional dance . . . of Grassland . . . and make her to enjoy my traditional music. . . . I bring her traditional dresses, yes. . . . I really, like, take my time to teach her the Cameroon culture. She speaks Pidgin . . . That is street language, you know, it is the language that most [middle-class Cameroonian] parents don't want their children to learn . . . And often people ask me, "Why do you talk Pidgin to her?" I say, "So that she should not be lost."

Iris's final comment, "so that she should not be lost," is telling. Iris is less concerned with ensuring that her daughter can speak a lingua franca during visits to Cameroon, than that her grounding in Cameroonian culture enables her to face challenges with pliant vigor.

Parents understand that they are giving their children tools toward future resilience and that their children cannot *yet* stand up for themselves.
This is particularly so when dealing with authorities rather than with play-
ground bullies. In such situations, a mother's understanding the codes of an
educated, middle-class presentation of self is crucial to counter teachers' and
school administrators' stereotypes of uneducated and helpless Africans. Hélène's situation is a case in point.

I had known Hélène for decades, since my early fieldwork in Bangangté.
Then, she had been a school girl; now she had become a married mother of
three, with two master's degrees. When I learned that Hélène and her husband had made a life for themselves in the southern German technology belt,
I phoned to catch up, hearing about her family life and experiences with German schools. Hélène told me how important it was for her to talk to her sons'
teachers so that the children are not immediately categorized as those worthy
only of *Hauptschule* (the stigmatized, lowest level of several German forms
of secondary school).[23] One son, a fifth grader, had just entered Gymnasium,
the college-preparatory track. Hélène's younger son, bilingual in French and
German, had recently entered first grade—a year of multiple school-entry
assessments. When his teacher complained about the little boy's imperfect
German grammar, Hélène visited the school, frightened that her son would
be misdirected to a remedial track. "It makes all the difference," she told me,
"to go present oneself as a highly educated parent, speaking German fluently.
The teachers are surprised." When I asked what happens to the children of
less educated parents or those without the courage to speak up, Hélène answered, "Oh, Pamela, I've decided one has to have courage."

Cameroonian migrant parents of school-aged children readily share stories, with me and with each other, about the hardships of life that they have
endured and that they know their children will endure. They narrate ways
their young children's self-confidence and feeling of belonging in their German school milieu are undermined by teachers and schoolmates alike. They
describe experiencing everyday acts of aggression and thoughtlessness, based
on common stereotypes that mark African immigrants as poor, illegal, unruly, and ignorant. Through their stories, mothers paint a picture of life as
struggle. Mothers also develop a repertoire of strategies to help their children
face this struggle. Preparing their children for high academic achievement—
being better at school than one's classmates—is one strategy. Cultivating their
children's emotional identification with their Cameroonian origins is another.
Tessy, Iris, and others view the maintenance of Cameroonian belonging as a
basis that builds resilience in their children, who face the complicated—and
sad—situation of never being fully accepted as German.

Mothering Teens: Discipline and Emotion Work with an Accent

Cameroonian immigrant mothers place a high value on discipline in the home. Along with imparting a self-confident sense of cultural roots and connectedness, and emphasizing high academic achievement, enforcing discipline is these mothers' third strategy to prepare their children for the difficulties of life. In mothers' perception, discipline is closely related to both cultural belonging and academic achievement. Discipline enforces respect, which mothers name as a cultural attribute. And many Cameroonian mothers remarked that discipline is valuable because it helps their children to succeed in school. Mothers' intense cultivation of their children's academic skills, knowledge, and experience continues throughout children's school careers. Because migration weakens social capital—in the form of resources embedded in network ties (Lin 1999)—Cameroonian mothers view human capital (Becker 1993; Bourdieu 1983) as a necessary, protective force.

The Cameroonian mothers I met in Berlin perceive discipline in terms of respect for the authority of elders.[24] Through respect, mothers anticipate that their growing children will gradually learn self-discipline and the value of hard work; internalizing these values helps children to become independent, accomplished young adults.[25] We saw that training for respect and discipline begins with preschoolers and young schoolchildren. Barbara's children say "please" and "thank you" and greet adult guests with all due formality before scurrying off to play. Long after her friends have finished dinner, Bih's child stays at the table without complaint until all her food is eaten, following her mother's command not to "run while chewing." Mothers expect children's obedience, and usually receive it.

Mothers' expectations for obedience and increasing self-discipline pose particular challenges for parents of teens. Because Cameroonians in Germany tend to be young, most of their children are infants, preschoolers, and primary school children. For the few with adolescents born or raised in Berlin as of 2012, mothers' descriptions of the importance of discipline often did not match the realities of their teens' lives. Agathe, an engineer, promoted her thirteen-year-old's education in an accelerated school. She described training him to be independent with his schoolwork, and indeed he received very good marks in school. Like many Cameroonian mothers, Agathe fostered bilingualism by speaking only French in the home. Nonetheless, I observed that her son Thierry completed his homework in front of the TV and clearly preferred speaking German over French.

When it comes to enforcing discipline, mothers feel handicapped by prevailing German ideas about children's rights, enforced by authorities such as teachers and child protection services. In chapter six we will see that many mothers equated regulations against corporal punishment as strictures against all sorts of punishment, leaving them feeling helpless about how to discipline their children. They worried that children "knowing their rights" limited parents' ability to discipline their children. Parents feel little privacy about the child-rearing strategies they employ in their homes. They are concerned about classmates' and teachers' interest in their lives because they worry about "being reported," about facing possible sanctions for raising their children the best way they know how. They also worry about the long-term consequences on their children of mothers' inability to enforce discipline. Brianna, reflecting on her encounters with mothers of older children, stated, *"My problem is here that the way I was brought up, if I were not brought up like that I would not be what I am today. So I want to make sure my child grows up in that way, to be something tomorrow."*

Like Brianna, Gisèle frets about her teenage son's diminishing chances to "be something tomorrow," and her ability to connect with him emotionally to set him on a safe path. Jean-Claude was born in Cameroon before Gisèle's migration to Germany. Married to, and then divorced from, a German, Gisèle brought Jean-Claude to live with her in Berlin when he was ten. He had previously been cared for by her mother, attending a French-language primary school in Yaoundé. She describes working hard with her son to help him integrate and speak perfect German. When I conducted the bulk of my research in Berlin, Jean-Claude was fifteen. He called himself Hannes, hung out with friends, and barely squeaked by in school. Gisèle was terrified that Hannes would not be able to stay in Gymnasium. This would be bad enough for the German child of academically ambitious parents striving to attain or maintain their German middle-class status; for the black African child of a now-single immigrant mother, changing schools would be a portal into increasingly narrowed pathways.

Gisèle desperately wants a warm and caring relationship with her teenage son. She explained, "It's just the two of us, we only have each other." Gisèle knows that Hannes observes more companionate relations between his peers and their parents than what she feels comfortable giving her son. Although warm and caring, Cameroonian mothers are more familiar with emotional boundary-keeping between generations. When Hannes comes home late, or fails to greet houseguests properly, Gisèle cannot resist scolding him.

When I visited three years later, Gisèle was relieved that Hannes was still in school, progressing toward the end of Gymnasium. But she had a new worry—like many mothers, Gisèle observed that her teenage son was responding to the siren call of German teen culture, wishing to not be reminded of his otherness

(Belinga Belinga 2010). With deep pain in her eyes, Gisèle told me that Hannes did not want to be black. She had discovered skin-lightening creams in his room. As an activist in the Afro-German scene, Gisèle was shocked that her son did not embrace his blackness. *"I am an activist! How can he do something like this?"* Gisèle further recounted that Hannes was rude to her Cameroonian friends but extraordinarily polite to her white German acquaintances and colleagues. Knowledge that such rejection of immigrant identity was not uncommon among 1.5 and second-generation children (Levitt and Waters 2002; Portes and Rumbaut 2001; Rumbaut 2004) did not diminish Gisèle's emotional pain. She felt personally rejected. Hannes's rude behavior also shamed her vis-à-vis her local Cameroonian acquaintances. Compounding her hardship, Gisèle described how difficult it is to express her feelings in German, to connect with Hannes when they do not share a preferred "first" language. Even more than Agathe, Gisèle struggles to do emotion work with an accent.

The difficulties of connecting emotionally to one's teenage children across linguistic and cultural divides are compounded in small families, like Gisèle's, that are geographically distant from supportive kin. We have seen that mothers of infants experience the thinning of affective circuits—the decreasing intensity and limited types of emotion-laden flows of care among kin—as being "all alone." Mothers of teens also feel alone, without the child's aunts, uncles, and grandparents to help enforce discipline. If they were present, mothers speculate, their teens would also be thoroughly embedded in a Cameroonian cultural milieu. Respect for elders would be normalized, and a less ambiguous sense of belonging would allow their children to face hardship with confidence.

Support from extended kin for the emotional work of guiding adolescents is even more complicated when families' affective circuits have been disturbed. Both Gisèle and Agathe described tensions between themselves and their kin living in Cameroon. Agathe's husband had sent money for her brother to buy a car and start a taxi business in Douala, only to discover that the money had been improperly invested. Following similar disappointments, Gisèle had also decided to send remittances solely to her mother, ignoring her siblings' demands. Rather than reciprocal moral support, discord flowed between Cameroonian kin and this small migrant family in Berlin, making Gisèle's "accented" emotion work with her rebellious teen all the more trying.

SHORT CIRCUITS? THE RARITY OF CHILD CIRCULATION

Comparing Cameroonians to migrants from the new African diaspora to other countries in Europe, it is surprising that difficult teens like Hannes are not sent "back to Africa" (Bledsoe and Sow 2011b), and that transnational fostering arrangements are so rare among Cameroonians in Berlin (Coe 2013; Åkesson, Carling, and Drotbohm 2012; Kamga and Tillard 2013). For Gisèle and most other Cameroonian immigrant parents, interrupting the pursuit of migration goals and returning to Cameroon seems impossible. Unemployment is rampant for professionals, particularly those in the humanities, affording the academically trained scant economic prospects in Cameroon. In Gisèle's particular case, disagreements over remittances had strained her relationship with her siblings. Strained relationships diminished not only Gisèle's motivation to return "home" but also her ability to call on siblings to care for Hannes should he return alone. Why do Cameroonians seem so reluctant to engage in transnational fostering arrangements, when migrants from Ghana, Cape Verde, Senegal, and Mali readily circulate their children to families and schools in their countries of origin (Coe 2013; Drotbohm 2009; Mazzucato and Schans 2011; Whitehouse 2012)?

Cameroonian parents in Berlin tell each other didactic stories about German-raised children who returned to their biological families and were unable to adapt to life in Cameroon. Stories of school failure, depression, and juvenile delinquency serve as warnings about the neglect of cultural transmission. These told and retold narratives also provide emotional support for Cameroonians' growing orientation toward permanent settlement rather than temporary migration. In Berlin, Cameroonian children's language of education is German, rendering the adaptation of returnees all the more arduous; return migrants from French- and English-speaking countries do not face the same linguistic difficulties and often have enjoyed a similar school structure to that in Cameroon (Kamga 2013). Returning to the specific case of Gisèle and Hannes, nearly all Cameroonian parents would say that Hannes had passed the point of no return—that it would be unlikely for him to once again become Jean-Claude and to adjust to the authoritarian Cameroonian school system. Parents struggle emotionally to balance the dangers of growing up black and foreign in Germany with the pain of parental separation and the risk of difficult adaptation upon return to Cameroon. Gisèle told me she would never consider sending Hannes back to Cameroon to attend a boarding school—for his sake, and for hers.

Transnational fostering arrangements from Berlin to Cameroon are also rare for younger children, surprisingly so in comparison with other immigrant experiences (Coe et al. 2011). The pattern of child circulation, particularly of grandmother fostering, reveals social stratification among the Cameroonian immigrant population in Berlin. All of the mothers (and one father) I met who had a young child remaining in Cameroon had borne their children out of wedlock and before migrating to Germany. Among migrants from other African countries, children born in the destination country are often "posted" back to their parents' country of origin to be cared for by kin.[26] In contrast, fostered Cameroonian children remained in the country of their birth, usually falling under the care of a maternal grandmother after their mother's migration. In most cases regarding young children born premigration, Grandma's care was part of a wider pattern of delaying young women's entry into *social* (as opposed to biological) motherhood (Johnson-Hanks 2006). The young mothers' migration plans merely reinforced an arrangement that most likely would have endured even if the mother had remained in Cameroon.[27]

The emotionally laden flows of advice and goods between migrant mothers and the Cameroonian grandmothers who fostered their children were particularly strong. Most mothers who had migrated to Berlin seem content with their children's care, focusing instead on the new families they had formed in Germany. But when affective circuits were abruptly interrupted when the mother had to flee political persecution, separation is emotionally painful. Eveline, for example, dreams of overcoming this separation. "*Well yeah, my dream is that someday I would perhaps be reunited with my family, because I have a family, but we are separated, we are not really linked. My dream is that we could . . . that we could one day be reunited together and really live like a family. Because now that's not the case. My son, he is thousands of kilometers away from me, and then I am just here.*" Eveline perceives her situation to be unusual, a heartrending separation to endure when most other Cameroonian mothers in Berlin have the privilege of raising their own children. In the same sentence, Eveline reveals the contradictions of her situation when she emphasizes that she indeed *has a family*, and that she simultaneously is not really tied to her son.

Earlier, I suggested that the ready availability of publicly subsidized child care diminishes migrant mothers' need to send their German-born children to be raised in Cameroon. Notwithstanding migrant mothers' concerns about social control, the organization of German public services, including early childhood education, enables migrant mothers to keep their German-born children with them while they work and study. In fact, German public institutions are venues in which mothers meet other Cameroonian migrants, develop networks of mutual support, and share information regarding how to navigate the next steps in their children's schooling.

I know of only one case of a child, Olivia, returning to Cameroon to begin school under the care of her aunt and uncle. Olivia was born in Cameroon but raised in Germany from the time of her first birthday. Olivia's mother,

Placide, had joined her husband in Germany in 2000, at a time when few Cameroonian migrants were having children; thus, she did not have more experienced predecessors from whom she could seek advice. Placide lacked confidence in being able to navigate the German school system and feared that Olivia would thus be disadvantaged vis-à-vis ethnic German schoolchildren. She sought a fostering arrangement in which Olivia would attend a private school in a major Cameroonian city along with her paternal cousins.[28] Placide's husband's brother lived in economically comfortable circumstances and was thus able to provide for Olivia. On several occasions, Olivia's mother expressed that this was an enormous emotional sacrifice that she had undergone in her child's best interest. "Sometimes, Pamela," she told me, "you just have to hold your emotions aside, and do what's best for the child."

Through communication with teachers, phone calls, and visits home, Olivia's mother constantly monitored her child's situation, adjusting to different developmental stages. When Olivia was ready to begin middle school, her mother decided that the preteen would be best served under the influence of close maternal kin. The mother traveled from Berlin to place Olivia in a boarding school in the English-speaking region of Cameroon, in the same town as her own parents and sisters. Olivia's maternal grandmother is now recognized as the responsible foster parent. Grandma keeps track of Olivia's school progress, hosts her during school vacations, and keeps her migrant daughter informed about Olivia's well-being. Rare cases, like Olivia's, of transnational child circulation underscore the sense of purpose permeating Cameroonian migrants' child-rearing strategies regardless of their decisions regarding fostering.

Conclusion

This chapter opens with a quotation from Ariane juxtaposing a familial sense of belonging with the emotional burdens of everyday microaggressions suffered by migrants whose difference is visible as well as cultural. Ariane worries about what growing up in an environment of strange looks will mean for her young son's development. She proposes that grounding her son in a strong identification with his familial and cultural roots will give him the resilience he needs, as a black boy, to move through the German day-care and school system.

The child-rearing strategies presented here are Cameroonian mothers' best attempts to ground their German-born children via an emotional identification with Cameroon and a network of social ties to fellow Cameroonians. Mothers seek to forge belonging (depending on the situation, as black

African, Cameroonian, or Bamiléké) for their children while simultaneously giving them the best chances to adapt, be successful, and even be upwardly mobile in a German environment. In their depictions of migrant parenting, Cameroonian mothers defuse the tension between the social reproduction of a culture of origin and social mobility in a destination society by defining attributes that contribute to adaptation and success as specifically Cameroonian characteristics.

The general story of a tricky balancing act between cultural continuity and adaptation is similar in other accounts of immigrant parenting and immigrant childhoods. Distinctions from a wider pattern emerge from the relatively small scale of the Cameroonian immigrant population in Germany, its youth, its high level of education, its geographic dispersal, and its visibly racialized difference. An additional contrast to immigrant families in other colonial metropoles—such as Britain, France, and Portugal—is Germany's short and truncated colonial history, an inglorious history that ended in 1916. The uneasy relationship between diasporic identities and assimilation poses itself in other ways where higher concentrations of Cameroonians live in former colonial metropoles sharing the same language and bureaucratic organizational forms (Bouly de Lesdain 1999; Kamdem 2007).

The feeling-tone of the tension between fostering a Cameroonian diasporic identity and encouraging accommodation to a new society is captured in two oft-repeated phrases that summarize themes from this chapter. "I have a German child" expresses mothers' ambiguous feelings regarding their children's socialization. "Where do you come from?" is reported speech in which mothers poignantly acknowledge challenges that their children encounter every day. Mothers are proud of their children's adaptability to German orientations and habits; I suspect they are also a tad envious of their children's easy fluency in German language. In many ways, they want their children to "belong," to feel comfortable and at home, in Germany. Nonetheless, mothers do not aim to raise culturally German children. They prefer to raise flexible, adaptable, successful Cameroonian children in Germany.

From mothers' perspectives, their children are Cameroonian by birth, regardless of their legal citizenship in Cameroon or Germany. Keeping their children Cameroonian implies two understandings of Cameroonian belonging: a performative aspect and an interior, social-psychological aspect. Children *perform* Cameroonian belonging, for example, when they act on Cameroonian codes of respect toward elders. Children *feel* their Cameroonian belonging when they view themselves—as individuals and in relation to other people—as Cameroonian. Mothers indicate that acting Cameroonian and identifying as Cameroonian are mutually reinforcing. For most mothers, following Cameroonian standards of good behavior is evidence not only of their children's character, but also of their identity.

The child-rearing strategies that mothers employ to make and keep their children Cameroonian reflect mothers' dual concern with felt identity and performance. As such, they provide a window into Cameroonian migrants' ideas regarding culture and cultural transmission. Through phone calls to Grandma, visits "home" to Cameroon, and arranging playdates with the children of their Cameroonian babysitting-swapping friends, mothers create conditions that foster identification with Cameroon. Much of this identification occurs through interacting with other Cameroonians, especially with kin and with friends who are close-like-kin. Exchanges of child care, food, small gifts, and communication carry with them positive sentiments that tie children simultaneously to other Cameroonians and to identification with their Cameroonian roots.

Cameroonian mothers build affective circuits not only to promote belonging, but also to prepare their children for the hardships of life. Imparting a self-confident sense of cultural roots and connection ideally makes their children resilient. Discipline and respect for elders gives them tools for academic (and later financial) achievement. Embedding children in meaningful social networks both reinforces Cameroonian identity and provides social capital for future success. When they employ these child-rearing strategies, mothers define the qualities that will lead to a healthy balance of individual achievement and group solidarity as specifically Bamiléké, Anglophone-Grassfields, or Cameroonian cultural attributes. In practice, these strategies represent ideals that are difficult to realize fully. Mothers adapt their child-rearing strategies to the new cultural and institutional environment that they find in Berlin, as well as to the changing developmental stages of their children.

Child-rearing strategies are an important element of coping with being a migrant mother. When mothers establish ties *for* their children, they simultaneously create and strengthen their own ties to other adults *through* their children. Kinship-based affective circuits build upon core values and everyday practices regarding what it means to be either Bamiléké or an Anglophone Grassfielder. Exchanges flowing along these circuits include expressions of care and emotion, nostalgic goods that remind of home, high-tech gifts that evoke European opportunities, and money that helps kin to manage the challenges of everyday life. These exchanges undergird the reproduction of belonging to a cultural group through belonging to a family, no matter how geographically scattered that family may be.

In the next chapter, we will examine another type of affective circuit that also helps to manage reproductive insecurity and foster a more formalized ethnic belonging, based in migrant community organizations. We will see that these community organizations are venues in which an ethnic diasporic belonging is fostered, practiced, and brought under scrutiny. Through these organizations, childbearing provides mothers with an opportunity to forge or deepen extra-kinship ties and to lay claims on community support. Migrant community organizations provide an arena for child rearing, anchoring children not only in emotional allegiance but also in an organizational structure.

Civic Engagement

The child is the responsibility of the whole village or a whole society, so we as an association, we feel the responsibility when a child is there. And there are some social
benefits; we try to support them, the parents . . . [But] confiding [about reproductive
or family problems], no. We can exchange matters about school, daily activities, just sit
and think about some things in Africa.

LOLA

Bearing a child and rearing it to become a successful, moral, and culturally an-
chored person is a task not only for mothers and their transnationally stretched
families but also for migrant community associations. Cameroonian mothers
interact in diverse and sometimes contradictory ways with place-based associations in the course of birthing and raising children. Lola (a nurse, mother of
five, and resident in Germany for sixteen years) explains that migrant hometown associations provide formal benefits to the parents of a newborn, simultaneously granting material support and encouraging a spirit of mutual responsibility at important life-cycle moments. Lola's compatriot KemKarine
told me that "*because we are in a strange land* we need people, we need to be
together. *We Africans, we have a lot of stress, the stress here, the stress back home.
So we need people to be beside to*" (emphasis in original). Building upon a rich
tradition of place-based associations, Cameroonians are motivated by the difficult context of migrant life to organize into groups based on familiarity and
togetherness. In these groups, members seek moral, social, and emotional support. This intangible form of solidarity complements and reaches beyond the
formal benefits that accrue with vital events such as childbirth or hospitalization. Lola reminds us, however, that the conviviality of meeting others from
a shared home place is counterbalanced by an underlying caution and reluc-
tance to confide about reproductive challenges.

If, as Lola states, the child is the responsibility of the whole village or whole
society, where and how do its members come together and create islands of
home in a strange land? In this chapter I focus on mothers' and children's
involvement in hometown associations. Throughout West Africa and among
transnational African migrants, hometown associations are a ubiquitous way
that people engage in local civic life in a highly mobile world.[1] We saw earlier

that in Cameroon hometown associations provide the organizational basis of belonging for rural to urban Bamiléké and Anglophone-Grassfields migrants (Feldman-Savelsberg and Ndonko 2010). In Berlin, they remain important reference points for immigrant Cameroonian mothers, helping them to manage the challenges of reproduction and settlement in a new land.

Hometown associations are formally organized, publicly registered groups whose members share an affinity to a particular homeplace.[2] A homeplace may be a village, a town, or an administrative district. It is thus a location of variable size that has meaning as the site of lineage and ethnic origins, where relatives may continue to live, and where one may return to be buried (Cohen and Atieno Odhiambo 1992; Geschiere 2009; Jua 2005; Smith 2004). Because so many transnational Cameroonians grew up in provincial capitals and major cities, some may have only occasionally visited their homeplace, if at all. Nonetheless, their sense of belonging to a rural homeplace is fostered by numerous practices. Families tell stories about their land, their compound, and past events that occurred in the homeplace. Families also experience a long history in which social life and mutual support are organized around shared allegiance to the homeplace. Finally, the attributions of others reinforce identification with a homeplace.[3]

In Berlin, hometown associations meet at regularly scheduled times and places—for example, every third Sunday at a neighborhood community center. Meetings are social occasions that combine pleasure with obligation (Mercer, Page, and Evans 2008, 6). The pleasurable sociability and formal obligations of hometown association meetings are immediately relevant to the major topics of this book—the construction of belonging, the management of birth and illness, and the challenges of cultural reproduction among a mobile, diasporic population.

Hometown associations are one of several avenues through which Cameroonians come together in an organized way. Nonetheless, hometown associations stand out in the landscape of more or less formal community life; each migrant could imagine joining a hometown association (or two), whether or not they do. Other affiliations are formed according to characteristics less widely shared, such as religion, profession, or political party allegiance.[4] The idea of joining an association in Berlin comes easily to migrants, because hometown associations are a familiar and ubiquitous presence in the Cameroonian locales from whence they migrate. Iris recounts that in Cameroon she *saw it like a must. Everybody that I used to know belongs to an association. The moment you get to an age of independence, you belong to an association.* Mrs. Black explains further that her family tradition of association leadership in Cameroon made participation in associational life in Berlin more attractive. "*Because in*

Cameroon we do that. Like my mother, she is like a president of [B Association] in Cameroon. And I have been from childhood, I have seen all these organizations and you know it is really okay. It is really nice."

Mothers forge extrafamilial connections when they maintain formal membership in associations, participate in monthly meetings, make claims on association resources in times of need, and in turn—as association representatives— deliver gifts and aid to others. They fulfill obligations of belonging through children when they "make fresh people" (newborns)[5] and throw an elaborate party honoring the new baby as a community member ("Born House" in Pidgin and *Jeunes Mères* in Cameroonian French). By bringing their growing children to meetings as well as to Born Houses, wakes, and organized cultural events, mothers seek to reproduce a sense of belonging to a community for their children. Mothers thus create extrafamilial ties for their children, give them a taste of Cameroonian-style sociality, and provide children with opportunities to perform Cameroonian manners.

Through a series of scenes from associational life, this chapter explores the creation and reproduction of diasporic community belonging for Cameroonian mothers and their children. A monthly meeting reveals a formal setting in which members attempt to build community after migration, creatively reformulating notions of "home" and "belonging."[6] An association's year-end party reveals parallel currents of conviviality and caution, as mothers commune with each other but avoid revealing family or health problems. A Born House celebration illustrates how migrant mothers maintain life-cultivating practices associated with "home" (Nyamnjoh and Rowlands 2013) while simultaneously accessing association resources. Observations on a "children's table" at a monthly association meeting and a grandfather's wake illustrate moments of children's involvement in the cultural activities of their parents' hometown associations. Taken together, these scenes reveal the interweaving of formal membership and emotional allegiance. Through their association participation and accompanying exchanges, mothers build up extrafamilial connections that support familial life-cycle obligations and embed belonging in an organizational structure.

Ngó Ndé, Ngó Ndé—Ngó Koni: An Association Meeting

On a cold and gray January afternoon, I slipped into the meeting room of a community center in Lichtenberg, a neighborhood in former East Berlin. There a meeting of the hometown association that I had been attending for four months had just gotten underway. For purposes of anonymity, we will call this Association D. Every month approximately thirty people, with roots in the administrative division (*préfecture*) D in the Bamiléké highlands of

Cameroon, met to discuss association business and to eat, laugh, and argue together. The previous October, Marthe's husband Alain had introduced me to the group, to which I felt particular affinity because I had conducted my previous research in this same Cameroonian homeplace. My husband, our children, and I shared common praise-names (in local language called *ndap*)—such as Tangun, So'nju, and Ntecheun—with members of the hometown association in Berlin. At association meetings, formal business and most informal conversation were conducted in Cameroonian-inflected French; members used local language only for an antiphonal greeting to announce their arrival or begin an important speech.

"*Ngó Ndé, Ngó Ndé [land of Ndé]*," I said in quiet greeting, shy to disturb the meeting underway.

"*Ngó Koni [land of love]*" responded the few people I passed on my way to an open chair next to Marthe's friend.[7] Recognizing me from the association's year-end party a month before, she nodded and smiled before turning back to a white paper easel where the "*Ordre du Jour*" was posted: attendance, summary of the previous meeting, autocritique of the year-end party, treasurer's report. The board officers sat gathered around a formica table placed next to the easel—four men and one woman—some with paper and pencil in hand, one with a laptop. Folding chairs were pushed all along the sides of the room, creating the largest possible oblong seating arrangement.

When I arrived, only nine men and two women in addition to the board were present; others trickled in over the next hour until about eighteen men, five women, and several babies filled the chairs. Some husbands and wives sat together, others did not. One side of the circle was occupied by a group of men who—with their unbuttoned collars, prominent sport shoes, and constant jostling—appeared slightly younger and less reserved than the married couples and students sitting closer to the windows. In Cameroon they may have been labeled "*chauds gars*"[8]—literally "hot guys"—who were still struggling for adult success. In Berlin they struggled all the more to obtain or retain legal residency, the basis of financial and personal—including reproductive—security. Just behind the circle, on a broad bench near the door, a half dozen children between five and eight years old huddled together around a Game Boy and shared coloring books, whispering together in German, periodically breaking out in giggles.

I remembered from a previous meeting that a discussion about attendance had devolved into a lively argument about association membership and into a metapalaver regarding giving people a chance to talk. Then, the woman sitting next to me had whispered, "*toujours en désordre*" (always disorderly). The assistant secretary, the only female office-holder, had given an impassioned appeal for using reasoned discourse and etiquette to set an example for the children and youth who were present. Arriving at the January meeting, I was curious how the gender dynamics would play out, and what informal commentary would accompany the association's formal proceedings.

Indeed, the gendered division of labor became the major theme of the autocritique of the year-end party. During this segment of the meeting, the association president and secretary gathered comments about refreshments, the organization of presents for the children, and the spirit of voluntarism. Women make up barely one-third of this association's membership, and they expressed feeling overburdened from cooking for the party as well as preparing food for the buffet that ended each monthly meeting. A few men proposed changes in the rotation of the reception committee, while two women begged for "real" as opposed to symbolic help. Their outspokenness at this meeting regarding unequal gendered responsibilities for the nourishment and social aspects of meetings and get-togethers contrasted with interviewees' descriptions of women's roles in association discussions. Previously Fanny had said of the women in her association: "*Most of them are shy, most of them are reserved not because they want to. Maybe their husbands or their boyfriends don't want them to speak out or they make them to believe that their place is not to talk in the middle of the people. Because sometimes some of them have ideas but they just say it from the background.*"

I noticed this "saying it from the background" during the election of officers at a later association meeting. The election was held with great concern for transparency; a committee of two women and one man explained the procedures—who has the right to vote, who is running for which post, and how much time the candidates had to present themselves. One woman on the election committee waved a stopwatch, repeating "*Two minutes, two minutes!*" Her gesture prompted a remark from the woman sitting next to me, "*The women are dangerous!*" When a female candidate for *Chargé Culturel* (Cultural Affairs Officer) began her speech by addressing her male opponent, the audience burst into laughter and another woman called out, "*She's attacking!*" With great merriment the relatively few women regularly attending association meetings presented themselves as tough enforcers of rule-abiding behavior, lending weight to their complaints about the unequal division of labor at association events. Although the women of Association D grumble about the burden, their work organizing year-end parties, providing refreshments for meetings, and even bringing people to order yields recognition, enhancing the emotional depth of their belonging.

Regardless of how women *feel* about their diasporic community allegiance, the rights, recognition, and obligations of belonging are formalized as association membership. Hometown associations are formal organizations with constitutions, elected officers, and membership fees. Members have rights to benefits in cases of births, major illnesses, or deaths in the family. Members participate in decision making regarding the association's activities in Berlin as well as its contributions to development projects in the homeplace. Reaching beyond one's personal day-to-day struggles by contributing to a common goal mitigates the feeling of being all alone, instead reinforcing a sense of belonging to a group. But because hometown associations are formal organizations, formal membership—according to criteria such as payment of membership fees and timely attendance at meetings—rather than common descent or personal sympathies determines who "belongs" to the association. This became evident when the January meeting of Association D turned to the treasurer's report.

The treasurer explained that the association's coffers were getting too low to cover the constitutionally guaranteed benefits for cases of illness, births, and deaths. In the past year, these hardship cases had occurred more frequently than anticipated. One member of the board began naming individuals who had not paid their "insurance" fee, calling them up to complete their payments publicly. Another board member began a conversation regarding the official start time of meetings and the need to introduce fines for late arrival, because there were "weddings, births, and illnesses in the community to take care of."

"*Ngó Ndé—Ngó Koni!*" A man from the group of *chauds gars* stood up, using the antiphonal greeting to introduce his explanation that he would like to join the association but did not have enough money to pay the insurance fee. A second man took the floor, protesting apparent misunderstanding about his payments, waving a stack of receipts, and asking two others to vouch for him. Discussions continued, deliberating over the wisdom of an additional annual fee to replenish the association's coffer for hardship cases, and how best to save for children's presents for the next year-end party. Veering away from financial discussions but continuing along the line of association membership and belonging, one person debated if another attendee was still a member and had the right to distribute messages through the association's e-mail list.

It took some effort for the assistant secretary—who had calmed a palaver at an earlier meeting—to steer the group to the next point on the agenda, collecting ideas for projects to aid development in the homeplace. To get the ball rolling, she suggested that the association buy balls and jerseys for the local soccer team. By that time, however, attendees were getting tired and hungry. Women stage-whispered to their friends and husbands that it was time to get the kids home and to bed, as the next day was a school day. One by one, people started getting up, putting on coats, or going to the kitchenette to fetch paper plates with boiled ripe plantains, greens, and chicken. Children rejoined their parents, and groups of friends pulled chairs together into small circles. In quiet conversation, they reminisced about schooldays in Cameroon and exchanged stories about making it through daily life in Berlin. Over the next half-hour, small groups left together for the tram.

As this hometown association meeting demonstrates, participants foster—and scrutinize—formal (institutional), performative, and emotional aspects of belonging. The association regulates belonging by setting formal criteria for membership, thus excluding some people who feel emotionally connected to the same homeplace. To be a member, a migrant must have grown up in or be descended from a lineage with origins in and allegiance to one of the villages, towns, or fondoms of D Division. A member must also pay dues, contribute to various accounts within the association, and attend meetings with sufficient regularity.

The boundaries of belonging—in the form of association membership—are maintained through formal accounting, but not everyone can meet the criteria.[9] At the meeting described above, one man begged for an exception because of his inability to pay. Money is just one hindrance to maintaining association membership. Several of my interlocutors spoke of their difficulty, as mothers with primary responsibility for young children, of finding time to attend meetings regularly. Sophie, a thirty-year-old student in a master's degree program, has one young child and is hoping to conceive more soon. She explains, "Ja, *I belong to two [associations], but at times they have a monthly meeting I cannot make it to all the sessions . . . If—there are times—I have time I will do that, but if there are months that I can't, I won't.*" Women working on weekends as nurses, home health aides, or hotel chambermaids have further difficulty attending regularly, and may even drop their memberships. Lola observed how the issue of time, and thus involvement in hometown associations, is linked to a mother's life-course: "*How do I put it? Some of them they now have grown-up children and have enough time or a little bit of time that they can offer to do something for Grassland.*"

Community belonging through membership in hometown associations does not extend to all Cameroonian immigrants.[10] Sophie and Lola's statements show that this form of belonging excludes the most vulnerable—those lacking the means to pay dues, and those whose type of work and family obligations leave them little time for regular participation. The latter are mostly women. The gendered division of wage labor most often places women in service-sector jobs with irregular and/or weekend hours. Moreover, the gendered division of household labor still gives Cameroonian women major responsibility for child care and food preparation. The effect of the gendered division of labor on time available for civic engagement is reflected in the low proportion of women (less than one-third) among Association D's members. My interlocutors described that women are almost always a numerical minority in the mixed-gender hometown associations of Bamiléké and Anglophone Grassfields peoples in Berlin (see also Beloe n.d.). Finally, additional types of vulnerability may diminish a woman's sense of ease in a crowd. So'nju first attended a meeting of Association D when she was living without legal papers; her boyfriend, who was then married to a German woman, had instructed her to stay inside and mistrust the advice of fellow migrants. Thus, So'nju felt nervous, uncomfortable, and unwelcome at an association meeting and never returned. Likewise Rose—a young woman whose failed marriage, upon which her visa depended, temporarily catapulted her into illegality—stated that she avoided most fellow Cameroonians, and particularly hometown associations. Rose still suffers from the emotional trauma of being without papers; she prefers to avoid situations where she may feel judged or become the subject of gossip.

Conversely, belonging-as-membership in hometown associations may also select out the most settled (and most prosperous) among Cameroonian immigrants. Here, my interlocutors give me a mixed picture, for both women and men. On the way to my first encounter with Association D, Marthe's husband Alain explained that the association was founded by students in 1998, and that students as well as asylum seekers searching for contacts continue to make up the majority of members. He explained that while some professionals remain involved in the association, others get busy and start having other priorities. Alain mentioned that he is getting increasingly involved in a group that raises money for the Université des Montagnes, a private health sciences university that opened in the Bamiléké town of Bangangté in 2000. Other examples include Dr. T., a political consultant with roots in Bangangté whom I met while attending a panel discussion on the social integration of African migrants in Germany; he founded a large pan-African religious and social-service organization. Ntecheun, a physician who had lived in Berlin for two decades and had recently opened her own private practice, said of hometown associations, "*It's never been my thing.*" She prefers direct engagement in projects such as the establishment of a palace museum in her kingdom of origin. Agathe, an engineer, explained that nonprofessional women seek both company and the material benefits of the association, while as a secure professional she had no need for those material benefits. Instead, Agathe experienced association membership as a drain on her scarcest resource—time.

Iris, the filmmaker, eloquently assesses the differences between professionals who no longer belong to associations and other Cameroonian migrants who continue to seek connections in associational life.

But now when they come to Germany, why is [it that] some of the people don't belong to the association? Because they . . . think they are self-sufficient . . . They come to Europe, they are economically satisfied, they have health insurance, if they are sick, they go the hospital, they pay the hospital bills. They don't need this association. They don't need to feel so [much] belong[ing] . . . When you come to Europe, your mentality changes. You start accepting that death is death. If I die, if nobody was there for me, I can be burned and my ashes can be thrown somewhere and I am gone and gone. So why should I go and hook myself in an association? Okay, if I am working I want to celebrate my child's birthday and I am capable of doing that alone without collecting some little-little contributions from the association.

In describing reasons that self-sufficient professionals who have settled in Germany may avoid Cameroonian associational life, Iris points out the importance of the benefits of membership for others—the feeling of belonging, repatriation of a body or financial support to attend a funeral in Cameroon, and contributions toward life-cycle events. Iris goes on to explain:

First the mentality in Africa or in Cameroon is that when you belong to an association, when you have . . . financial problems, you can go to this association, borrow money from the coffer. When you have money, people will come and dance, will come and be with you and in the midst of this, there are people from this association. If you die . . . your corpse cannot be left on the street, they will bury you. So that is why most people in Cameroon see these associations as something that is very, very important . . . if you die, . . . they will even give some rest of the money to your family and your children to send them to school.

Indeed, the benefits and rights of formal membership encourage participation while they recursively foster emotions of belonging. Having one's voice heard through public deliberation at meetings and the association's online forum, and voting for association officers is a mode of performing belonging. Likewise, claiming gifts reaffirms that one is among one's people, that one is cared for and that one belongs. The performance of belonging through the exchange of opinions, claims, and goods generates attachment and loyalty while creating a new affective circuit.

Just as association membership is regulated through a system of accountability, belonging through claims-making is limited by rules that circumscribe what counts as a legitimate claim. Association members confirm hospitalizations, often visiting the sick before delivering the association's cash contribution. They verify births and weddings before delivering gifts. And they narrow the range of kinship relations for whom members may claim funeral benefits.

The most valued forms of aid from hometown associations relate to death. Both Bamiléké and their English-speaking Grassfields cousins retain a strong moral obligation to return the dead both physically and spiritually to the land of the ancestors. When a Cameroonian migrant dies in Germany, the association helps arrange and finance the return of the body to Cameroon. Likewise, associations support their members following the loss of a parent in Cameroon. They attend and make cash contributions to wakes held in Berlin and help finance the bereaved's voyage to Cameroon to attend the funeral. Anticipating such benefits motivates migrants to join associations. Sandra Star tells us: "*When I just came to Germany, something happened. I remember, one Cameroonian died. I decided that . . . this guy died, I said, 'No, it is not good to be alone.' When you are somewhere, look for where your people are. Because if something should happen tomorrow, you are sick somewhere and nobody knows where you are, or you're dying somewhere, this is not really good. Go to your people! Sometimes there is a problem, they will help you out.*"

In Bamiléké tradition, children are obliged to be present at a biological parent's funeral. To accommodate migrants, relatives preserve bodies in morgues—sometimes over weeks and months. Increasingly over the past decade, burial and death celebrations—grand ceremonies presenting the heir to the public, usually held a year after death—are combined in one event to facilitate the participation of globally scattered family members (Flavien Ndonko, pers. comm. 2014). Indeed, throughout the Grassfields region, delayed burial combined with elaborate death celebrations have become demonstrations of migrant success (Jindra 2011; Nyamnjoh and Rowlands 2013). They not only mobilize material and emotive resources of the hometown association (Page 2007), but also become part of larger dramas combining the demonstration of privilege and the politics of belonging (Geschiere 2005; Jua 2005).

Among Cameroonian migrants in Berlin, hometown associations regulate which kinds of relationships count as valid parent-child ties for claiming funeral benefits. In their concern to limit expenses and avoid the abuse of claims, hometown associations redefine kinship boundaries. Benefits are paid only to allow attendance at a biological parent's funeral. Because child fostering is common within Cameroon, a migrant may have been raised by another relative or foster parent and feel greater emotional closeness to the foster parent than to his or her biological parent. For the association in Berlin, such relationships are difficult to confirm. In addition, because any single person may have multiple foster parents from different stages of his or her life course, claims for attending foster parents' funerals risk multiplying out of control. Alain described how he was unable to attend the funeral of his mother's brother, who had raised him and upon whose death he felt "pain in his heart"; but he received support from his association to attend his biological father's death celebration. Association accountability practices thus contribute to redefining family according to biological descent and toward a nuclear family model.

Using a routine association meeting as a springboard, I have emphasized how the organizational rules of hometown associations shape who becomes or remains a member, and what that membership entails in terms of the obligations and benefits of belonging. The monthly meeting of Association D also reveals performative aspects of belonging, in the ways that members interact with each other. In effect, participants "perform belonging" through their use of an antiphonal greeting in the local language, Medumba, conversing in Cameroonian-inflected French, and participating in meeting oratory. By contributing to mutual aid funds and to association-sponsored development projects, members show themselves and others that they are part of the moral economy of this group. Finally, informal streams of interaction such as commenting on procedures, serving food, and even pulling someone else's toddler up on one's lap all contribute to the conviviality of associational life. Building upon formal rights and duties and the public performance of belonging, the pleasure of spending time together fosters emotional attachment to the homeplace and to one's fellow migrants. This conviviality, and its limitations in producing trust, was particularly evident in the association's year-end party.

SERVING GRANDMOTHER'S RECIPE: CONVIVIALITY AND FLEETING TRUST AT A YEAR-END PARTY

I waited in nervous anticipation for Alain and Marthe to accompany me to Association D's year-end party. Rather than slogging through the snowy streets and taking the usual tram to the association's meeting place, we were travelling together by car. The day before, my research assistant Magni had described what to expect: "*People usually go to the end-of-year party to relax, eat and dance. I know about four such parties this weekend.*" Members prepare for the event with both material outlay and the time and effort involved in nurturing bodies and souls through exchanges of cooked food and the personal acknowledgement of small gifts. At an earlier meeting, Association D's members had discussed contributions to buy holiday presents for members' children. Alain explained that parents also buy presents for their own children but give them to the association officers, who then pass them out as if they came from the association. This helps children build a positive relationship to a cultural group that reaches beyond immediate kinship ties. I climbed into Marthe and Alain's car, prepared with a wrapped stuffed animal that I anticipated would become part of a collection of children's gifts.

FIGURE 5.1. An Afro Shop, or African grocery selling produce, foodstuffs, cosmetics, hair products, and medicinal items that are familiar from African homeplaces. Afro Shops serve as informal meeting places where migrant mothers exchange observations and advice about getting along as an African in Berlin.
Credit: Pamela Feldman-Savelsberg

Marthe had arrived in Berlin only one year previously, joining Alain just before giving birth to their daughter Yvonne. During the ride to the event, Marthe straightened Yvonne's fancy bonnet, wiped her drooling mouth gently, and told me that she was looking forward to seeing her friend Solange, a member of Association D, at the party. While Marthe had not visited the association before, she had earlier befriended Solange when they had met shopping for taro and ripe plantains at the local Afro Shop. They often pushed their babies in strollers, chatting together on sunny days. Solange's son, Elias, was just a month younger than baby Yvonne.

Once we arrived at the event, this way of building closer acquaintance-ships through socializing outside the context of association meetings became evident in how people chose to sit during the party. For a moment, Marthe stood by the door, holding her breath and scanning the room; then she ex-haled, tugged my hand and—negotiating an obstacle course of chairs, bags, and winter coats—made her way to Solange. I sat with the two women and their not-quite-toddlers in a small cluster of chairs. The room looked as if it may have first been set up for a meeting, with chairs pushed to the edges of the room. But instead of neat rows along the walls, the perimeter of the room was full of small groups of chairs drawn together, with coats, hats, and presents stuffed behind them. Walking by these groups, I heard the hum of casual conversation ebb and flow. I overheard that a new Afro Shop had opened in one neighborhood. Someone told of an unpleasant encounter with a lab instructor at the technical university, while those in another group conversed about an upcoming trip to Cameroon. People greeted and chatted in French, making brief references to the occasional ways in which their lives overlapped outside the association's monthly meetings. Where there was less common experience, people could always comment on soccer clubs and on the display of food set up on tables in the center of the room.

Holding baby Yvonne on my lap, I leaned in to participate in Marthe and Solange's conversation. In low tones, Marthe filled Solange in on the latest developments in a month-long saga of Yvonne's feeding problems. Since early November, Yvonne had been refusing solid food. Marthe told us about her consultation with the pediatrician, who assured her that Yvonne is healthy and developing properly. "This happens sometimes with babies and then resolves itself," the pediatrician had pronounced; "after a short time the babies start eating again." Despite Yvonne's chubby cheeks and alert behavior, Marthe remained worried. She told us about consulting with some relatives in Cameroon whose child had similarly refused food for a few weeks. But Yvonne had continued her refusal of solid food longer than her Cameroonian cousin. Solange clicked her tongue, empathizing with Marthe's concern.

Two other mothers joined our little group. Their warm smiles of greeting were accompanied by handshakes formal enough to indicate that these were once-a-month acquaintances—women known only through their common affiliation with the hometown association. Almost in midsentence, Marthe changed the subject. She and Solange both straightened up, tugged at Yvonne's knitted sweater, and told the newcomers about the tips they had just exchanged about finding high-quality but inexpensive children's clothing. Solange told us that she wanted her son Elias to be well dressed when she and her husband traveled next week to present the baby to their families in the large port city of Douala. Would she bring the baby *au village*, to Bangangté, to see the red earth and blue-green hills of his ancestors? No, Solange replied, she rarely travels *au village*. Both her grandparents are long since deceased, and her grandmother's sister, who was like a grandmother to her, has also died. Rather than living "back home," Solange's parents have been well established in Douala for decades. Thus, there is no one to visit in the countryside. But the *koki* she cooked for the year-end party potluck, a bright yellow steamed pudding made of black-eyed peas and palm oil, is her grandmother's recipe. "Ahh!" came a chorus of appreciation from the nodding, smiling faces. Marthe nodded along brightly, no trace of her earlier worried expression.

Within a few minutes, the definition of the setting had shifted from backstage confiding to front-stage chattiness—before moving on to an invocation of ancestral ties. In adapting their presentation of self to a new audience (Goffman 1959), Marthe and Solange revealed that the year-end party—and diasporic associational life in general—was a setting marked simultaneously by conviviality and caution. We are reminded of Lola's description of communication patterns at hometown association gatherings: "*No, confiding [about reproductive or family problems], no. We can exchange matters about school, daily activities, just sit and think about some things in Africa.*" Formal interactions at monthly meetings, in which conversations about membership dues and duties sometimes lead to arguments, demand no revelation of personal problems other than the shared shortage of funds. Informal interjections commenting on the gender relations of formal proceedings are characterized by public posturing and banter rather than what may be confessional. In contrast, the less formal setting of the year-end party creates a treacherous mixture of intimacy and distance.

Clearly, participants were enjoying themselves at this party. Neither open conflicts nor grandstanding interrupted the buzz of simultaneous conversations. Toddlers and young children flitted from group to group, taking breaks from chasing each other to grab a hug or spend a moment on a parent's lap. A brief interruption of speeches did not dampen the general good cheer. The president stood and called "*Ngó Ndé, Ngó Ndé*" several times until he had the group's attention. First he and then another man gave brief speeches in French about mutual support and responsibility, their message emphasized by calls of "*c'est ça!*" and applause from the audience. A third man delivered a speech in Medɨmba, the language of Bangangté, receiving polite attention. I was not sure if all the adults could understand him, and I asked Solange about the children. "*No, the children do not understand Medɨmba. After all, they were born here!*" Once the speeches were over, people returned to their conversations or refilled their plates with food.

Sharing food and drink contributed to the feeling of togetherness. Participants had made great efforts to find and prepare dishes reminiscent of the homeplace: Solange's koki, another's *egusi pudding* (made of ground pumpkin seeds), a platter heaped with boiled ripe plantains, a large stew of bitterleaf greens and beef. In their interpretation of the role of nurturing in Cameroonian migrants' associational life in Cape Town, South Africa, Nyamnjoh and Rowlands (2013) suggest that providing and consuming food and drink together is a moral act of "good eating" that nourishes and unifies (*njɨ* in Bangangte, *dzie* in Mankon).[11] Ritual occasions of commensality, organized by migrant associations, "reiterate migrants' sense of belonging and self-consciousness . . . [and] also depict them as people firmly attached to their culture" (2013, 145).

By preparing her grandmother's recipe, Solange evoked memories of childhood visits "home" to the village and kept alive an intergenerational tie that by now linked this young migrant mother to an ancestor. Sharing koki with her fellow association members nurtured them in this connection through the lineage to common cultural roots. The koki tasted and felt authentic. Eating grandma's recipe together became a mutual demonstration of belonging. Because Cameroonian migrants' experiences in Berlin rarely reaffirm their sense of self, this mutual performance of belonging was all the more precious. Nyamnjoh and Rowlands describe this as an "'escape' by withdrawing the conditions of life to within the 'home,'" domesticating and privatizing "the cultivation of life as everyday practice . . . within settings [such as associational meetings] that are treated in some sense as 'home'" (2013, 141).

But hometown associations in Berlin are not really "home," nor do they create sustained face-to-face communities, despite everyday reference to "the Cameroonian community." While common affiliation through the hometown association may initiate new connections or deepen existing relationships among Cameroonian migrant mothers, most members meet infrequently, if at all, outside of monthly meetings.[12] As Marthe's husband Alain explained, "*The fact of meeting in an association, from the same hometown, does not mean that the members really have personal ties with each other.*" Strained by constant reminders of their foreignness, my interlocutors yearned for and savored the familiarity found in the shared food and conversation of hometown association events. And yet, because contact is relatively infrequent, familiarity in these settings does not breed trust and intimacy to confide about aspects of private lives such as childbearing and illness.[13] Henri, a journalist and president of another Bamiléké hometown association, contrasts trust with the experience not of home, but an *island* of home. "*People go to their meetings to have an island of home, to be comfortable and laugh with others. But trust is a different matter. We rarely talk about our private lives at meetings.*" At the year-end party described above, Marthe confided about an aspect of her private life—her infant's feeding problems—sotto voce, leaning heads together in a small group of three. When two less familiar acquaintances joined our tiny circle, Marthe and Solange collaborated in quickly switching the subject to neutral ground.

The cautious communion of associational life limits mothers' ability to mobilize their fellow migrants for advice, moral support, and even material or practical help in the case of a reproductive health crisis. These care-giving activities draw people together into ad hoc, case-specific "therapy management groups," central to the social dynamics of health and illness, particularly in African societies (Janzen 1978, 1987). For Maria Mar, whose love story appeared above, hometown association meetings are arenas where prudence must be exercised but also occasions to observe people who, over time, can give friendly support when facing a vital event or health crisis. Suffering from doubts surrounding the loss of her first pregnancy through a therapeutic abortion, Maria selected female friends from among her hometown association and her small *njangi* (a rotating savings and credit association) to seek referrals to a new obstetrician. The advice of these friends, and particularly her new physician and the hospital midwife, gave Maria the knowledge and confidence to get through three more pregnancies and one bout of postpartum depression.

Why, though, do most women avoid revealing private matters among association members and other contacts through place-based organizations? For one, the size of the Cameroonian population in Berlin affects both the composition of and interactions among association members. Berlin hometown associations draw together people with origins in an entire division (equivalent to a large county) in Cameroon, contrasting with hometown associations in Cameroonian cities like Yaoundé, which draw together members from the same village or neighborhood. Because most transnational migrants hail from urban centers, they may have never lived in their division of origin, or known each other before migration to Germany. Added to that is the geographic dispersal of Cameroonians throughout Berlin (see figure 1.3), making it difficult to maintain routinized, daily contact with fellow association members. In contrast to hometown associations in Cameroonian cities with large Bamiléké diasporas, such as Yaoundé and Douala, Berlin cannot support sex-segregated associations; this adds a layer of guardedness to men's and women's public interactions, since each feels observed by the opposite sex. Thus, demographic features of the diasporic population mean that associations give people affiliations of acquaintanceship rather than intimate communities of trust. Building upon Evans-Pritchard's analysis of structural distance in Zande witchcraft accusations (1976), one can explain that association members are close enough to be relevant in one's life, but not close enough to confide in.

Current and remembered vulnerabilities combine to develop a self-perceived Bamiléké trait of "prudence" in revealing private matters. In Cameroon, children are trained to avoid practicing hearsay and to reveal only minimal information about family life to others. Fear of witchcraft and historical experiences of repression by the French colonial administration and by Cameroonian secret police encourage this collective, learned caution (Feldman-Savelsberg, Ndonko, and Yang 2005). Ntecheun described to me how her mother and an elderly friend, visiting in Berlin, embodied these memories,

crouching in their chairs and whispering when they recalled frightening inci-
dents from their childhood during the guerrilla war fought between the UPC
(Union des Populations Camerounaises) and French forces during the late
1950s. Likewise, a male participant in Association D explained his *méfiance*
(mistrust) toward my role as a foreign researcher, declaring, "*After all, we are
the Black Jews,*" playing simultaneously on Cameroonian stereotypes and the
symbolic weight of Jewish victimhood in history-saturated Berlin.[14]

Ariane later related his comment to the vulnerabilities that members felt
regarding their immigration status.

> *Because, you know, here there have already frequently been cases that no one
> knew how to explain. Sometimes a Cameroonian who . . . is perhaps at a party
> or visiting a friend or even just at home, and suddenly the police come, there is
> a simple control, and then they arrest and take the person and repatriate them.
> This is a way to say that there are . . . events that frequently happen where one
> can't say where they come from. That's why there is this mistrust.*

Immigrants know that the circumstances of life make it all too easy to travel
back and forth across the invisible boundary between legal and illegal residence. Changes in marital status, child custody, matriculation into or out of a
school or university, or a delayed renewal of a visa can have profound effects
on one's ability to build a life or maintain a family. An unspoken norm pre-
vents migrants from describing such vulnerabilities to relatives back home in
Cameroon (Alpes 2011).

When one is uncertain about how information about one's private life will
be used and transmitted—particularly by those close enough to spread gossip
among friends of friends and thus to be relevant—shared place-based identification is not enough to establish the trust to confide in members or mobilize
them in cases of medical need. Ironically, shared place-based identification
is sometimes a basis of mistrust, due to fear of transnational gossip circuits
and their simultaneous effect on connections to kin back home as well as on
ties among other migrants in Berlin. As with Latin American migrants in Berlin (Huschke 2013) and Malagasy migrants in southern France (Cole 2014, 281,
283), highly valued companionship can easily turn into sabotage.[15] Even when
such occasions are rare, knowing they are possible encourages caution, or "*prudence,*" as Cameroonians often told me.

Cameroonian migrants' hesitancy to reveal personal information occurs
in place-based religious communities as well as in hometown associations.
Congregants at a Cameroonian Pentecostal church I visited sought communion with one another, but talk of God superseded and even deflected from

confiding about and seeking support in the face of reproductive challenges. Along with her husband, Lily, the mother of three whom we encountered above, founded a church-based rotating credit association of fellow Bamiléké who are also Pentecostal Christians. The action of common prayer and "sharing the word of God" affords Lily a sense of communion with her fellow association members. Nonetheless, it is a cautious communion from which Lily would never think of seeking help for reproductive or medical issues. Word about one's private business spreads quickly and uncontrollably within the Cameroonian community, as Lily told me: "*Especially when in Europe, it's difficult to hide. Let's take an example: If you see a Cameroonian somewhere, naturally someone knows your history, what it is that you do. Whether you do good or bad, people know about it . . . especially if you attend certain groups. Naturally, and then the people who are there, one says they are just there to gather information [for gossip].*"

Mobilizing a social network to seek support when facing a pregnancy, birth, or any sort of family problem requires a woman to engage in self-revelation, and thus to risk vulnerability. For migrants, the affective dimension of trusting someone with confidential information about oneself is accompanied (and often heightened by) potential legal and reputational consequences. Rose was traumatized by her period of undocumented residency following the breakup of her marriage, as well as by her tarnished reputation vis-à-vis her parents and former in-laws in Cameroon. When I asked about association membership and casual contacts with fellow Cameroonians, Rose claimed that she "doesn't know anybody" in the Cameroonian or Bamiléké community, and "doesn't want to." Instead, she relied on counseling through *German* community and church-based initiatives providing social and medical support to undocumented migrants and women in distress. Rose explained that she sought out these initiatives based on their professionalism, and also because their independence of place-based identification provided her with more privacy.

Place-based hometown and religious associations provide regulated support for particular, prescribed life-cycle events (birth, marriage) and crises (hospitalization, death). For other challenges, such as struggles with infertility, an abortion, or chronic illness, some women turn to new forms of sociality. For example, in self-help groups (such as the organization for people affected by HIV/AIDS for which I volunteered), women develop new discourses about the need to put one's troubles into words and to share them in a group of fellow-sufferers. Léonie, an African-born social worker, told me that most African migrant women seek out self-help groups founded by migrants who are *not* from the same country of origin (see also Nzimegne-Gölz 2002,

21–22). Another social worker, Frau Ehrlich, who works at a family-planning center in a heavily migrant neighborhood, speculated why this may be. She explained that her Cameroonian clients

> *are so self-controlled, and therefore there's also this mistrust with one another. Perhaps they are afraid that the family in Cameroon will learn [for example] that they are not really studying here. What are they doing here [the family might ask]? Nah, there's just such a big [gossip] network there, I presume . . . When they are here for a particular purpose and their parents are naturally waiting on them . . . "Oh, God, am I fulfilling their expectations? I've made all this effort to get to Europe and I'm supposed to become something." And the fear of failure . . . Cameroonians are the academics [students, the educated] here, you see.*

Despite the many reasons for caution within a network close enough to be able to spread gossip but too distant to confide in, migrants overcome their mistrust and continue to seek out conviviality within their diasporic community. In addition to year-end parties, hometown associations contribute in various ways to special occasions that bring community members together. These special moments of conviviality often center around the regeneration of life and of life-ways, ranging from birth, to childhood socialization, to managing death and mourning.

"Shake Your Shoulders with Us": A Born House Celebration

Born House, the celebration of the birth of a child, provides an occasion to practice ways of living together and foster mutual well-being. Hometown associations provide an audience for Born House festivals, contribute speeches, blessings, and dances, and present the parents and child with a substantial gift. They allow mothers to access community resources, and provide children the opportunity to enjoy themselves within their parents' diasporic community setting.

Knowing of my interest in the social management of reproductive events, Magni offered to bring me along to a Born House celebration organized by a couple from her hometown association to honor the birth of their baby daughter. The family waited until they had gathered enough funds to stage the celebration, in the end combining it with the child's first birthday party. The association participated in the event in an official fashion—sending a delegation of past and current officers, providing speeches and blessings, presenting a large wrapped gift and a cash donation, and performing traditional dances to the drumming of two members. Magni herself was to dance, and

I was eager to observe. On our way to the event, I could see the patterned Cameroonian fabric of the long wrap-around skirt, or wrapper, that would serve as her costume peeking out of her shoulder bag.

At 9 p.m., a gust of November wind pushed us through the door of the rented hall. The entryway pulsated with sounds, smells, and sights. Recorded music mixed with excited sounds of greeting, "*How [are you]?*" "*Long time!*" Newcomers removed their winter wraps to reveal brightly colored suits and dresses, mostly in European style. A few women changed their footware from boots or flats into stiletto heels. A long set of tables on the left, decked with food, and a well-stocked bar on the right formed a corridor through which arrivals squeezed to enter the large, open space of the hall. A silver dance-hall mirror ball sent reflected flashes of light across the dance floor. About twenty children, ranging in age from approximately fourteen months to ten years, danced to the music of Cameroonian bands such as Petit Pays et les Sans-Visas and X-Maleya, Nigerian musicians such as Flavour-Shake and the R&B duo P-Square, and ubiquitously popular Congolese music. These little ones were dressed to the Ts like small adults in suits and ties, or oversized flouncy party dresses. The children had been in the hall since 5 p.m., enjoying a child-oriented birthday party as a prelude to the adults' Born House festivities. Princess, in whose honor the festivities were held, seemed to be enjoying her first birthday, bouncing up and down in place to "dance" before throwing herself in the arms of one of the older little girls. A few parents milled around the dance floor, occasionally scooping up an overtired toddler who needed a break from dancing.

Most adults were young, in their twenties or early thirties. They sat at a series of smaller tables set up to the right of the bar area, facing the dance floor, moving about from time to time to chat with people at other tables. Looking around, greeting and being greeted, Magni and I noted overlapping connections among the attendees of the Born House party. Because the event was co-sponsored by Magni's hometown association, we were not surprised to see the past and current male presidents of the association and their wives. A bit later, Magni's cousin—the association's vice-president and drummer of its dance group—arrived from his job at a major local hospital. But not all present were members of Magni's association or hailed from her home village. We chatted a bit with Barbara, whom we knew as Bih's close friend and a keen observer of subtly racialized messages at the Kita. I recognized three members from the ethnically mixed Cameroonian Pentecostal church that I had attended with Lily. And Magni was familiar with the Congolese hired band that had previously performed at similar events.

Magni, Barbara, Shelly (the wife of the association's past president) and I struggled to converse above the music. Nibbling on the shrimp chips and chickpea-sized cookies of fried dough set out on each table, we compared Born House celebrations held in Berlin with those put on in the English-speaking regions of Cameroon as well as among the French-speaking Bamiléké. In Cameroon, Shelly explained, a Born House celebration is generally held at the mother's house. The mother invites relatives, friends, and other well-wishers to see and hold her new child. The event is often staged shortly after the baby has reached its second month. At this point both baby and mother are no longer considered vulnerable to the risks of crowds.[16]

I reminisced that in the Bamiléké tradition, the child's umbilical cord is buried under a plantain tree just after birth. When presenting the child to the public, the gathering of women called *Jeunes Mères* eats a dish made of plantains harvested from this tree. "Oh yes," Barbara remarked, Anglophone Cameroonians do this, too, calling the dish "born house plantains" (Nyamnjoh and Rowlands 2013, 142; Angu n.d.). Prepared with bitterleaf and lots of bright red palm oil, the dish is full of symbols linking the child to the land of its ancestors (through the plantains grown in soil fertilized by the baby's own umbilicus) and to the mother's experience of birth (through the association of red palm oil with the blood of childbirth, and through traditional midwives' use of palm oil to lubricate the birth canal). "The old grandmothers know these things," I was told, "but we just strain to remember bits and pieces. We eat these things, and know they mean 'Born House,' but we don't know all the details or background."

Indeed, several of my interlocutors, including those at our little table that night, often look up details about Cameroonian ritual life on blogs posted by other Cameroonians. One blogger described a Born House she had just attended in her town in Anglophone Cameroon:

> The baby is first passed around for everyone to place a hand as a sign of blessing, and to have a close look at the baby. Then salt and oil is passed around for everyone to have a taste while wishing love, peace, and prosperity to the baby's family. Thereafter, there will be singing and dancing in jubilation of the child's life, in thanksgiving for the child's parents and in hope for an outstanding future. The well-prepared pot of plantain is then shared to everyone present, every single person present must [have a] taste of the food as a sign of a prosperous life for the baby. Most of the talking is done by elderly women of the family with experience in childbirth (Ndzelen n.d.).

As described above, passing a newborn around to be held and even bathed by well-wishers is an early method to socialize a child into community belonging.

Salt and oil are essential elements of cooking, ingredients that the husband must contribute to the wife to allow the household to grow.

The elderly women present at a Born House in Cameroon often include the baby's grandmother. Observed by Nyamnjoh and Rowlands, the visiting grandmother played a central role in nurturing practices at a Born House event held among Cameroonian migrants to Cape Town, South Africa. The Born House was scheduled to coincide with a grandmother's visit to see her new grandbaby. Holding the child, the grandmother gave a speech reminding the baby (and all present) that she would take his umbilical cord home, to be buried and kept with the ancestors. She called "on the ancestors to watch over him" and performed " 'fogho djwi-zo' on the child," pouring her breath, and through it that of the family and the ancestors, on the child as part of a libation (2013, 143). In her speech, the grandmother "welcomes the child into the world of the living and calls on him to stay and not go back to the world of the ancestors . . . As confirmation, the child is given a drop of liquid from the food prepared . . . to reassure him that he is among kin and kith who care about his well-being" (Nyamnjoh and Rowlands 2013, 143).

In Berlin, the challenges of obtaining visas and the costs of intercontinental travel make it nearly impossible for grandmothers to travel from Cameroon to attend Born House events. Likewise, because the migrant population is so young, there are no "elderly women" in Berlin who could pour their breath on the child or explain the symbolism of shared foods and practices. Attendees at the Born House that November evening in Berlin spoke about the foods and rituals of Born House with an air of nostalgia, like people trying to remember beyond the first line the lyrics of a song or the melody of a prayer heard long ago. Some practices were retained without explicit understanding of their meanings, while others were dropped and new ones added, as we will see below.

Migrants' apartments are too small, and their neighbors are too concerned with noise, to allow for an exuberant celebration in an intimate, family setting. Instead, Born House ceremonies are elaborate civic events drawing together diverse community members in a semipublic space. Parents organize the event, expending enormous resources in time and money to rent and decorate a hall, buy food and arrange help in preparing it, print and distribute invitations, staff the bar, rent or borrow sound equipment, and hire a band. In the same way that mothers felt all alone with the stresses of pregnancy and caring for a newborn, parents preparing a Born House event have no locally available or extensive network of supportive kin that they could mobilize. Thus, not all parents manage to put on a Born House celebration, or to arrange one for each of their children. For those who are able, the complexity of the task means that

Born House is often delayed until the child's first birthday, giving the parents time to save and plan. This is exactly what Princess's parents had done, combining her Born House and first birthday party.

The birthday-girl's parents were helped by their hometown association. I learned about hometown associations' roles in staging Born House celebrations from several interlocutors, including Lola. *"[We get involved] in my association in times of sorrow, in times of happiness, for example, birth of a child. The child is the responsibility of the whole village or a whole society, so we as an association, we feel the responsibility when a child is there and there are some social benefits we try to support them, the parents. Born House is like the presentation of the child to the society or the association."*

Informally, Princess's parents recruited helpers—fellow cooks, decorators, and bartenders—from among the association's membership. Past and present hometown association officers provided speeches honoring the new child, encouraging mother and father in the task of good parenting, and extolling the virtues of community belonging. The association's small dance troupe performed, enlivening the party and giving the event an air of authenticity. Finally, the association's constitution set the parameters for its formal contribution, in cash and kind, to the celebration. How did this interaction between family and association involvement play out over the course of the evening?

When we arrived at 9 p.m., some women from the association and friends of the mother were still adding to the display of food on the long tables near the bar. In addition to dishes of Born House plantains, *achu* (prepared from cocoyams), and *eru* (a forest vegetable), they brought platters of chicken wings, roasted meat on skewers, and attractively arranged salads with shredded lettuce, carrots, tomato wedges, and sliced boiled eggs. One platter held fried rice. A few bowls held flavored potato chips and oriental shrimp chips. Another dish held homemade fried donut balls, known in Cameroon as *beignets* or *gâteaux*. The mixture of African dishes and European party food attested to the hybridity of the event. Adaptations to the availability of ingredients, the larger and more public scale of the event, and a diasporic party culture were evident even on these long and narrow tables. A large sheet cake, iced and decorated, added to the event's birthday-party tone.

Bit by bit, couples and groups of women sitting at the small tables got up to fill their plates from the generous spread of food. Around 11 p.m., Magni's cousin arrived, famished, from work. He received a mixture of sympathetic looks and teasing jibes at the amount of food he took, and how quickly he ate it. Half an hour later two women arrived, balancing a large wrapped box between them. Nearly one square meter in volume, the box contained the association's present to the parents and new child. Barbara whispered into my ear that laundry soap, or even a car seat, were common presents. Magni added that parents can choose their present, being aware that the monetary size of the gift is set in the association's by-laws. The association then purchases the item, giving the parents an envelope with any remaining cash. On this night it took some time for a third designated association member to arrive with the cash gift, breathless from rushing through the early winter air. Only then could the dancing and official handing over of gifts occur.

The association president motioned to a young woman dressed coquett-ishly in a short turquoise dress and stiletto heels, the Master of Ceremonies for the evening. Reaching for a large microphone and struggling with occa-sional feedback from the sound system, the MC welcomed all who had come to this joyous occasion, celebrating the wondrous birth and first birthday of little Princess. She nodded to the mother and father standing next to her, and to baby Princess, who by then was snuggling on her dad's arm, visibly tired. Unexpectedly, the MC asked Magni for a prayer to bless the assembly. The adults all bent their heads, murmuring "Amen!" at the end of the short bless-ing. The MC announced the band of musicians from the Congo, exchanging a bit of bilingual French-English banter with them, thanking them for "animat-ing" the occasion. She announced a few speakers—the association president, a "Cameroonian sister" (close friend) of the baby's mother—who simulta-neously addressed the new parents and the assembled audience. A child is a blessing, and brings joy to its parents. The parents should raise the child so that it grows strong and smart. They should think about their child's future, helping her to take advantage of new opportunities. Sometimes parenting is hard, but father and mother should persevere, giving love to reach prosper-ity in the end. Above all, the child should know where it comes from, that it *has people*. It is part of a wider community, living in the solidarity of give and take. Cries of "yes, yes" and applause rounded out the speeches.

Shortly before midnight, members of the association's dance troupe, in-cluding Magni, retired to the little entrance corridor to put on costumes of matching blue-and-ochre Cameroonian printed fabric, wrapped on top of their street clothes. The first few drumbeats started. Thus cued, the MC mo-tioned to the crowd, which immediately quieted down. A line of some seven women and two men entered the dance floor, the women dancing and the two men drumming. The MC quickly placed two chairs in the middle of the dance floor, so the two drummers could sit. The dancers formed a circle, dancing around the drummers. The past and current presidents joined the circle, as did the father, mother, and baby daughter. The dancers sang call-and-response songs extolling the love and solidarity of the association, and the blessings that children bring. Soon the MC announced that anyone who wanted could

FIGURE 5.2. "Shake your shoulders with us," dancing at Born House, Berlin 2010. Family and home-town association members dance together at a celebration in honor of a newborn infant. Hometown association members wear matching *pagne*, or cloth wrappers. The association's gift to the baby's parents shines in the glaring lights of the rented hall in Berlin.
Credit: Pamela Feldman-Savelsberg

join the circle. "*Shake your shoulders with us!*" she urged. Shelly, as wife of the past president, shimmied up and slipped into the circle, matching her steps to those of the other dancers.

Following the dance troupe's performance, the MC and association president presented a large wrapped present and an envelope with cash to the parents. "Use this well, raise Princess well. Let her know that she has people." Individuals then had a chance to come up and hand personal gifts to Princess's mother. Most of these gifts were, like mine, clothes or small toys for Princess, rather than the practical diapers and OMO laundry soap that I had witnessed at similar occasions in Cameroon. The festivities continued until 2 a.m. An a capella gospel choir, in which one association member sang bass, performed movingly. Attendees ate from the buffet, chatted, took care of the by-now over-tired children, and danced to the beat of the Congolese band.

Princess's parents, their friends, and their hometown association collaborated in staging a laughter-filled, enjoyable evening of togetherness. In exchange for blessing the community with a new member, providing special foods, and throwing a good party, the parents received both material and moral support. In this way, giving birth and arranging a Born House event gives parents and children access to community resources. Even if the event itself costs the same as or more than the official gift from the association, the Born House celebration opens up a circuit of exchange between the association and the young family. Among Bamiléké associations, the mere announcement of birth prompts an official visit and a gift for the child, as Ariane describes.

> When you give birth, for example when I gave birth, someone announces it at the [hometown association] meeting and then the association members come . . . they delegate people [from the association] who will come greet the child at the house. So . . . they bring along a small present for the baby. One can only rejoice when there is a birth, and all. It's the association that gives the present . . . They come, they visit you. If you need help, you can also let them know.

Among Anglophone Cameroonians, resources from the hometown association flow primarily to those mothers who put on a Born House celebration.

Drawing upon extrafamilial networks, Born House pulls together participants with overlapping ties, who each contribute in some way to the event. In the absence of the kin- and neighborhood-based ties that one would have in Cameroon, even this momentary encounter helps community members build enduring multiplex relationships (Gluckman 1967, 96). Blessings and exhortations for community solidarity stretch from the child to its parents, and outward to all who are present. The home association provides both formalized entitlements (e.g., gifts specified in by-laws) and less-formal organizational support preparing the party. The association also helps to animate the Born House event with food, song, dance, and good cheer. Born House is an event of conviviality, publicly linking the birth of a child and the socially reproductive practices of parenthood to the positive emotions of belonging.

Even more than at association meetings or year-end parties, children are central players in Born House celebrations. They witness their parents' hometown association in action, and in a joyous setting. Mothers later remind their children of the provenance of Born House gifts, as a means of fostering identification with the homeplace and its associational representative in the diaspora. The next section explores a number of scenarios through which mothers attempt to forge children's belonging through participation in associational life.

The Children's Table and Verses for Grandpa's Wake: Easing Children into Associational Life

One afternoon, meeting at the local university library for tea before going to pick their children up from Kita, Barbara and Bih chatted with me about

child-rearing and associational life. I had seen Barbara at the Born House celebration, so she knew of my interest. I had observed children interacting with
each other and with their parents at Association D's meetings, the year-end
party, as well as at the Born House cosponsored by Association B. Barbara and
Bih suggested that I visit an association with an organized children's program.
Both women's husbands belonged to the large Highlands Region Cultural Association,[17] and until recently this association had supported an active children's program. Barbara's husband often took their two older children along
with him to attend meetings. Barbara offered to accompany me so I could see
firsthand.

We met at the subway stop the following Sunday evening, traveling together to the so-called Afrikanische Viertel (African quarter) in Wedding,
a historically working-class neighborhood of Berlin. This part of Wedding
received its nickname from the streets named for German colonies lost nearly
a century before.[18] Ironically, Kamerunerstrasse (Cameroon Street) sported
two Cameroonian restaurants. The Highlands Region Cultural Association,
at the time between leases for a more permanent assembly hall, was meeting
temporarily in one of them. Barbara said that it was best, as two visitors, for
us to arrive once the meeting was already underway.

The restaurant space was crowded with attendees. Several tables had been
shoved together in the anteroom, filled with crayons, coloring books, and
snacks. This was the Children's Table. Three mothers hovered around the table,
quietly settling squabbles over sharing favorite colors. They passed out juice
boxes to the dozen children around the table, speaking in loud whispers. It
was hard to do much more, because late-arriving adults attending the association meeting used the space as an overflow room, crowding around and
straining to hear what was going on in the main room. I recognized Lola and
Sandra Star, both of whom I had interviewed. Two of Barbara's children were
at the table, coloring away; they had arrived earlier, accompanying their father.
Happi, whose *Einschulungsparty* I had attended the previous summer, gave me
a huge grin of recognition. Before we left, Happi and her sister presented me
with pictures they had drawn—a bucolic scene with tree, lawn, house, and a
kitten; flowers and butterflies; and a portrait of the fairy Princess Lilifee.

The Children's Table that evening served as a way to occupy a bunch of
kids who had accompanied their parents to the meeting. The children had
fun coloring with friends whom they saw only at community events or at
special occasions such as Born House celebrations or birthday parties. A few
designated association members—all women, all mothers—supervised them.
In the midst of the meeting hubbub and the crowded space, there was no
room for a special program dedicated to the transmission of "Cameroonian

cultural traditions," as Barbara put it. According to several interlocutors, however, this was a state of exception, due to the transitional period in which the association found itself.

Sandra Star, a vivacious thirty-year-old single mother and former student, described a longer tradition of a more focused monthly children's program, held separately from the adults' association meeting.

> I have been in this association for more than three years . . . oh this [Highlands]
> House organized a children's program. We try to teach them how to play drums,
> sing African songs or teach them English, how to introduce themselves. Because
> most of the children we have there . . . they mostly spoke German, the German
> language. So we try to teach them a little bit of English, so that they could at least
> know these two languages. So that was always the first Saturday of the month,
> it was Children's Day.

Lola likewise recalled a period of more formal programming for children, including preparing dances and songs for special events, like the annual parade of Karneval der Kulturen (Carnival of Cultures).[19] Even without special programming for children, Lola insisted that bringing children along to Highlands meetings brought many benefits. "*The joy of meeting other people. Exchanging our experiences here in Germany or giving advice. The children getting to know other Cameroonian children, playing with them and where they can practice English or French or whatsoever. For them to realize O.K., maybe I am the only one in my school, but there are other children from Cameroon too.*" Like several other parents, Lola pointed out both cognitive (learning and practicing languages from "home") and emotional (overcoming isolation) benefits to forging ties with other Cameroonian children under the aegis of associational life.

Parents belonging to a variety of hometown associations described similar reasons for bringing children to events sponsored by place-based community organizations. Iris explained that becoming familiar with her roots gives her daughter the tools to move more easily—and critically—between multiple cultures. "*I take my child there because I want my child to know her roots. And I want my child to know her roots and languages—we speak Pidgin there. And taking her there also . . . shows her a different mentality. And she already knows that very well, because she used to tell me everything she sees, she compares it to the German society and the German ways of doing things.*"

Hannah likewise brings her children along to meetings to "meet people from T and hear the dialect." Alain emphasized that it is important for children to witness that their parents come together to organize meaningful projects through the association, something more than just eating together. Kem-Karine turns attending meetings into a pleasurable family outing. "*I go with them, so that they should feel free. Because being only in the house they need a change at times. From the meetings we come by and eat at McDonalds before we come back. And then they say thank you for taking us out. And there they meet other children, so they play together."*

KemKarine explained that her children could feel free because they were among other Cameroonian children who shared their experiences; at association events, they did not stick out as the only black child in their class or day-care group.

Sophie belongs to a large Anglophone hometown association with a network of branches in other German cities, in the United Kingdom, and in the United States (cf. Mercer, Page, and Evans 2008, 83). Each year, the Berlin branch stages a "cultural weekend" to which it invites members of other branches in Germany. Sophie describes how a woman from her association prepares the children for a dance and storytelling performance at the cultural weekend. *"The children will be dancing and telling a story in our dialect, then sharing of the culture . . . We have a lady that tries to teach the children some things, and she tries to tell them the story in English, in German, and in the dialect so they can try to understand . . . Most of them speak German and English . . . [and then learn the local language from this lady] just a bit."*

Sophie encourages her daughter to participate in such events because this is a way to forge connections and create a set of childhood memories that will later contribute to her daughter's ongoing sense of belonging. She explains, *"It is the culture. To know her parents belongs to these associations. Like she likes dancing . . . she really knows that she is from M and she grows up with this identity in her . . . I know that each time she goes to the M association there is eru to eat and she likes that a lot. And she knows that she will meet friends there and after eating they will play. I am sure she remembers."* Maria Mar, a member of Highlands, echoes Sophie's concern with building memories. Maria incorporates explicit reminders of community belonging into her daily child-rearing strategies, claiming that it is important to *"tell the child that this thing comes from [Highlands]."*

Lily, whose place-based associational life centers on her church, is warmed by children's participation in the newly imported ritual of the baby shower. A woman in her church association returned from a visit to Cameroonian relatives in Takoma Park, Maryland—an area with a relatively high density of Cameroonian immigrants. There she had observed several mixed-gender baby showers. Lily's acquaintance was particularly amused by a game in which the men placed balloons under their shirts, and had to bend over to pick up items from the floor without popping the balloons. Upon return to Berlin, she introduced the baby shower as an alternative to Born House events. When Lily was expecting her most recent child, her church-based association hosted a baby shower for her, involving her older children in a surprise.

When they put on my baby shower, the children came, because the children, like, were already going to church, and they—without my being there—they prepared something [to perform at my baby shower]. Because when they came, I hadn't been to church perhaps for two or three weeks. Thus they had had time to prepare something to surprise me. The children sang; they presented me with their songs and all. So the kids did something, they participated, in fact, they participated. That's it, it was sweet and all. They came together, they sang and all . . . it warmed my heart.

Cameroonian migrant parents have not always had such an easy time finding opportunities to introduce their children into associational life. Justine, a close friend of Barbara who has lived in Berlin for over a decade, explained that Cameroonians in Berlin started forming associations only in the late 1990s and early 2000s. During those early days, not as many Cameroonians remained in Berlin for long, or were old enough to be raising children.

I think that much has already been done and there are opportunities there to raise our kids, with this feeling of belonging or not to lose their culture . . . Things are changing because people are growing up because at first I knew just students and now things have changed, they have families, kids, they are coming up, and that's a different image and a different responsibility . . . I think [the younger people who have just arrived] are coming to a better environment because they have people to turn to ask for information and they have associations that they can go to and get information.

It is a new generation, Justine told me, with more Cameroonians in the city, with people raising children. Thus Berlin now has people from whom one can ask advice, people who collaborate to build a diasporic community to which children can belong.

In addition to hometown association meetings, Born House celebrations, and the year-end parties and cultural weekends sponsored by associations, wakes—following the death of an association member (or more frequently, the death of a member's parent)—occasionally provide an opportunity for parents to expose their children to the supportive role that associations play at vital events. We have seen that death benefits and support at "wake-keeping" are central reasons motivating migrants to join hometown associations. Wake-keeping, which is generally adults' business, continues into the wee hours of the morning, accompanying the bereaved family through a sad and difficult

night. Speeches are made, Bible verses read, songs sung, food and drink are
shared, tears are shed, and donations are made for burial and transport. The
bereaved hold the wake in their house or apartment, without the presence of
the body. For those who are unable to travel to Cameroon for a funeral, the
wake is often held in Berlin on the same day that the burial occurs in Cameroon. Those who can travel to Cameroon hold the wake before the funeral; it
serves not only as a way to manage grief, but also as a send-off and fundraiser
for travel and funeral expenses.

After the Born House and year-end events had shown me more joyous
sides of conviviality, Barbara's father-in-law died in Cameroon on a late January day. Bih, who knew Barbara from the Kita, told us first, with tears in her
eyes. With siblings and step-siblings scattered throughout Cameroon, Germany, and the United States, there was much for her friend's husband to organize. The funeral was set for mid-March, to allow the scattered family time
to assemble and to stage a funeral worthy of their dear father (and of their
means as migrants or bushfallers).[20]

In the meantime, Barbara and her family held a wake one Saturday in February. Friends came to the apartment to pay their respects. The family held a
little service, permitting their children to be involved. The two older children,
both in primary school, read Bible verses aloud. Later Barbara told me that
the baby of the family, still attending the Kita, was not very aware of what was
going on, but cried when others cried. In addition to the comfort experienced
in this time of bereavement, Barbara expressed that it was important to her
that their children see how the community comes together to support their
family. Participating in wake-keeping is one way for children to learn about
how life-cycle events are managed through an adapted tradition within their
community.

Children observe their parents' joy at occasions to celebrate belonging—
year-end parties, baby showers, and Born House events sponsored by place-
based community organizations (D'Alisera 1998). They witness their parents
working with others to prepare public diasporic events (such as association
floats for the Carnival of Cultures parade) and to coordinate development
projects in the homeplace. Within the limits of their young understanding,
children also share in their parents' sorrow at the death of loved ones. Children sense that their parents' sorrow is deepened by geographical distance;
they overhear their parents' mournful conversations about lost links to a
dearly held former home. At the same time, children note the community
coming together to buoy their family in this difficult moment. They recognize
faces familiar from the happier occasions of their parents' civic engagement
in migrant associational life.

FIGURE 5.3. Members of Highland Region Cultural Association dance at the *Karneval der Kulturen* (Carnival of Cultures) parade, Berlin 2011. Mothers encourage their children to participate in the preparation for such events, hoping to instill a sense of Cameroonian belonging.

In recent correspondence, Magni reflected on the importance of fostering children's connection to community organizations. From her dual perspective as a social scientist and migrant mother, she wrote:

> From my experience and those close to me, it helps when children are immersed in cultural activities of associations as early on as possible. This helps them gain familiarity with it and gives them [an] anchor in their identity. Living in a dominant (German) culture, children show less interest in their parents' culture if they are introduced to it at a much later stage, for example in their teens. The main idea behind this is to enable the children to fit in either of these cultures depending on where they find themselves. It is important as migrants to be able to integrate in the society of residence without losing a sense of self and identity.

Magni's words indicate purposeful strategizing on the part of parents. Belonging needs to be cultivated. Parents know that interactions with other Cameroonians do not occur with enough quotidian regularity to allow identification with a broader community to emerge organically. They also want their children to see the many ways that Cameroonian migrants actively organize themselves in extrafamilial, goal-oriented associations. Parents, especially mothers, socialize their children to become agentic adults who are civically engaged in promoting ties to a distant homeplace. Engendering such identification is no simple matter, because children's daily activities occur within a dominant German cultural setting. As Justine told me, to keep children from losing their culture, "*It's now the challenge for the parents. The parents have to act now, the other part cannot be done by regulations. It's the parents, it's their duty to be able or to have the time to do it.*" Associations—with their rules about membership, claiming benefits, and participating in mutual aid—help forge belonging, but cannot do so without considerable parental, particularly maternal, effort.

Conclusion

We have seen that associations foster multiple types of belonging. Associations regulate the boundaries of belonging-as-membership, selecting who can become or remain a member from among the population of Cameroonian migrants and their family members. Associations allow members to assert their belonging by participating in decision making, by offering gestures of solidarity to compatriots in need, and by making claims upon the association's resources. Associations set limits to belonging-as-claims-making, by circumscribing the types of kinship relationships for which one can receive benefits as well as by defining the size of those benefits. Finally, associational life provides an arena for members to practice belonging-as-performance, through engaging in expected forms of social interaction and reciprocal exchange.

In formal monthly meetings, specially organized life-cycle and cultural events, and the informal interactions that surround them, migrant associations generate overlapping streams of interaction for Cameroonian migrant mothers. These streams of interaction are both formal and informal. They involve formal accountability regimes for membership fees, benefits, and obligations, as well as the informal remarks, looks, and gestures that build sympathies and animosities. Streams of interaction among women occur at monthly meetings as well as at special events sponsored by associations, but also while waiting together at tram stops after these events. The interactions can be supportive or distressing. Sometimes these streams of interaction occur parallel to each other in the same time and place, for example when the rule-bound open annual election of association officers is accompanied by the buzz of informal conversations among clusters of people sitting together. In other circumstances, separate streams of interaction occur during discrete moments in various venues. Through these diverse interactions, women connect with other Cameroonian mothers via their common relation to a home association.

Becoming civically engaged through migrant place-based associations allows mothers to develop extrafamilial ties. These connections are circuits infused with the emotions of attachment as well as the practical aid that flows along them. Acquaintances built at meetings, year-end parties, and cultural festivals sponsored by the association serve as a basis for developing deeper and more frequent ties. Associations allow migrants to add layers of connection to other occasional meetings in the neighborhood, at markets, or at the Kita, making relationships multiplex and thus more enduring.

Describing her relationships with women in her association, Sandra Star nicely conveys the mixture of conviviality and seriousness at the Highlands Regional Cultural Association:

> [My relationship with other women in Highlands] is a very cordial one, very flexible, very sweet. Because when we come together, we crack a lot of jokes, we speak slang, we laugh. And it is also a serious one, because we plan seriously on how to change . . . our old habits which were really draining the house down . . . like late coming and staying too long in the meeting, where children are getting hungry and they need to sleep and prepare for school the next day.

Sandra Star points out that women's participation in associational life is shaped by motherhood. Women struggle to promote rule-abiding behavior at association meetings to set an example for children and to manage time in a way compatible with children's bedtimes and school schedules.[21] Mothers also have an interest in creating children's programs to transmit folkloric and linguistic elements of culture. Lola speaks to these interests when she characterizes women in her association by saying, "*First, they are mothers.*"

Women's very attendance at meetings and events is constrained by familial demands and irregular schedules of service-sector jobs. Sophie tells us, "*I think they are more concerned with their families or with their kids than being engaged in the association's issues. That is because the kids, they need more time and they would be there running around. They would not have the issues to take care of*"—in other words, the children would distract the mothers from engaging in association business.

Nonetheless, women transcend the constraints of family demands to join hometown associations. Doing so, as Iris states, helps mothers to overcome isolation and deal with financial issues.

> Most women join associations first for the . . . social networking, meeting friends, it's a room for them to chat. And because sometimes in their homes they are stressed up, people don't visit them, and so when they go to the association it creates for them a forum to meet, at least to laugh and this kind of thing. And then they enter the association also for the reason . . . to be financially secured

*a bit, because they don't know what can happen. The man today or tomorrow
can leave, they might have some troubles, they can only go to this njangi, to this
association, for help, to save something, you know.*

Friends provide moral support, even if it is just to encourage each other to
attend meetings. Sandra Star recounts:

*I have very good friends in the association that, at least before we even come to
the meeting, once a month, we already call each other, "Are you coming for the
meeting? Bring this or bring that. I am waiting to see you." We even encourage
others . . . like you may call your friends, if she is not really in the mood, maybe
she is sick or feeling down, she will be encouraged, okay, you are coming, my
friend is coming, okay, then . . . sometimes we even come for the meeting, because
you are happy to come and see your friends.*

Monthly meetings, year-end parties, cultural showcase events, Born House
celebrations, and even wakes are all occasions in which mothers can build
overlapping ties in a spirit of conviviality. They work hard to involve their
children in these positive experiences of living together with and in a community; mothers seek to thereby anchor their children in a positive identity, helping them establish social ties and attachments that will sustain them
through future hardships.

Observing these events, however, has taught us that conviviality in migrant
community associations has its limits. From maintaining personal reputations
to concerns about possible irregularities in immigration status, Cameroonians
have several reasons for caution when seeking pleasurable sociality at hometown association events. For example, the year-end party was an occasion to
relax together in a momentary "island of home." Yet as we learned from Marthe's presentation of her baby's feeding problems, that venue simultaneously
called for vigilance about revealing personal information. Fellow association
members are likely to be connected to members of one's personal and family
networks both in Cameroon and in the diaspora, and thus could spread gossip
among those who matter. In this case, not only goods, advice, and moral support flow among affective circuits, but also potentially harmful or malicious
information. Even in this generally relaxed setting, an individual cannot be
sure that the relatively infrequent, public, and largely formalized interactions
of hometown association meetings are trustworthy.

Commenting on trust and mistrust among association members, Ariane
told us about Cameroonian migrants' experiences of betrayal. Anonymously
reported for immigration infringements, some migrants found themselves
deported. Stories of their fate circulated through migrant networks, from the
association outward to friends, family members, even casual encounters while

buying plantains at the local African grocery. Even for those with relatively secure immigration status, such stories had a chilling effect. In the next chapter, we explore Cameroonian migrant mothers' encounters with the German regulatory regime. We will see that notions of family and care are reshaped in response to these encounters, as part of a newly emerging legal consciousness. In the process, mothers develop strategies to build their families within a field of multiple belonging.

6

In the Shadow of the State

Sorry to interrupt, I have to go to my lawyer. That's how it is with us here.
L I L Y , Berlin 2010

Lily Runs to Her Lawyer

Lily apologized, she would have to cut our appointment short. Lily assured me that she had been looking forward to this second of a series of interviews. But her lawyer had called, requesting a meeting that would begin only an hour after I had arrived at Lily's apartment. *"Sorry to interrupt,"* Lily explained, *"I have to go to my lawyer. That's how it is with us here."* I sensed both urgency and regret in Lily's voice. Because our relationship was still new—we had met at her church, and again for an interview about childbirth experiences—I did not yet dare intrude into Lily's life to ask the reason for her sudden appointment with her lawyer. Only several years later did I learn that Lily had set off on the long path toward achieving German citizenship for her and her children. But the feeling that hung in the air that day was clear. There were so many things to sort out in life, so many legal rules to follow, even half a decade after migrating to Germany one needed a lawyer's help. New legal difficulties could take one by surprise. It was common knowledge that this was the fate of migrants. *"That's how it is with us here."*

Interacting with the law and living in the shadow of the complex rules and organization of the German state is a big part of "how it is with us here." The shadow of the state affects the connections that Cameroonian migrant mothers maintain with their relatives in Cameroon, with their newly found families in Berlin, and with the fellow migrants they meet in hometown associations, churches, and neighborhood markets. As in many countries of the so-called Global North, German immigration, labor, and family law is part of an audit culture based on a fundamental mistrust of immigrants from the so-called

Global South (Coe 2013, 104). African mothers notice that the burden of documentation is on them; immigrants need to verify that they are worthy of living, working, marrying, and bearing children in Germany, that they are not taking jobs or social resources away from "real" Germans.[1]

This underlying mistrust of immigrants spreads beyond the state, in a mutually reinforcing cycle among policy, opinion leaders, and public opinion. While suspicion of immigrants is countered by pro-immigrant civil society organizations—such as ProAsyl—and prominent political voices calling for tolerance and inclusion—such as the current and past German presidents (Gauck and Wulff)—these countervailing voices are barely heard in the everyday lives of African immigrants. Mistrust of immigrants is evident in African mothers' daily interactions in public places—the stares and comments of strangers who find black skin or foreign accents unfamiliar and disturbing. These microaggressions take their toll on the emotional as well as practical lives of African migrant mothers. In her collection of short stories, the renowned Nigerian author Chimamanda Ngozi Adichie writes, "At night something would wrap itself around your neck, something that very nearly choked you before you fell asleep" (Adichie 2009, 119). This invisible "thing around your neck," like a snake or demon choking its victim at night and impossible to shake off, is the burden of difference and strangeness that wears down Africans living in the diaspora.

My Cameroonian interlocutors hinted at this same, diffuse burden of not-belonging. Contrasting her foreignness as a Cameroonian in Germany with her imagination of what it feels like to belong, Ariane evokes the alienation she feels in Berlin despite the support of her loving fiancé, the laughter of her sweet toddler son, and the satisfaction she draws from being part of the board of her hometown association. "*[I feel] not strange or foreign, no weird looks from others, no system [to deal with] that's really new for me.*" Instead of feeling at home ("*chez moi*"), Ariane senses the piercing stares and bureaucratic confusions that underscore her foreignness in Berlin.

In this chapter, I address a particular aspect of Cameroonian mothers' not-belonging: the shadow of the state. In my choice of metaphor, I draw inspiration from anthropologist Gerd Spittler's now classic article "*Streitregelung im Schatten des Leviathan*" (1980)—("Dispute Resolution in the Shadow of the Leviathan")—proposing that it is the wish to avoid the coercive, law-and-order mechanisms of the colonial state that motivated Africans to resolve disputes through customary means. For Spittler, the Leviathan (the law-and-order state) casts a threatening shadow. For African immigrants to Germany, however, the state is more than the Leviathan; it is part of a regulatory regime that categorizes people, demands obligations, and provides or denies rights and services. I attempt to look at the shadow cast by the German state from the perspective of Cameroonian migrant mothers. When is the shadow dark and threatening? When is it more like a heavy mist that infuses the organization of social service agencies, schools, and clinics that mothers encounter in their everyday life? When does the shadow of the state provide protective shade?

Through its complex set of laws, regulations, and organization of social services, the German state casts a shadow upon the ways Cameroonian mothers give birth, rear their children, and make connections to others while living in the diaspora. At times the shadow is threatening, particularly when it comes to immigration law, residency rights, and the threat of deportation. In everyday life the shadow casts a pall over the ways Cameroonian mothers move through life. This diffuse shadow is felt through the ways that German laws and regulations constrain how Cameroonian mothers make families, rear children, and maintain connections to other Cameroonians. The diffuse shadow of German regulations shapes the types of interactions Cameroonians entertain with authorities, teachers, physicians, and service providers. Even when less threatening than the shadow cast by the Leviathan, it affects the emotional tenor in which migrant women build new lives in Berlin. To push the metaphor further, another type of shadow is evident when the German state gives protective shade to migrant women, when they can use the law and the instruments of the state to pursue their interests.

This chapter explores three types of shadows—threat, diffuse pall, and protective shade—cast by the German state upon Cameroonian migrant mothers' pursuit of building families and forging a sense of belonging. Visits to the Foreigner's Office and the Welfare Office provide an opportunity to understand the web of control spun under the Leviathan's dark shadow. Conversations with mothers reveal that regulations create an overwhelming labyrinth that women must navigate following the birth of a child. They also show how the state and its charitable nongovernmental extensions simultaneously provide shelter and create risks for mothers seeking documents, but also make it difficult for service providers and Cameroonian mothers to establish more than formal, short-lived relationships. Revisiting mother's accounts of their relationships and marriage and their child-rearing challenges allows us to see that the shadow of state regulation recasts affective circuits among kin, and constrains mothers' autonomy in caring for their children. Finally, in cases of serious marital disputes, we witness Cameroonian mothers turning to the protective shade of the German state.

In the Shadow of the Leviathan

When Cameroonian mothers migrate, the legal and cultural norms they carry with them regarding how to form relationships, give birth to children, and care for them appropriately confront new realities. These new realities include the legal norms, rituals, and organization of the German state. German legal norms and their regulatory apparatus carry within them German cultural ideas about partnerships and marriage, childbirth and child rearing. Law regarding citizenship, families, and care is not only affected by culture but is part of culture. In the making of migrant families, multiple (legal) cultures come into play, at times existing side-by-side, at times in conflict, and at times prompting compromises of adaptation. When Cameroonian migrants and their German interlocutors meet, they select from their cultural and legal toolkits (Swidler 1986) and reshuffle schemas and repertoires regarding family life and the movement and separation of persons (Coe 2013; Sewell 1992). In the process they reveal the utter creativity and indeterminacy of culture (Moore 1978; Moore and Myerhoff 1977). At the center of these legal and cultural adaptations are the migrant mothers, fathers, and children who build families in a new place.

A good three decades ago, Spittler's Leviathan article investigated the mutual influencing of two legal cultures in a situation of legal pluralism (1980). These two legal cultures—African customary law and European colonial law— were brought into contact by a specific form of global mobility, namely European colonialism. Putting aside for the moment a rich debate regarding the colonial invention of "customary law" (Moore 1986), Spittler aimed to explain the effectiveness and validity of indigenous forms of dispute resolution, even when local leaders' and communities' ability to impose sanctions had been greatly curtailed by the colonial state.

Spittler proposed that earlier anthropological explanations of the enduring force of customary law were insufficient because they largely ignored the context of the colonial state and its alternative to local dispute-resolution mechanisms. Spittler argued against the idea that indigenous forms of dispute resolution are effective because village societies are held together by a Durkheimian organic solidarity (Durkheim 1984). He also did not find social structural features of African societies—for example, the complex web of enduring multiplex relationships, which puts parties under pressure to avoid tearing apart a wider social fabric (Gluckman 1967, 96)—a sufficient explanation for the efficacy of home-grown dispute-resolution mechanisms in African colonial and postcolonial states. Instead, the parties to a dispute, their social networks, and the traditional authorities who mediate the case all share an interest in avoiding the colonial and postcolonial court system. They operate in the shadow of the Leviathan—a state that seems remote, opaque, and often hostile. It is the threat of going to the next higher instance—of submitting to the norms, procedures, and punishments of another legal culture—that motivates parties to collaborate, resolving disputes within their local group.

What happens to Spittler's expectations when global mobility flows in a different direction, from Africa to Europe? Cameroonian migrants to Berlin do indeed live in the shadow of a European legal Leviathan. Nonetheless, this does not make them preserve or consistently turn to the legal norms and procedures of their ethnicities of origin. How *do* Cameroonian migrants' legal norms, rituals, symbols, and procedures travel? Do migrants avoid other forms of law (such as German immigration and family law), resist them, or use them to serve their needs?

One way we can approach these questions is through the theoretical framework of legal consciousness. Legal consciousness refers to the understandings and meanings of law that circulate in social relations, the same social relations that form affective circuits. We could call legal consciousness "law from below." Legal consciousness operates at the microlevel of social action. People engage with the law through the routines of everyday living, and then exchange stories about their interactions with legal rules and institutions. Their storytelling occurs in situations of secular ritual (Moore and Myerhoff 1977), in which key gestures take on the quality of authoritative symbols. The meanings thus circulated become patterned into collectively shared, habituated legal orientations (Mauss 1979 [1938], Bourdieu 1977). Through these situations, the understandings of law become more collective and binding. In this way, legal consciousness is constitutive of legal culture as a macrolevel phenomenon.

Following Ewick and Silbey's analysis of American legal consciousness (1998), we identify tentative patterns among Cameroonian migrants to Germany. Migrant women stand in awe *before* an inscrutable state law, learn to work *with* the law, and learn to *avoid* the law. Each of these patterns represents a different normative ideal (law as objective, as a game, or as arbitrary) and a different type of action (conformity, tactical maneuvering, or resistance).

The legal consciousness of Cameroonian migrants is further complicated by the multiple legal cultures that serve as reference points for Cameroonian family formation. Each ethnic group in Cameroon forms its own legal community, consisting of rituals and symbols that organize and give shape to dispute-resolution processes and norm enforcement. Among the Bamiléké, law-finding at least throughout the twentieth century was embedded in political and religious practice (Kwayeb 1960; Malaquais 2002). In 1986 while doing fieldwork in the Bamiléké kingdom of Bangangté, for example, I witnessed a case of dispute resolution when parties to a family dispute came before the fon, each stating their complaints and understandings of the situation. The fon then referred the litigants to ritual specialists associated with the court, the People of the House of God (*Ba Nda Nsi*). These actors from the king's court employed royal symbols and ritual—including bathing their feet in purifying "cooked" palm wine—to enforce reconciliation in this family dispute.

German, French, and British colonial rule introduced new symbols, rituals, and norms into Cameroonian state law, which incorporates both statutory and common law elements. Cameroonians can be quite creative in their dealings with plural legal regulations. For example, prosecutors apply state law regarding grave desecration only when it offends against traditional rules governing inheritance and the treatment of ancestors.

Migration to Germany engenders contact with yet another legal culture, with new legal norms, rituals, symbols, and organizational carriers (Gephart 2006). Cameroonian migrants interact with German legal institutions in the course of making families—to obtain visas, get a marriage license, and to register a child's birth. Sharing stories of everyday encounters with German officials is an important element of Cameroonian migrants' sociality. Migrants exchange stories in family settings and at community meetings, within the same networks along which migrants provide care and forge belonging. Recently arrived migrants learn from those who are more settled and experienced with the German system (Kohlhagen 2006b). Migrants' stories, told with ritual aplomb and authority, crystallize into collectively held ideas about getting along with and in spite of the law in a new place. This is the essence of legal consciousness as a process of meaning-making in which legal cultures are formed, contested, and interwoven. Next, we witness how this process occurs through Cameroonian mothers' encounters with German officials in a labyrinthine legal-bureaucratic system.

Encounters with the Legal-Bureaucratic Labyrinth

When a Cameroonian mother arrives in Germany, finds an apartment, or plugs in a television set, she needs to interact with German authorities. When she gives birth to a new baby, brings it for a pediatric checkup, and registers it for day care and school, she must travel from office to office, gathering certificates and stamps. Her journey is such a prominent feature of German life that it has its own term—the *Behördengang*. Reminiscent of an obstacle course, this word is directly translatable as "authorities course," lending a distinct flavor to a mother's dealings with government agencies. Our Cameroonian mother is familiar with unwieldy bureaucracies from her homeland, but what she finds in Berlin is a new and unfamiliar labyrinth. The pressure she feels to navigate the uncertain terrain of the unending Behördengang casts a shadow of insecurity over the mother's daily life and family-making.

Germany's unique way of organizing social services contributes to the labyrinthine nature of dealing with government agencies. Germany is a relatively generous welfare state, investing 26.7 percent of its gross domestic product (Giehle 2014)[2] in a comprehensive system of health, pension, accident, long-term care, and unemployment insurance as well as a combination of child benefits and tax concessions meant to equalize the burdens of raising a family. Germany's social welfare system is based on the subsidiarity principle, meaning that responsibility for problem-solving and implementation regarding social problems should be undertaken by the smallest, most local level possible; the federal government, as a central authority, plays a subsidiary role, performing those tasks that cannot be dealt with effectively at a more immediate level. Thus, "Germany does not provide its citizens with . . . social welfare benefits through a centralized state-run system. Rather, it provides these benefits via a complex network of national agencies and . . . independent regional and local entities—some public, some quasi-public, and many private and voluntary" (Solsten 1995). Because the social safety net in Berlin is provided by such a diverse mixture of public and private agencies, services are scattered among multiple units, which themselves are geographically scattered throughout the city. It is up to individuals to find their way from office to office.

My Cameroonian interlocutors made frequent reference to the responsibility to navigate the Behördengang, often wending their way across major portions of the city, as a major annoyance of everyday life. They spoke about the need to get their "papers" in order, and how very many papers those were. Lily observed what it was like for her fellow Cameroonians who lived as unauthorized migrants: "*When you find yourself in a country without papers, for example, you don't feel right in your skin . . . a person feels down and out, she just stays there in her corner, and her thoughts become dark.*"

Obtaining documents is a central purpose of the long, winding path that Cameroonian mothers take through the German bureaucracy. Documents are keys to services, to welfare aid, to temporary protection from deportation, and to regularizing immigration status. Migrant mothers submit to what Lavie in another context (the struggles of single Mizrahi mothers in Israel) has termed "bureaucratic torture" (Lavie 2014) because the services and protection they hope to receive will enable them to stay and raise their families in Germany.

When it came to life in Germany, many mothers felt as if the traces of themselves that were captured in documents, rather than sociality, were what made them real.[3] One's type of visa or passport determined the ease or possibility to get a job, find an apartment, and register one's address (a civic requirement in Germany, as in many European countries). Without a registered address, it is impossible to open a bank account, get a library card, or sign up one's children for school. In addition, papers in the form of a diploma—an official credentializing document—seemed to matter more than experience in being chosen for employment. As Brecht wrote in his *Refugee Dialogues* in the early 1940s, a passport is "recognized, when it's good, but a person can be oh so good and nonetheless still not recognized" (Brecht 2000, 7, translated by author).[4]

On those occasions when Magni accompanied me, once the interview was over, mothers asked Magni's advice on how to best deal with the Behörden-gang. Jucal, for example, asked Magni to look over the documents she had prepared to apply for a course of study as a social worker. "*I gave all my documents to [Magni] because I just thought it might be [close to] sociology.*" Jucal hoped that Magni could help her to access the various social services that would allow her to return to school after having dropped out because of fertility treatment and a difficult pregnancy. And indeed, Magni was able to tell Jucal which papers to get stamped first at which office before checking off that hurdle on her legal-bureaucratic odyssey.

I know of their experiences through their conversations and the stories they shared with me, and through the way women's interactions with authorities affected our ability to meet. Lily had to cut an interview short due to an appointment with her lawyer. Just before our first meeting, Jucal called desperately from her cellphone, asking me to meet her in the hallway of the city registry office; she did not dare lose her place in line. Because I only rarely met my Cameroonian interlocutors at government offices or service providers, I need to use other sources to describe face-to-face encounters with the German bureaucratic labyrinth. I combine mothers' accounts of their journeys from office to office with my experiences as a foreign researcher seeking a residence permit, and observations from my volunteer work as an interpreter for a young African refugee.

A VISIT TO THE FOREIGNERS OFFICE

On a cold December morning, I climbed the stairs out of the gloomy Amruner Street subway station, on my way to the Foreigners Registration Office.[5] Calling a central number nearly two months earlier, I had been assigned an appointment with the caseworker handling my application for a residence permit. At the time, while waiting on hold, I remember thinking, "Thank goodness I can speak German!" Without such skills, even making an appointment would be a challenge. At the top of the subway stairs, I blinked at the bright daylight, confused about which way to turn. I finally found the street sign for Torfstrasse and was on my way. Walking past working-class housing, tiny African groceries, and the inviting windows of the Africa Media Center, I wondered what this walk toward the Foreigners Office might feel like for a newly arrived Cameroonian immigrant. If her German were still weak, would she be able to get directions from the public transportation website or ask a passerby? Would she understand the various residence titles listed on the official website, and the conditions attached to them? Would she have the money for the fees, generally over one hundred euros?

Even I was a bit nervous, because the appointment I was able to obtain was well after the three-month grace period for citizens from Australia, Israel, Japan, Canada, the Republic of Korea, New Zealand, and the United States of America, all of whom can enter Germany without a visa. What would it be like for a young African woman, without the privilege of citizenship in a favored country—mine is the United States—two prestigious research affiliations, and a German-citizen spouse to boot?

Cameroonian writer Priscillia Manjoh ends her novel *Snare* with a scene of the protagonist emotionally unable to walk over the bridge at the end of Torfstrasse on her way to the Foreigners Office. She sits on a bench, scribbling her woes—her desperate need for *doki* (papers)—in the form of a Pidgin poem, crumpling the paper and throwing it in the canal (Manjoh 2013, 216–18). Crossing this same bridge, I left the lively world of immigrants' shops to enter an industrial strip along a canal separating the Berlin neighborhoods of Wedding and Moabit. Among the edifices along the canal was an imposing set of four brick buildings, the Foreigners Registration Office complex.

Entering this complex, I discovered that each building was dedicated to applicants from different regions of origin, with a separate entrance for those seeking asylum and visas on humanitarian grounds. Following the yellowing charts and arrows, I found the section dedicated to the Americas and sub-Saharan Africa, wondering why these two world regions were combined in one section. While waiting outside my assigned door I saw a single man waiting by a door down the hallway, and a couple with careworn faces waiting by yet another door. Everyone fidgeted with their papers, looked at their watches—and no one spoke.

Once inside, I realized again my privilege as an American researcher, paid by an American foundation, with no need to seek employment during my stay in Germany. I was further privileged by my marriage to a German citizen. Frau Eiche (Mrs. Oak),[6] my caseworker, pooh-poohed my concerns about the late date of my appointment, and quickly completed all the necessary steps to issue me a one-year residency permit. We even had time to chat about her experiences working in the Foreigners Office.

Frau Eiche explained that she and her colleagues need to specialize regionally because different regulations apply to foreigners originating in different parts of the world. In addition, caseworkers need to develop knowledge about country conditions in the place of origin to assess each individual's case. Frau Eiche described her education in a technical college for administrative sciences as akin to an abbreviated law degree, because of the knowledge of immigration law necessary to deal with the cases that came across her desk. Frau Eiche told me that she exercises some discretion in decision making, as allowed by the law, and that she makes use of that leeway whenever she can. Through her demeanor and facial expression, she seemed to indicate that she used the discretion available to her to help people to stay in Germany. Scholarship on migration to Germany and other European Union countries reveals that bureaucrats' discretion can cut both ways—being helpful or punitive, facilitating or restricting access to legal residency (Alpes and Spire 2013; Alt 2003; Ellermann 2006; Mau and Brabandt 2011). Comparing visas issued and denied in European Union states, Finotelli and Sciortino (2013) find an asymmetric visa regime, in which discretion works to the detriment of migrants crossing the Mediterranean (i.e., from the African continent).

In public and private settings, Cameroonian migrants share stories with each other that tell very different accounts regarding the discretion of immigration caseworkers. At a public event on the fate of African migrants cosponsored by the mayor of the Lichtenberg district of Berlin and a Catholic charity, one man mesmerized the audience with a horrifying tale of bureaucratic indifference and downright cold-heartedness—seemingly a case study of Herzfeld's definition of bureaucratic indifference, "the rejection of common humanity . . . [and] the denial of identity, of selfhood . . . Everyone, it seems, has a bureaucratic horror story to tell, and few will challenge the conventions such stories demand" (Herzfeld 1992, 1, 4). The man had arrived in Germany from West Africa years before as a student in one of Berlin's prestigious universities. Falling ill with cancer, he had to drop out of his degree program and thus lost his visa status. While still in the hospital, he was evicted from his apartment, losing all his papers, notebooks, and even childhood photos. His caseworker, he claimed, never lifted a finger to help him.

Only through the help of a refugee aid organization was he able to obtain a new residency permit and complete his medical treatment.

In contrast, Maria Mar related that she originally came to Berlin seeking a six-month internship, with the intention to return to Cameroon to pursue studies in history. To her surprise, Maria found that she used up the time allotted by her first visa on language classes to learn German. Maria returned to the Foreigners Office to extend her visa so she could finally start her internship. Her caseworker, however, encouraged her to ask for a longer stay and to study at a university here rather than merely seeking an internship. After all, Maria had already gone to the effort of depositing nearly eight-thousand euros in a mandatory German escrow account to obtain her student visa (DAAD 2013).

> So [when] I came, my purpose was not even like staying here for long . . . Even though I had a student visa I really even didn't want to study at that moment. I wanted to do like [a] Praktikum, internship somewhere. I just wanted to be here for six months or a year. So when I came I had to study [German] language for a short time before I get place for my internship. But then I went to the Foreigners Office sometime after extending that six month [visa]. Because first I got three months, after renewing that I went a second time, by then I was just about finishing with my language, I didn't have an internship place [yet] then. So I went to them; I only need a visa now for my internship. And the man I met was so nice to me. "But why just internship?" he said, "you already, you have studied to an extent already, why don't you [go to] a university and then try to get . . . a student place and then you can stay and study, for as long as you want." That is the advice he gave me. So he gave me another six months . . . You know, it wasn't in my head but he gave me the advice and I took it. So I tried, I applied in one or two universities. I got a place at the University of Potsdam.

Thus, in Maria's case, a German bureaucrat's advice rather than her original life planning encouraged her to extend her stay in Germany. Maria's caseworker thus initiated a chain of events that led to education, employment, family formation, and permanent settlement in Germany.

At the Foreigners Office, caseworkers' discretion can work to the benefit or the detriment of migrants. Whether out of kindness or meanness, thoroughness or overwork, social engagement or *Dienst nach Vorschrift* (working by the book), low-level officials' decisions are consequential. They determine whether an immigrant can stay in Germany legally, or must either go underground or return to his or her country of origin. Through the types of residence permits they issue, Foreigners Office employees also determine whether a migrant mother is allowed to work or receive social benefits.

ESCORTING MAIMOUNA

Finding safe haven in Germany with access to social services and health care were of life and death importance to Maimouna. I met this young West African refugee through my volunteer activities with African Embrace,[7] an African self-help organization that provides social work and HIV-prevention services to migrants. Our first encounter was in early spring, a bit more than halfway through my fourteen months in Berlin. Maimouna had arrived in Germany the previous autumn from a West African country, unnamed here to protect her anonymity. Merely seventeen years old and fleeing an involuntary marriage in which she had been abused by her senior co-wives, Maimouna ended up in Berlin's only public hostel for unaccompanied minors.

Maimouna's hostel is administered by the *Senatsverwaltung für Bildung, Jugend und Wissenschaft* (Senate Administration for Education, Youth and Science). As of August 2014, Berlin had five government-run reception centers (Aufnahmeeinrichtungen) and thirty-three further contracted residences housing nearly ten thousand adult asylum seekers and refugees (Glaeser 2014.). Even more adult asylum seekers are housed in fenced barracks located in small towns in the surrounding state (Bundesland) of Brandenburg; there they must apply for permission to see a doctor or to leave the county to visit Berlin. Unaccompanied minors arriving from abroad are treated differently from adult refugees and asylum seekers; German lawmakers and service providers recognize that children and youth like Maimouna are vulnerable, and offer them more care than adults.

After a medical exam revealed that Maimouna was HIV-positive, the government home for unaccompanied immigrant minors contacted African Embrace in Berlin to request social work services and counseling for this young woman. Maimouna's situation was quite different from the Cameroonian women I had met—most of whom were educated, spoke English or French as their first language, and had been raised in urban settings.[8] Maimouna was younger, grew up in a village speaking a local language, attended only four years of school, and had a relatively weak grasp of French. She was married at sixteen, had fled that marriage with the help of a friend of her deceased mother, and had no children. I share Maimouna's story because it reveals something about the shadow cast by the bureaucratic labyrinth confronting Cameroonian migrant mothers, as well as the network of caseworkers, teachers, and volunteers who help immigrants find their way.

When I met Maimouna, she had just turned eighteen and had just received asylum on humanitarian grounds. Both events changed the combination of cash benefits and vouchers she would receive for living expenses and required her to attend an integration course (for language and civics). Maimouna was still living in the home for unaccompanied minors, but with her new status as an adult asylee she would soon need to move out. Her social worker at African Embrace asked me to escort her to the welfare office (Sozialamt), to serve as interpreter while providing some moral support. Maimouna and I met at the office of the African self-help organization, to get to know each other and to arrange where to meet.

On a lovely spring afternoon, I met Maimouna in the subway station at Turmstrasse. In the seven months that Maimouna had lived in Berlin, she had become familiar with the subway system and with cellphones. Breathless, ringing me to say she was coming, Maimouna ran down the platform to greet me. She was rushing from the German-as-a-second-language course she attended for two hours every afternoon. Because Maimouna had minimal formal education in her homeland—only four years of a village school, and that with frequent interruptions—she was learning not only a new language but also basic literacy skills in her German course. By the subway station kiosk, Maimouna thanked me for the copy of the French-language newspaper I had bought for her, regretfully telling me that she could not read it herself. Then we noticed that we were almost late for the appointment. Luckily Maimouna had a great spatial memory; after only one prior visit to the Welfare Office, she knew exactly where to turn. Grabbing my hand, she pulled me along. We ran across the street like two teenage friends chasing through the sunlight.

Ironically, our rushing merely meant that we had hurried up to wait . . . and wait, and wait—for two hours. We used the time to practice reading the numbers we had drawn for the waiting room, and to get acquainted. Maimouna told me that her village is dry, dotted with the shade of baobab and mango trees. Maimouna spoke nostalgically about the few avocado and papaya trees in her village, but then shook her head. "*My village is a village. It is not pretty.*" Maimouna's parents had both died when she was quite young, so Maimouna was raised by her mother's sister. When Maimouna was sixteen, her aunt arranged that she be married to an elderly man as his fourth wife. "*It wasn't good*," Maimouna repeated, because even if her husband did not beat her, her elder cowives did. Because it was such a bad situation, Maimouna told me, a friend of her deceased mother arranged for her escape, traveling with her to Germany. Arriving in Berlin, the friend abandoned Maimouna in a train station. Afraid and crying, Maimouna overheard a woman speaking her language. This stranger took her to an asylum-seeker's home. Ever since, she has been a ward of the system caring for unaccompanied minors.

Finally Maimouna's number flashed on the screen, with an indication of the room in which we would find Frau Amt (Mrs. Office), her caseworker. Frau Amt invited us to sit on two plastic chairs in her crowded office, apologizing for the heavy caseload that had made her so late that day. By then it was after 7:00 p.m., the time that Frau Amt would normally go home. She congratulated Maimouna that her asylum claim had had such a positive and quick outcome. She complimented Maimouna on being calm, smart, and "nice," expressing her confidence that Maimouna would "find her way well." Frau Amt encouraged Maimouna to work hard learning German, because language is the key to "integration." Frau Amt explained that this would be Maimouna's last visit to her at the Sozialamt, because now, with her new status, Maimouna would be taken care of by the JobCenter, the Employment Office that is also responsible for general welfare benefits. As a recognized refugee, Maimouna's benefits would now be paid at a higher rate than those for asylum seekers. Frau Amt explained the new benefits (monthly allowance, apartment vouchers, health care vouchers) and the address of the JobCenter in Marzahn—a neighborhood in the easternmost part of the city—to which Maimouna had been assigned. Maimouna was a bit frightened at the prospect of needing to deal with a new office and find an apartment. We agreed that I would accompany her to the JobCenter the following month, once she had made an appointment through the social worker at the African self-help organization where we had met.

Indeed, one month later Maimouna and I met at the Springpfuhl S-Bahn (rapid rail) station. Despite our relatively brief acquaintanceship, Maimouna hugged me warmly, like a long- lost family member, and then pointed to a small, dark-haired woman talking on a cell phone, Maimouna's "*maitresse*" (her German language teacher). Maimouna's teacher then turned to me and introduced herself as Anoush. Following an early retirement, Anoush began a part-time career teaching language to newly arrived immigrants. Describing herself as inspired by the challenges her Armenian ancestors had experienced in their exile from Turkey following the 1915 genocide, Anoush is a highly engaged teacher. She accompanies several of her language pupils on their way through the bureaucratic labyrinth, complaining that her pupils do not know their rights, and that poorly informed officials often create hindrances.

The appointment at the JobCenter was prompt and businesslike, lasting only fifteen minutes, despite the time required for interpreting between French and German. The caseworker was mostly concerned that Maimouna establish a bank account into which her welfare payments could be deposited. The quick appointment was hardly conducive to creating a personal relationship between Maimouna and her caseworker. Our continuing interaction with Anoush ended up being much more interesting.

Leaving the JobCenter, Anoush complained to me that the amount of German language instruction required by the state for immigrants to continue to receive welfare benefits was just not enough for newcomers to learn sufficient German to get along in German society. Three months, she said, was inadequate, especially for people like Maimouna, with relatively low levels of literacy. Anoush jumped ahead of herself in her thoughts, listing for me training courses that might be suitable for Maimouna once her German skills were up to par. Anoush clearly wanted to set Maimouna on what she viewed as a productive path, one that would give Maimouna a basis for financial independence and personal satisfaction.

It is striking that both Anoush and Frau Amt emphasized the importance of learning German to integrate and get along in German society. Georg, the secretary at the African-led self-help organization that had connected me with Maimouna, made a similar point about language. "Even with the educated, it's a problem. So many come thinking that English will get them everywhere. But really, you can't get along here if you don't speak German. Speaking German well is the key to independence, to getting a job, to understanding your rights." Indeed, language learning is closely related to the multiple, highly disputed meanings of the term "integration" in German society. The importance of immigrants learning German seems to be the one area of agreement among Germans across the political spectrum.

In contrast to common US-American usage of "integration" as the opposite of racial segregation (e.g., in schools or neighborhoods), common German usage denotes migrants' adoption of cultural orientations and participation in German social and economic life. Integration was a hotly debated topic when I first arrived as a researcher in Berlin. A demagogic book had just been published by the Berlin politician Thilo Sarrazin, *Deutschland schafft sich ab* (*Germany Is Abolishing Itself*) (2010). The ensuing controversy reignited the media frenzy that began in 2006 with reports about schoolyard violence at the Rütli school, located in my neighborhood of Neukölln. Newspapers, talk shows, and public town hall events became arenas for people to express either resentments or counterarguments regarding the failure of foreigners to integrate. In a 2009 interview with the cultural affairs magazine *Lettre International*, Sarrazin famously stated that "integration requires effort from those that are to be integrated" (Sarrazin 2009).[9] Not only heated media discourse but also protocols of deportation hearings use language that distinguishes among the integration-willing and integration-refusers (Schwarz 2011, 56). Progressive activists countered that responsibility lay with the receiving country—Germany—to provide not only the legal and economic means for immigrant integration but also a welcoming attitude.

Immigrants' responsibility to integrate is codified in law, as part of the Residence Act (Aufenthaltsgesetz). In his study of integration discourse and asylum law in Germany, anthropologist Tobias Schwarz (2011) describes that chapter 3 of the Residence Act focuses on the "promotion of integration." At the turn of the millennium, immigrant integration became a cause célèbre among prominent conservative politicians; Edmund Stoiber, a leader of the conservative Bavarian party Christian Social Union (CSU), stated in 2006 that "immigrants should accept German everyday culture—*Alltagskultur*" (cited in Schwarz 2011, 61). Chapter 5, paragraph 55 of the Residence Act was amended in 2007 to include the lack of integration as grounds for deportation (§ 55 Abs.2 Nr. 9–11 AufenthG, cited in Schwarz 2011, 53).[10] Schwarz explains that while the law itself does not use the term "integrationsfeindlich" (resistant to integration) that had been popularized in some German media, the official commentary on the law explains that the grounds listed in the law for deportation represented "serious violations against the obligation for integration" (BT-Drs. 16/5065, 180, 183) (Schwarz 2011, 54, my trans.).

In the eyes of the law, integration means learning German language and civics. Bureaucrats at the local Foreigners Office determine—on the basis of their impression regarding German fluency—whether an individual receiving a residence permit is obliged to attend an integration course. Caseworkers at the JobCenter can also decide if a recipient of unemployment insurance needs to take an integration course. Integration courses are primarily language courses divided into several modules for a total of 660 lessons, plus an orientation course that teaches German history and civics. Students pay fees calculated per lesson (792 euros for the complete course of 660 lessons), although the fees are waived for those demonstrating economic need. Integration courses become part of the legal-bureaucratic labyrinth, because immigrants must first receive a certificate of eligibility from the Foreigners Office and then choose among an array of course providers listed on a website of the Federal Office for Migration and Refugees (BAMF). The path through the labyrinth is even longer when seeking a fee waiver.

Among frontline government bureaucrats (and much of the general public), language learning, the major focus of integration courses, becomes a shortcut for a more multifaceted sociological definition of integration. More variegated understandings of integration—including but not limited to German language acquisition—are buried in the research departments of federal agencies and in academic writings. For example, a BAMF survey identified three areas of integration benefits gained by participants who have learned German in integration courses: guiding their children's school education, using German-language media, and frequency of contact with Germans (Lochner,

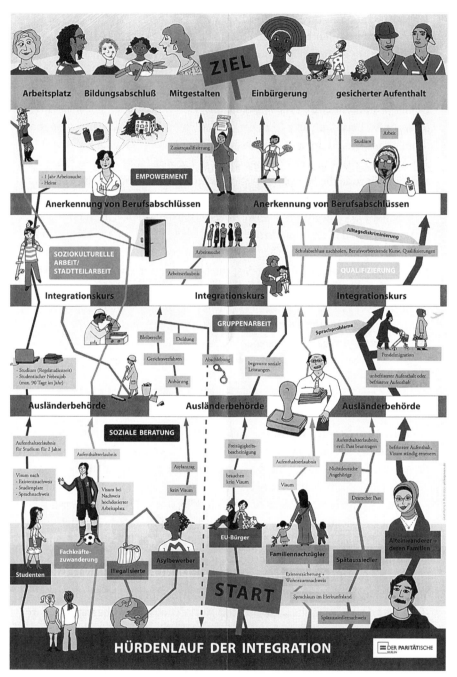

FIGURE 6.1. A poster hanging in the Africa Embrace office, portraying the bureaucratic obstacle course (literally "hurdle race") facing immigrants seeking social integration in Germany.

Büttner, and Schuller 2013). The authors of the survey also mention increased employment opportunities, daily communication between parents and children, and expressions of growing attachment to Germany. In his quantitative study about social integration of African-origin residents of Germany, Benndorf focuses on macrolevel indicators: participation and status in the labor market, academic and vocational training, political participation (through voting, as regulated by law), and engagement in civil society (e.g., political parties, unions, civic associations) (2008). Benndorf describes both macro-and microlevel impediments to integration, from the side of the migrant (low competence in German language) and from the side of the receiving society (restrictive regulations, lack of acceptance by civil society).

Most German discussions of integration focus on migrants' assimilation or at least adaptation to German cultural and social arrangements, including language. I spoke with several German social workers, language teachers, family-planning nurses, and physicians who provided counseling and services to Cameroonian migrant mothers. To them, immigrant integration means speaking German well, working and paying taxes, and following German customs regarding child rearing, religious expression, and even noise levels in apartment buildings. Focusing mainly on immigrants' direct interaction with native-born Germans, these German service providers tend to ignore African migrants' social integration and civic engagement in migrant community organizations, such as hometown associations, savings clubs, and Pentecostal churches (Karagianni and Glick Schiller 2006). At least, migrant social integration in *diasporic* life seems either irrelevant or merely a stepping-stone for integration into *German* life.

In some ways, we could consider becoming a German citizen as the ultimate integration in German society. Becoming naturalized as a German citizen is expensive for families (255 euros per adult, and 51 euros for each dependent minor child naturalized along with a parent) and demanding (Federal Ministry of the Interior 2014). Cameroonian parents seeking citizenship for themselves and for their (often German-born) children must not only pass a citizenship test (introduced in 2006), but also show evidence that they have sent their children to German child-care centers and schools and that their children speak German. Cameroonians who become German citizens—by 2005 nearly 10 percent of people of Cameroonian origin living in Germany (Benndorf 2008, 338)—gain all the rights, security, and access to the job market as German ethnics who are citizens. Cameroonian interlocutors who had become citizens, as they said, "for the sake of the children," reminded me that citizenship does not protect one from everyday slights, or even from violence. Indeed, Benndorf addresses the bodily cost of exclusion; between 2004 and

2005, people of African origin were victims of xenophobic and racially motivated violence in far greater numbers than their proportion of the population would predict (2008, 350).

Anoush was well attuned to precisely this danger of violence confronting so many African immigrants. Switching to a slower tempo and simpler vocabulary so that Maimouna could understand, Anoush warned Maimouna not to look for an apartment in Marzahn. Maimouna's familiarity with the immediate neighborhood surrounding her hostel for unaccompanied youth—like the JobCenter also located in Marzahn—did not dissuade Anoush from expressing the strictest possible warning. Like many politically progressive Germans, Anoush was horrified by reports that particular neighborhoods in Berlin had a reputation for racially motivated violence. And like many Germans who had grown up in West Germany before unification, Anoush found it easy to believe reports regarding right-wing extremism in former East Germany, including in the neighborhoods of former East Berlin. Even if the fall of the Berlin wall "marked the collapse of a symbolic system" (Borneman 1991, 10), the symbolic division between East and West was continually—if only partially—reconstructed through xenophobic violence and its representation as an East German phenomenon.

Indeed, radical-right extremist groups, including those associated with the extremist political party NPD (Nationaldemokratische Partei Deutschlands), began promoting so-called "national liberated zones" or "no-go areas" in the 1990s, shortly after German reunification (Novotný 2009, 596). Right-wing militants used intimidation and violence in their attempt to make no-go areas free of "undesirable" elements (foreigners, Jews, people of color). When Germany hosted the soccer World Cup in 2006, the African Council (Afrika-Rat) of Berlin-Brandenburg and the International League for Human Rights published a list of dangerous no-go areas to warn "dark-skinned" visitors and fans (Gerhäusser 2006). Setting off a flurry of media attention, this announcement included the neighborhoods of Lichtenberg (where many Cameroonian students currently live), Köpenick, and Marzahn-Hellersdorf (Novotný 2009, 592)—the very area that Anoush warned Maimouna against.

Hate crime statistics only partially support Anoush's fears (and prejudices about the impoverished areas of East Berlin). A 2007 government report on right-wing violence in Berlin reports that violence against foreigners is concentrated in the boroughs of Lichtenberg, Pankow, Friedrichshain-Kreuzberg, and Treptow-Köpenick—not in Marzahn (Senatsverwaltung für Inneres 2007, 64). Marzahn, however, is home to a greater number of right-wing hate crime perpetrators than would be expected from its population size (2007, 15). Anoush took it upon herself to guide Maimouna through a difficult system and to protect her from a potentially dangerous neighborhood.[11] Like a doting mother or aunt, Anoush stroked Maimouna's cheek and kissed her goodbye, all the while repeating that she would be fine and would do very well on her own.

BIRTH AND BUREAUCRACY

Wending one's way through the legal-bureaucratic labyrinth continues beyond a migrant's initial period of registering with the Foreigners Office and regularizing one's immigration status. Mothers of infants are overwhelmed with a veritable flood of applications and visits to German authorities and physicians. These errands just add to the unending to-do list that Ariane complained about above, a list of "you must, you must" that can make women rethink their fertility goals, settling for a smaller family.

The German welfare state—from an American perspective—is generous, offering maternity leave, day-care and housing vouchers, and cash benefits to parents and children. German laws guarantee health insurance to legal residents, which covers home visits by a midwife and even help with household chores. But to access the entitlements of the German welfare state, mothers must take steps with at least five different offices before the child is born, and many more after the birth. A mother must establish the newborn's legal personhood and legally recognized kinship relations through applying for a birth certificate and obtaining recognition of paternity from the baby's father. Adding to her long pathway of administrative errands (Behördengang), a new mother must take her infant to a highly regulated series of pediatric checkups. German law establishes these pediatric examinations as the child's right to health care. At the same time they are an obligation for the parents. Each visit is centrally registered through a bar code in the child's pediatric checkup booklet (the *Untersuchungsheft*, colloquially referred to as the "yellow book"). Missed visits are thus automatically reported to Youth Protection Services (the Jugendamt), prompting investigations that in the most drastic scenarios can lead to a mother's loss of custody.

Traveling through the legal-bureaucratic labyrinth is even more consequential, and risky, for mothers without regularized immigration status. Being undocumented means not having the right kind of documents. Ironically, being undocumented means that to access services and to work toward regularizing one's status, one has to carry around "a slew of documents" (Ticktin 2011, 196), including a passport or birth certificate, a diploma, a prescription for medication, an attestation from a refugee-support organization, a rent receipt, or a utility bill showing a street address. Being undocumented also means

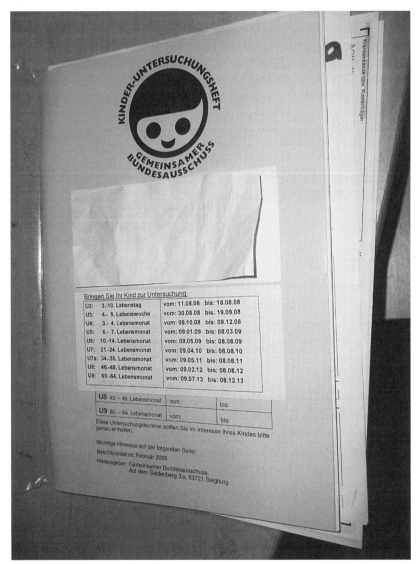

FIGURE 6.2. The child's pediatric-checkup booklet, nicknamed the "yellow book," of one of my interlocutor's children. The booklet tracks attendance at pediatric visits as well as health and development indicators. It embodies the combination of bureaucratic control with highly praised thoroughness of care.

that one is constantly on the lookout for opportunities to change one's documentation, to get newer, different, better, safer documents—in other words, to change how one is categorized in that documentary character of administration that Weber called "administration on the basis of [legal] documents" (Weber 1972, 126).[12]

The birth of a child can be simultaneously a risk and an opportunity for an undocumented mother. On the one hand, searching for prenatal and obstetric care can expose a woman who has been living "underground." The Residence Act "mandates that persons residing illegally in Germany be reported to the authorities if they seek services at public facilities" (Castañeda 2008, 344). Physicians rarely (if ever) follow this "denunciation rule." But pregnant women without a proper visa may become visible to immigration authorities in two ways. If they seek emergency medical services stipulated by provisions of the Asylum Benefits Act (§4 and §6), the Social Services (welfare) Office "that handles reimbursements is required by § 87.2 of the Foreigners Act to relay information to the authorities, which may lead to arrest and deportation" (Castañeda 2013, 228). Thus, unauthorized migrants are reluctant to share the detailed information and supporting documents required by claim forms; claims are thus declined "due to insufficient 'evidence'" (Huschke 2014a, 9), leaving hospitals with uncovered costs for treating undocumented migrants. In these cases, and when pregnant women choose not to draw upon government-funded social services and then find that they cannot pay for their obstetric care, pregnant undocumented migrants attract the attention of hospital billing departments who may then report them.

On the other hand, pregnancy and childbirth render migrant women deserving of help in the eyes of medical charities, immigration activists, and the law. Pregnant women make up around 20 percent of the patients at Berlin's largest medical charity clinic for the uninsured (Castañeda 2008), directed by a physician with the pseudonym Dr. Fritz. Through this charity, migrant mothers also come in contact with social workers, clothing banks, and other social services. Religiously based service providers for "women in distress" and this medical clinic refer clients to each other in a reciprocal relationship grounded in religious social teachings of charity toward the needy. Being pregnant, needing obstetric care, and seeking vaccinations for one's baby also allow migrant mothers to access the aid of citizen activists who coalesce around providing medical services to unauthorized migrants. For these German citizen activists, medical aid is an act of protest rather than of charity; fueled by the current "heightened self-consciousness of German efforts to be seen as a 'normal nation among nations'" following the Holocaust (Mandel 2008, 13), these activists take a critical stance toward the German state's treatment of foreigners (Castañeda 2013, 228, 232; Ellermann 2006). Pregnancy becomes one way that migrant women perform deservingness vis-à-vis humanitarian health-care providers (Huschke 2014b). In terms of law, pregnancy and childbirth offer undocumented mothers protection from deportation for three months prior and three months following a birth—as decided by Berlin's municipal government in August 2008 (TAZ 2008). This legal protection, however, comes with risks, as I discovered through my volunteer activities.

At the African migrant-led community organization where I volunteered, a large binder labeled "pregnancy" included handwritten notes on "illegals and pregnancy." Through this I learned that once a woman is seven months pregnant, she can visit one of the many city Centers for Sexual Health and Family Planning to obtain a document testifying that a person cannot travel (a *Reiseunfähigkeitsbescheinigung*, or Certificate of the Inability to Travel). She needs to get papers ready to apply for her baby's birth certificate—including a valid passport from each parent and a certificate from the father claiming paternity. Through the principle of protection of pregnant women, she can also apply for a certificate of suspension of deportation, called a *Duldung* (literally, toleration). A Duldung temporarily gives the mother access to social welfare (including a cash allowance and maternity clothes), to health care, to baby equipment and clothing, and to publicly subsidized child care. To apply for a Duldung, however, the mother must bring to the Foreigners Office her maternity care medical record booklet (the *Mutterpass*, or "mother's passport"), her certificate that she cannot travel, and two passport photos.

By applying for a temporary stay of deportation, the pregnant woman secures up to six months' legal residence but simultaneously makes herself known to authorities, increasing her risk of later expulsion from the country. Cameroonian mothers warn each other about such risks, leading many to forgo medical and legal services to which they have a right. Dr. Wohlgemuth,[13] a physician at a family-planning center serving a substantial immigrant population, explained how this works among her patients: "*[Pregnant] women without residency permit or health insurance in any case have a right to medical care six weeks before and after their delivery date. And with this we have already noted that despite [this rule], women do not necessarily register themselves and take advantage of this care, because they think that they will then be documented or registered—and what happens then six weeks later?*" I can only imagine what it must feel like for an undocumented pregnant woman to enter the hallways of the imposing Foreigners Office buildings, seeking the documents that will give her only temporary protection.

Documenting illness provides another pathway for mothers to at least temporarily regularize their immigration status; such documentation involves yet another journey from office to office through the legal-bureaucratic labyrinth. In interviews with officials at the national German AIDS organization (Deutsche AIDS Hilfe), family-planning and conflict-pregnancy centers,[14] social workers, and legal aid at the Afrika Center, I learned that severe illness (such as AIDS or cancer) can be the basis upon which an otherwise deportable individual can receive a stay of deportation on humanitarian grounds. Frau Gmeinder,[15] the head of migration services of the national AIDS foundation, described how some immigrants use this stay of deportation to buy time, hoping to stabilize both their immigration status and their access to care: *"And by now, with an HIV infection—including with illegal migrants—one of the first steps they can take is to get a stay of deportation. Through this they naturally also gain time. In this time anything can happen, they can get to know a German man or whatever."*

Frau Gmeinder went on to tell me that by taking advantage of this humanitarian provision in German immigration law, HIV-positive women face similar legal risks as pregnant women, as well as additional social and medical risks. When the Foreign Ministry decides that HIV therapy has become sufficient in the patient's country of origin, the person will be sent back.

A woman's perseverance and web of social relations play crucial roles in accessing temporary legal protections. The mother must visit a physician to document her illness. She must then overcome stigma to reach out to self-help and/or humanitarian associations. By mobilizing her newfound humanitarian network, a woman can then obtain the help of experts who can officially document lack of treatment for that illness in the country of origin. These multiple forms of documentation obtained through the Behördengang can then generate new documents, temporarily securing the residence of the previously undocumented migrant.

In her book *Casualties of Care: Immigration and the Politics of Humanitarianism in France*, Miriam Ticktin illustrates the central role documents play in the medical lives of the so-called undocumented. In France as well as in Germany, documents change the quality of communication and symbolize—more than spoken words—a person's fate and her deservingness of public and private aid, as well as simple human sympathy.

> Amina handed over a slew of documents, both medical and legal—the unruly pile of papers that all those who are "paperless" must carry wherever they go . . . After the nurses thumbed through the majority of her documents [and discovered that Amina and her baby were HIV-positive], their attitude suddenly changed from mild annoyance to care and concern . . . They promised her papers and told her to take care of herself and the baby, to be sure to take the medication (Ticktin 2011, 196).

Through documents, initially annoyed and impatient public health nurses suddenly recognized Amina's humanity.

Lily, whose words introduce this chapter, understands completely about situations like Amina's, carrying around a slew of documents. Lily had first arrived in Europe as an unauthorized migrant to France, what the French call *sans papiers*. Although she had been legally resident in Germany for seven years by the time we first met, the lived experience of giving birth to her first child while being undocumented remains deep. *"Without papers, one is uncomfortable in one's own skin. Perhaps things suddenly will go well, and I can get my papers. But maybe it takes a long time . . . All you can think about are your immigration problems."*

Lily presents getting and losing papers as contingencies or "luck." We learn from Lily that not only the state of having or not having documents but also the uncertain process of searching for papers affects one's psychological state as well as one's relationship with others, the "atmosphere one transmits."

More specifically, Lily describes what it is like to be pregnant and give birth in the absence of documents:

> When you arrive pregnant, the European state will take care of you . . . In France you can receive l'Aide Maladie [health insurance], which allows you to deliver [in a hospital] and receive all necessary medical care, whether you have papers or not . . . But once you've given birth, if you still don't have papers, the state . . . might take care of the baby, but it doesn't give you much to live on. You need to fight for your papers. You need to know people to get informed, have a passport and an address. Even the homeless are given an address. For pregnant women, that's the law in Europe.

Being pregnant may render even unauthorized immigrants deserving of state aid and medical care. But, particularly in Lily's understanding of the law in Europe, this deservingness ends once the baby is born.

Lily not only laments being "all alone," but also gives us a glimpse into her legal consciousness. When she retells her experiences with managing legal stipulations—fulfilling duties and claiming rights as a pregnant woman and young mother—Lily's myriad encounters with French and German bureaucracies crystallizes into narratable orientations toward the law. Lily narrates the documentality of social structure (Ewick and Silbey 2003; Ferraris 2013) when she tells us about the benefits one can and cannot access when undocumented, and how even the undocumented are "documented" through an address.

I have used my own encounters—as a foreigner and as an escort and interpreter for a young African refugee—as an entry point to understand the legal-bureaucratic context that made Lily sigh, *"that's how it is with us here."* Through the legal labyrinth surrounding pregnancy and childbirth, the shadow of the state renders the lives of pregnant African immigrants and young African mothers difficult. We have seen, though, that some women take advantage of humanitarian provisions in an otherwise exclusionary set of immigration laws. With its risks and benefits, the shadow of the state is both nebulous and ambiguous, seeping into myriad aspects of life, simultaneously casting threatening darkness and protective shade on individual women's unique lives and circumstances. How does this two-faced shadow of the state reshape central categories of family life?

Redrawing the Boundaries: Family, Marriage, and Acceptable Care of Children

Living in the shadow of the German state encourages Cameroonian migrant mothers to redraw the boundaries of the family, to alter expectations regarding marriage, and to rethink the proper way to raise a child. Through its immigration laws and diverse forms of regulation, the state "divides families . . . through its definitions of 'family' itself," thus delineating and regulating kinship relations in ways that diverge from immigrants' often more expansive sense of familial obligations (Boehm 2012, 60). Cameroonian migrants learn to adjust their ideas about family life to the exigencies of living as a foreigner in a new environment. Sometimes these changes occur incrementally, nearly imperceptibly to the actors involved. At other times—in moments of difficulties and conflicts—these redefinitions of the contours of family life come into consciousness (Coe 2013, 127ff; Sewell 1992; Swidler 1986). Mothers bring their redefinitions of what it means to make and grow a family when they process difficulties and conflicts through storytelling. I witnessed these redefinitions through the accounts that Cameroonian mothers shared with me during our interviews and encounters in Berlin. I now revisit some of the characters and cases presented above, in light of what it means to form new intimate relationships, maintain affective circuits with family, and care for their children as they see fit. These cases illustrate ways that legal cultures travel and articulate with other legal cultures, as Cameroonian migrants work *with*, *against*, and *in spite of* the law in the course of forming families (Ewick and Silbey 1998). I pose three questions: what counts as family, what counts as marriage, and what is the proper way to raise a child?

WHAT COUNTS AS FAMILY?

In Cameroon the Bamiléké and most other Grassfields people define family broadly. Customary law and lineage affiliation determine the obligations that living descendants have toward their deceased paternal and maternal ancestors, reflecting local ideas about relationships between living and dead family members and the powers of the dead over the well-being of the living. Customary law regards certain members of the same lineage as equivalent legal persons; these particular kin may serve as proxies for each other in customary legal proceedings, including marriage. Caring for children is often distributed among many actors in several households, providing the child with multiple opportunities and experiences. Notions of mutual obligation, sentiment, and parenting thus reflect an expansive conceptualization of family in Cameroon.

In German immigration law, family reunification rules work with a more narrow definition of family. The law allows only specified relatives of a legal migrant—spouses and dependent children—to join him or her in the new country of residence (Breyer 2011; Fleischer 2012). European Union states set temporal and biological limits on who counts as a dependent child. Fostered-in children do not count as dependents, and an immigrant's biological children may age out of dependent-child status. Some European countries, such as Spain and France, use bone density and DNA to determine age and biological relatedness (Bledsoe and Sow 2011a). Adult children, siblings, aunts, or uncles do not count as family for immigration purposes, curtailing their freedom of movement. But these are exactly those relations most likely to provide practical and moral support to a new mother and to help care for a young baby.

The legal definition of family in immigration law makes fulfilling the strong cultural expectation for female kin to help out following childbirth nearly impossible. Kin in Cameroon find it difficult to obtain visas, particularly for longer visits. Above, we heard numerous laments that being pregnant and caring for infants in Germany "all alone," is hard. Here we see that mothers' loneliness is partly a consequence of law.

In our chats about childbirth, Lily contrasted her mother's birthing experiences in Cameroon with her own in Berlin:

> In Cameroon, there is always a lot of help . . . in the house, to cook, clean, wash the baby . . . As for advice, in Cameroon, the mothers are there, they have their experiences, and that helps a lot. But even us here in Europe, we need the experience of our mamas, who can tell us if we need to do this, do that . . . Here, your church members might come for a formal visit, but it's just [only] that. One is closer to the family, it's your mother, your sister, your girl-cousin . . . but they are far, far. The telephone, even Skype, it's not the same. Who will hold your baby for you, buy the groceries? You have to do it all yourself. It's hard being a mother here.

Lily juggles the birth of her third child with the demands of her own education, supervising her children's homework, caring for her husband, and singing in the choir of her Pentecostal church. Considering her many obligations, we can well understand the weight of having "*to do it all yourself.*"

Through sharing such stories, migrant women create a common orientation and vocabulary that organizes their experiences into the two ideal-typical spheres of a highly social and supportive Cameroon and an overwhelmingly complex and lonely Germany. Framing this in terms of legal consciousness, women like Lily and Christine use such contrasting images to make sense of the consequences of law.

The legal environment of transnational migration makes it difficult for migrants to maintain relationships with extended kin, which in turn transforms ideas about family among Cameroonian migrants. More and more, Cameroonian migrant mothers aspire toward companionate marriage (Hirsch and Wardlow 2006) and increasingly focus on the nuclear family. Gazing together at Lily's photo album of wedding portraits and baby snapshots brought our conversation to the ambiguity of family ties. "*Sometimes one confuses things a little, frequently putting family in front of one's proper family . . . The husband will look after his mother too much in relation to his wife and children. That's a little bit the problem one has among Africans. They don't manage to make this distinction . . . But nonetheless, I think that family is very important . . . I have great relations with my mother, my sisters, my brothers.*"

Here Lily expresses the lived tension between the needs of the nuclear family and migrant spouses' emotional and material obligations toward their families of origin and extended kin.

The customary law of Bamiléké and other Grassfields peoples reflects the wide lateral connections among kin related to a common ancestor. Distant cousins share social and ritual obligations to honor their common ancestor. Their common vertical tie engenders lateral expectations for mutuality among extended kin.

But in Germany, family is defined differently; two legal cultures interact for those in the diaspora. Due to restrictions on travel caused by legal definitions of family in immigration law, relatives scattered across continents cannot easily enact the duties of kinship. Legal strictures contribute to migrants redefining the "proper family" as the coresident nuclear family. Nonetheless, "family," meaning one's family of origin—including parents, siblings, aunts, uncles and cousins—is "very important." In Lily's words, we note that this transformation in Cameroonian norms regarding the boundaries defining family is unsettled (and unsettling).

WHAT COUNTS AS MARRIAGE?

Cameroonians perform three types of weddings—traditional rites, civil marriage, and church weddings. Personal choice, family expectations, and available resources determine how many ceremonies a couple performs. Cameroonian family law recognizes all three types of marriage, including both monogamous and polygynous versions of civil marriage. In Germany, couples can conclude only a monogamous civil marriage (Dethloff 2012). When Cameroonian forms of marriage are not legally recognized in Germany, Cameroonians living in Germany find that their spouses' immigration and social welfare rights are constrained.

Recall the love story of Maria Mar and Paul. Of the three possible types of wedding ceremonies, the traditional wedding rites were most important *socially* and *emotionally* to Maria and Paul. Maria termed these rites *"the necessities,"* in contrast to the civil and church weddings. Traditional wedding rites forge material and emotional exchange among a wide set of actors and are thus a central part of establishing and strengthening affective circuits through marriage. Maria felt strongly that the two families should perform the traditional wedding rites before she and Paul concluded the civil and religious rituals. But Maria was still a student with nothing more than a part-time job and a small scholarship. In addition, she and Paul were not yet legally married in Germany. Travel to Cameroon to perform the traditional wedding ceremony was both too expensive and created too large a bureaucratic headache at that time. Thus, Maria and Paul adapted the rituals and timing of their wedding ceremonies to the financial and legal constraints of transnational migrant life.

Maria and Paul innovated, performing a marriage-by-proxy. The public exchange of bridewealth, vows of solidarity between family members, and blessings for the newlyweds were performed in Cameroon despite Maria and Paul's absence. Through a myriad of phone calls and wired money transfers, Paul arranged for key family members to be present. Full siblings—children of the same father *and mother* who are part of the same *pam nto'* or uterine group—can serve as proxies, making the ceremony legally binding. Maria's sister made vows in Maria's name, pouring libations of palm wine to seal her promises of fidelity. Maria's sister—standing in for the bride—was anointed with palm oil and camwood powder to symbolize the blessings of fertility and protection that would now accompany the newlyweds. As Maria explained, *"with us before the legal marriage we must do the traditional rite, the necessities. So my husband did that and that could be arranged without us. . . . I had to choose one of my sisters to stand on my behalf to represent me [as the bride] and give my word that I agree."* In customary marriage, the exchange of vows, bridewealth, and ritualized actions by legally recognized actors—in this case proxies—seals the union regardless of the presence of the bride or groom.

In highly mobile populations, a video of the marriage-by-proxy ceremony serves as proof of the validity of the legal relationship. In the same manner that legal consciousness emerges from the circulation of narratives, couples play and replay wedding videos in their living rooms. They thus relive in the presence of friends the details of the wedding's protocol. By watching the seriousness of the ceremonial acts framed by the jovial interactions of the participants, the bride and groom share the emotions of their wedding with their fellow viewers in the diaspora. The video documents the ritual performance of a legal act, while simultaneously recording and recreating its emotional import for family members separated by immense geographical distance.

In German law, a wedding performed in the absence of bride and groom would not be valid. Realizing this, and perhaps wanting to get married "in the modern way" by performing all three types of weddings, Maria Mar and Paul concluded a civil wedding in Germany. Maria told me, "*We got married legally here in Germany, and then we went back to Cameroon and then we did the wedding there.*" Maria explained that several years later, when both she and Paul were employed in Germany, they travelled to Cameroon. During this visit home, the couple completed the traditional rites in person, being anointed with palm oil and camwood powder and receiving blessings directly from their parents and other senior kin. Maria and Paul also used their visit to Cameroon to stage a "white wedding," a church wedding with formal dress followed by a big party. Maria showed me photos of her and Paul, dressed respectively in a white wedding gown and dark tuxedo. Finally, their marriage was ceremoniously and normatively validated for the three distinct audiences most relevant for the couple's sense of security and social embeddedness—their family in Cameroon, their religious community as Christians, and the German state.

German legal actors question more than the validity of Cameroonian marriage-by-proxy. A recent law on "sham marriages" (§1314 II Nr. 5 des EheschiRG) questions the validity of marriages concluded to gain a more favorable immigration status. Government registrars are the frontline actors who get to decide if a marriage appears "legitimate." Registrars thus practice great discretion as control agents. In her detailed demographic ethnography, Annett Fleischer (2012) found that recently arrived Cameroonian immigrants respond to the constraints of "Fortress Europe" by orienting "their marital and reproductive lives in Germany more toward Germans than toward their compatriots," finding no other way to regularize their immigration status (Bledsoe and Sow 2011a, 184). My research indicates that Cameroonians who either arrive without a visa, or overstay a tourist visa, may indeed initially seek to regularize their immigration status by marrying a German citizen or legal resident, or by bearing a German-citizen child.

For example, Mrs. Black explains that the circumstances of her marriage were shaped both by her need for documents and by regulations regarding the act of getting married:

> I came like a tourist first. Then I met my husband, then we have to go back to Cameroon, get married, because it was so difficult to marry here . . . When I came I took a tourist visa and you know tourist visa, those don't last long. So later the visa got expired and it was not . . . you know . . . [people were] telling me to seek asylum but I did not want to do that . . . lucky enough I met my husband before the visa get expired. So the only way I was supposed to stay in Germany is to get married and with the tourist visa I can't get married. So the lawyer told us that the only way was to go back to Cameroon, get married and then I can come back, I can be really legal with my husband . . . I stayed there [in Cameroon] again three months, did all my documents, then I came back again like a married woman.

The lengths to which Mrs. Black and her husband went to get married underscore that "marrying is a matter of the accumulation of documents before, during, and after a certain ceremony, and these documents are inscriptions of acts without which the marriage has no legal value" (Ferraris 2013, 286). The path Mrs. Black took to document her relationship through the legal, ritual, and bureaucratic requirements was circuitous indeed. Her story became one of many biographical tales that Cameroonian migrants circulated to understand how the connections work among marriage, bureaucracy, and legal documentation in various European Union countries. Its telling and retelling thus contributed to the ongoing production of a transnational legal consciousness among African immigrants to Europe (Schwenken 2013).

While the narrative of migrants marrying German nationals to "get documents" looms large in public perception, only four of the Cameroonian women I met were married or had been married to ethnic Germans. I noted that longer-term Cameroonian residents of Germany tend to seek out relationships with fellow Cameroonians. In the five love stories above, Cameroonian mothers who arrive and stay legally, especially students and highly qualified professionals, either come to Germany already married to a Cameroonian, or meet their Cameroonian partner once they have been living in Germany for some time.

Among the migrant mothers I came to know, a substantial minority were married or in long-term cohabitation with Cameroonian male partners who had previously been in relationships with ethnic Germans. The men's relationships allowed them to gain ever-more secure and permanent legal status. So'nju's story detailed the effects that men's marriages to Germans had on the migration experiences of their Cameroonian girlfriends. So'nju joined Nya—her boyfriend and father of her baby—in Germany on a tourist visa after Nya had regularized his status by marrying a German woman. Because Nya wanted to remain married to his German wife until he had obtained a more permanent residency status, he did not want his German wife to learn of So'nju's existence. Not only would the German wife be angry, but the German state would not recognize that Nya could be married simultaneously to his German wife and to So'nju. (Unlike in Cameroon, polygynous marriage is illegal in Germany.)

This precarious social and legal situation forced So'nju to live "underground," as anonymously as possible, for several years. Nya's working "with the law," manipulating binational marriage to obtain legal security in Germany, resulted in So'nju living in spite of or "against the law" (Ewick and Silbey 1998). Through this circuitous pathway, the shadow of the state had a lasting effect on So'nju's ability to build and maintain ties that would help her to belong simultaneously in German society and in her Cameroonian diasporic community. So'nju's vulnerable legal status and dependency on Nya isolated her from her German neighbors, preventing her from learning German and thus from becoming more employable and less conspicuous in public. So'nju's situation while waiting for her boyfriend to stabilize his immigration status also isolated her from her fellow Cameroonian migrants, separating her from potential avenues of advice on how to get along in a new place.

While So'nju was relatively isolated socially, Mrs. Black was active within the Cameroonian diasporic community in Berlin. She was also an outspoken critic of the difficulties she faced within her binational marriage. On the one hand, the stories Mrs. Black shared with her Cameroonian friends illustrated the daily compromises that could make a marriage between a German and a Cameroonian endure. After all, she had been married for seven years and counting. On the other hand, Mrs. Black's stories of everyday life served as a warning to her Cameroonian friends of the difficulties of binational marriage. Mrs. Black and her husband sometimes disagreed about her sense of financial obligation to her Cameroonian kin; instead of saving toward major purchases, such as a car, Mrs. Black regularly sent remittances to her parents and siblings.

Not only was Mrs. Black's husband "*not really into it*" when she sought fertility treatment; Mrs. Black also had a gnawing feeling that she would never be completely accepted by her German in-laws. When she chose her pseudonym for our interviews and this book, she declared, "Call me Mrs. Black, because this is how they see me. First I am Black, and only later am I a person."

Because their family ties are stretched across continents, couples like Mrs. Black and her husband are not embedded in a network of face-to-face, enduring multiplex relations that, as Gluckman proposed, would encourage them to resolve marital disputes (1967, 96). Cameroonian migrant mothers' stories about differing norms regarding family boundaries, obligations, and autonomy in binational marriage crystallize into shared, future-oriented ideas about working with the law and—as So'nju's testimony points out—also working to avoid the law. In various adaptations of marriage to the constraints of migrant life, we witness emerging patterns of legal consciousness.

WHAT IS THE PROPER WAY TO RAISE A CHILD?

In addition to the delimitations of family and adaptions of marriage, practices surrounding the care and socialization of young children reveal ways the shadow of the state engenders change and promotes a newly emerging diasporic legal consciousness. Through case studies, we can observe how African parents respond to the bureaucratic regulation of infant care and behavioral-health screening of young children. We also see how the shadow of youth protection services affects how migrant mothers care for their children by enforcing discipline.

For Cameroonian parents living in Berlin, the proper way to raise a child is to root it with a feeling of belonging to a Cameroonian community. Belonging, they say, is the basis for resilience when facing the hardships of migrant life. Mothers engage in a difficult balancing act between forging Cameroonian belonging—through bodily practices and enforcement of respect toward elders—and fostering adaptation to the German environment. They face host-country norms regarding male circumcision, the definition of preschoolers' rambunctiousness as illness (attention deficit hyperactivity disorder—ADHD), and proper relations between children and adults that seem strange and disturbing. Government bureaucrats and the physicians, teachers, and social workers who provide state-mandated surveillance and care to immigrant families appear to misunderstand or distort migrant mothers' relationships to their children. Mothers confront these situations with a combination of pragmatism and consternation. Using tales of their own and others' experiences, migrant mothers forewarn each other about ways state actors make them redraw the contours of appropriate child-rearing.

Bodily practices, such as the circumcision of young boys, mark belonging. In societies where the circumcision of male infants is common—such as in Cameroon or the United States—being circumcised means being normal, while being uncircumcised marks one as different. Male circumcision carries even more weight as a marker of belonging in Judaism and Islam, where it marks a covenant with God. But in mainstream German society, circumcision is anything but a matter of course. We saw how Jucal explained what she viewed as a German cultural peculiarity, that Germans believed circumcision is dangerous, exoticized, and *"not a tradition . . . here in Germany."* Dr. Fritz proved Jucal's point, when she opined: *"Christians wouldn't do anything like that [circumcision] . . . I'm personally no fan of circumcision—I find it to be bodily harm of the child. There's no medical necessity to it. There are lots of complications, depending upon where it's done."*

Like many other Cameroonian mothers I spoke to, Jucal had a difficult time articulating just what made circumcision part of being Cameroonian or Bamiléké. Most Bamiléké combine either Roman Catholic or Calvinist Protestant Christianity with vestiges of traditional religious beliefs. In Bamiléké and other Grassfields traditions, male circumcision is considered a prerequisite to becoming an adult man, but it is neither ritually marked nor practiced at any particular age. While oral histories I collected in the 1980s indicated that male circumcision may have been tied to puberty rituals in the distant past, most Cameroonians now have their sons circumcised at a hospital, sometime between birth and age three. Jucal thus described male circumcision not in religious terms, but rather as a custom that is taken for granted.

> I don't just know. It's just like it is something in the brain. Every male in Cameroon is circumcised. So I don't know whether . . . I just know it's something. Although here they say it might [be] there is dirt inside, people don't know how to clean it so well so it's good you cut it in order to be clean. But I just know that every man should be circumcised. Not should but where I come from they do that . . . even if you are undressing in like in beach or whatsoever, people will be looking.

Jucal explained that biomedical reasons (cleanliness, tight foreskin) were the sole justifications for covering male circumcision as a medical expense. Of much greater import to Jucal, however, was the potential social ostracism of her son remaining uncircumcised in the Cameroonian context. She was adamant that circumcision was an essential, early step in raising her son as a Cameroonian.

Jucal's son was still an infant when we met in 2011; her son's circumcision was thus very much on her mind. Jucal dealt pragmatically with the contrast between Cameroonian ideas and German regulation of infant male circumcision—regulations that were about to change. In 2011, insurance did not cover circumcisions that were considered elective for "cultural" reasons rather than medically indicated. Jucal received addresses for pediatric surgeons from her pediatrician, *so many addresses, so I just called, it's business, you pay them [200 euros] for their services.* At the time, health insurance companies, rather than physicians or courts, served as arbiters for conflicting norms. Insurance companies decided which cases would be covered; for those circumcisions termed "cultural," insurance companies' denial of coverage made access to the procedure difficult for those who could not afford to pay out of pocket.

In 2012, the legal standing of circumcision of male children became a hotly debated topic. In June of that year, a local court in Cologne ruled that circumcision constitutes "bodily harm" (*Körperverletzung*). Initial critiques of the ruling (e.g., *Die Welt, June* 27 and 29, 2012) were based on religious grounds (e.g., *Express* 2012; *Süddeutsche Zeitung,* July 5, 2012), pitting ideas about the protection of a child's bodily integrity against freedom of religion. Turkish and Jewish organizations in Germany, as well as the major German churches, spoke out against the ruling. Some op-eds even made reference to the Holocaust (*Süddeutsche Zeitung* July 16, 2012), engaging in a representational practice known as "analogic bridging" (Alexander 2002, 44; Savelsberg and King 2011, 125–28). Within a month, extended journalistic commentaries appeared in major print outlets regarding legal-cultural dilemmas, medical opinions, and the nature of religious identities (e.g., Rabinovici 2012; Sachsenröder 2012; Polke-Majewski 2012). These were followed by editorials describing male circumcision as an archaic form of bodily harm (e.g., Ehrmann 2012; Kelek 2012; Schmidbauer 2012), even calling circumcision "amputation of the male foreskin" (cf. Fraczek 2013).

By late December of 2012, a new law, §1631d *Beschneidung des männlichen Kindes* ("circumcision of the male child") was passed to clarify the legal status of male circumcision.[16] This new law grants parents the right to seek and permit the circumcision of their infant son. Before the baby turns six months old, the circumcision may be performed by a trained practitioner, whether a religious authority (such as a Jewish *mohel*) or a surgeon. After the baby boy has reached six months of age, the procedure may be performed only by a medical doctor (Scholz 2012).

The concerns of mothers like Jucal were left out of this debate. Cameroonian circumcision practices are based on custom rather than on the doctrine of a world religion. And as the debate continues to rage despite the attempted Solomonic solution of the December 2012 law, the only recognized "right" to circumcision is based on the religious laws and membership of the child's parents (Fraczek 2013). The circumcision debate leaves no room for circumcision based "merely" on custom, regardless of immigrant parents' conviction that this practice is part of providing the best care possible for their baby boys.

The intersection of medicine, law, and immigrant parenting becomes apparent during the behavioral-health screenings that occur when mothers register their children for first grade. Because immigrant mothers are concerned about how their children's school placement will affect their future success, these are high-stakes encounters. The pediatricians, educators, and social workers who fulfill state mandates regarding screenings usually see prospective school-starters and their accompanying parent (usually the mother) on only one occasion. Unfortunately, these encounters among African mothers, their children, and unfamiliar German officials often lead to misunderstandings.

When immigrant mothers are highly educated and articulate, such misunderstandings between German officials and African parents may be "merely" insulting. Barbara was concerned about her second child's preparation for the ubiquitous school-readiness screenings. During a parent-teacher conference at her child-care center, Barbara spoke to the teacher about bad behaviors young Kemayou was picking up from her classmates. After all, big sister Happi was doing so well in school, standing out both intellectually and through her polite manners. Instead of taking Barbara's concerns about Kemayou seriously, the teacher retorted that perhaps Kemayou was not getting enough attention at home, "because you Africans have such large families."

When immigrant mothers are less educated, they are more likely to get caught in a web of linguistic and cultural misunderstandings, sometimes with harrowing legal consequences. I heard of one such case from Evangeline, the lead social worker at the community-based organization African Embrace. Evangeline was helping a working-class African immigrant mother of four who had lost custody of her twin six-year-olds following their school-readiness screening. The client, Constance, was shocked when the pediatrician at the screening diagnosed her rambunctious twins with ADHD and suggested medicating them before they could start school.

When Constance refused this treatment, claiming that her children were "not sick," Youth Protective Services (the Jugendamt) intervened. Constance was declared unfit because she did not recognize her son's hyperactivity as "illness." With only rudimentary German reading skills, Constance had to sign papers—documents that she believed would allow her twins to attend a boarding school. Constance did not realize that these papers instead would take away her custody of the two boys and send them to a state-run group home (Jugendheim). By the end of my fieldwork in Berlin, the six-year-old twins lived in the group home, attended school there during the week, and visited their family on the weekends.

Evangeline supervised the boys' weekend visits home, documenting Constance's interactions with her sons to help her regain custody. Evangeline described that the boys were quite aggressive during their weekend visits. They were unhappy at the group home and angry that they had to live in the Jugendheim while their siblings were living at home. The twins also asked why their father did not pick them up from the group home. According to Evangeline, Constance answered that their father was not allowed to pick them up for weekend visits because one of the boys had once told a youth services social worker that his father had locked him in his room for misbehaving. During another weekend visit, the boys were roughhousing with their older brother, and one got a black eye; Evangeline reported that Youth Protection Services naturally asked about the black eye, making insinuations about violence in the home.

Evangeline is frustrated by her meetings with representatives of Youth Protection Services. She feels that they seem to understand neither the situation of a mother whose children have been taken away, nor the deleterious effects that the group home and separation from their parents and siblings were having on the two young boys. Evangeline acknowledges that employees of Youth Protection Services became particularly skittish after a few notorious cases of children dying in abusive families. But Evangeline also feels that these employees worked hard to construct a case in which the mother, Constance, is always shown to be unfit. They are upset with Constance for arriving late to meetings, and overly exacting about details of reported conversations between Constance and her sons. During one weekend visit, one of the boys complained that the group home wasn't good and asked why he and his twin have to go there. In Evangeline's account of the situation, Constance answered that "they have to go to school, and yes, she understands that the *Heim* [group home] isn't good, but still he must go there." Evangeline told me that the Youth Protection Services employees used this incident as evidence that Constance manipulated the boys to be negative and aggressive in the group home. For her part, Evangeline worried about such labeling increasing the boys' ADHD and aggression.

For nearly a year, Evangeline built rapport and modeled positive interactions by engaging Constance and her sons in craft activities and baking cakes with the family. Finally, after many months of documenting the children's visits home, Evangeline saw some movement in the case; Constance seemed to be on a path toward regaining custody of her twins. Youth Protection Services had made arrangements for one of the boys to attend a therapeutic school for children with behavioral problems. They had diagnosed the other twin as mildly mentally retarded and were planning to send him to a special education school. Evangeline reported that Constance felt that the boys' separation from their family had caused their behavioral problems. Even more strongly, Constance found it difficult to accept the diagnosis that one of her children was "handicapped," and was upset that he would be sent to a school with children who have visible handicaps. Nonetheless, Constance had learned that going along with the Youth Protection Services' labels was the only way for her to regain custody of her children.

Constance's heartrending encounter with Youth Protection Services may be out of the ordinary, but cases like hers serve as exemplars warning other Cameroonian mothers to beware of an intrusive government agency. The threat of intervention by Youth Protection Services—and the fear that this intervention may result either in loss of child custody or loss of a secure immigration status—hangs over Cameroonian parents' decisions regarding child discipline like Spittler's shadow of the Leviathan (1980). When they meet to drink tea, to braid hair, or to swap babysitting favors, mothers simultaneously share and comment on stories about people like Constance. They develop an impression that Germany is an environment in which children "know their rights," to the detriment of their African parents' attempts to keep them in line.

Cameroonian parents like Barbara, Bih, Jucal and Brianna despaired that their children would pick up disrespectful manners from their German peers at child-care centers and schools. Bih, for example, said that she worries that her child might become more like German children, talking back to their parents and misbehaving. Bih disciplines her child strictly, because German society fails to provide the standards or support for fostering respect that Bih could expect in Cameroon. Like Bih, Brianna worried that the long-term effects of prevailing antiauthoritarian parenting styles in Germany would diminish her child's chances to "be something" in life.

From cases like Constance and her sons, and discussions at parent-teacher conferences, Cameroonian mothers learn that corporal punishment—legal and common in Cameroon—is strictly limited and controlled in German law. Mothers fear that teachers or even the German parents of their children's classmates might report them to authorities. As Iris explained, "Even with their friends when they are playing [and ask each other], 'What did you do yesterday?' . . . The children [are] talking, talking, talking. Before you know the teachers know . . . what is happening in your house, how your parents are treating you in the house." Iris was concerned that a child's complaint about strict rules or what she considered a mild spanking could be blown out of proportion by overly vigilant teachers, who would then seek the involvement Youth Protection Services.

Not only did Iris and other mothers like her mistrust teachers' interest in their lives as suspicious intrusions, they also commented that their children learned from classmates that corporal punishment was forbidden. As Jucal told me, "*You can't do anything to the child because they know they have their rights.*" In fact, Jucal's statement reveals how parents also learn about the law from their children, developing an exaggerated view in which all forms of discipline, from time-outs to spankings, are off-limits.

Iris recounted that Cameroonians circulated information and personal accounts about children invoking the right not to be punished. "*We always say, you know, in the African community that these children here are born with rights. They are born and they just know their rights.*" Note how Iris introduces her comment with "*We always say . . . in the African community.*" Parents worry *together* about the long-term consequences of their inability to enforce discipline. Through the retelling of cautionary tales, these mothers' individual experiences coalesce into a shared Cameroonian discourse of drastically limited parental rights to discipline their children. We learn from the legal consciousness approach that people develop collective orientations to the law through the circulation of exemplary personal stories. In the case of disciplining children—setting the boundaries of how to best rear one's child— Cameroonian mothers do not avoid or work against the law, but instead are frustrated by what they view as its intrusive power.

Turning to the State: Intimate-Partner Violence and Other Disasters

Following Spittler's proposition that the shadow of the Leviathan fosters the success of alternative forms of dispute resolution (1980), we might expect Cameroonian migrant women facing marital problems to turn to "customary" dispute-resolution mechanisms within migrant community associations. After all, the state casts a shadow that redraws the boundaries of what counts as marriage, family, and appropriate child rearing. Instead, I found that when facing intimate-partner violence and other serious marital disputes, Cameroonian mothers do occasionally turn to the organizations and laws of the German Leviathan, as illustrated by the experiences of Fanny and Rose.

We learned that Fanny's love story represented one variation on the ways that Cameroonian migrant women meet their partners and get married. Recall the difficult circumstances Fanny faced before finally meeting her Cameroonian fiancé, Cedric. Fanny had worked as an English-French bilingual secretary in Yaoundé for a German firm. She was content with her work and her life and had no intentions to migrate to Germany or elsewhere in Europe. But through her work she met and fell in love with a German coworker, whom she married. Under pressure from her German husband, Fanny left the stepmother who had raised her with love, and all of her remaining extended family, to migrate to Germany. *"I never wanted to come here but he insisted because we couldn't live distantly."* After arriving in Germany, Fanny learned that her German husband insisted on complete control. *"He became another person. We had to* Streit, *fight every day . . . And it led to so many problems, police getting involved, me running away from time to time and coming back home. That kind of life was difficult."* The only place Fanny's German husband would allow her to go was her German language and integration course.

The integration course proved to be a lifesaver, once Fanny's husband turned emotionally and physically abusive. Through conversations with her fellow integration students—immigrants from all corners of the globe—Fanny learned about the existence of women's shelters in Germany. Her language teacher gave her brochures and explained whom Fanny could call to access protection from her abusive husband. As Fanny said, *"I got to ask information from there . . . I was made to understand that . . . I could call the police or . . . go for help somewhere called* Frauenhaus *[Women's Shelter]."*

Fanny moved to a women's shelter and eventually resettled in Berlin. She considered returning to Cameroon, but several economic, emotional, and legal considerations kept her in Germany. Fanny had no job to return to in Cameroon, because she had resigned her position at the international firm when she moved to Germany. She feared that her abusive husband would talk to people at the firm, spreading "lies and gossip" that would prevent her from getting a new job in Yaoundé. Fanny also worried about returning to Cameroon facing the shame of a failed marriage. In addition, she was in the midst of an ongoing legal process regarding her husband's violent abuse. *"Actually I wanted to go back to Cameroon, but when the issue was at a level that the state had to go into it, they . . . decided to keep me here to see if things will go on well."*

In the end, Fanny could stay in Germany through a law protecting victims of abuse (Dethloff 2012, 89).[17] A paragraph in immigration law lifts the requirement that foreign citizens remain married to their German spouse for three years before becoming permanent residents—if they suffer "particular difficulties." The law specifically mentions intimate-partner violence, and that it aims to prevent people from remaining in a marriage characterized by domestic violence. Fanny became aware of this law when she received the court's report. *"I was surprised when they came to me to give me another report, changing my status to give me another status to stay . . . I was relieved that they could understand me.*" Having learned from fellow migrants that the law did not always treat immigrants kindly, Fanny was surprised and relieved that the authorities had understood and sympathized with her difficult situation.

Rose, who first arrived in Germany as the spouse of a Cameroonian with a student visa, also turned to a German organization and to German law when that marriage went sour. Like Fanny, Rose is a young Bamiléké woman who worked as a bilingual secretary in Yaoundé. Her husband received a scholarship to attend university in Germany. Once he was settled, Rose gave up her job to join him, arriving on a family reunification visa. Because Rose spoke no German, her job prospects were limited to the most menial labor—in her case, working as a hotel chambermaid.

Rose and her husband tried to conceive a child, but could not, due to male-factor infertility, as the couple later discovered. This was particularly upsetting, because Rose's mother-in-law asked, "Where is the child?" during every phone call. Although her husband was infertile, Rose was blamed for their childless marriage. When Rose had been in Germany for barely a year, her mother-in-law convinced Rose's husband to drive her from the marriage. He did so to cover up his own infertility, fearing the stigma that would result should his family reveal his secret. The end of their marriage, however, meant the end of Rose's claim to legal residence in Germany. Rose's visa was dependent on her marriage to her legally resident husband.

Rose entered a period of illegality, making her fearful that any contact could reveal her irregular status and get her deported. Returning to Cameroon, jobless and divorced on the basis of childlessness, would have been a shame too great to bear. During this period of trauma, Rose met another African migrant, a long-term legal resident, and became pregnant. The January 2000 Nationality Act permits a child born in Germany to noncitizen parents to acquire German citizenship if one parent has lived in Germany as a legal resident for at least eight years (Bundesministerium für Justiz und Verbraucherschutz 2014). When Rose's baby, Serge, was born, she made sure that his father signed paternity papers. Rose was thus able to obtain a German passport for her young son. This in turn allowed Rose to obtain a residence permit as the custodial parent. Baby Serge thus shaped his mother's relationship with German immigration authorities, rescuing her from deportability (de Genova 2002; Huschke 2013, 120).

Baby Serge also shaped Rose's relationship with German voluntary organizations. Many migrant women like Rose, whose qualifications are either not recognized or not considered useful in Germany, work as hotel chambermaids, as home health aides, or in elder care. Pregnancy and childbearing puts their service-sector jobs at risk. When Rose was eight months pregnant,

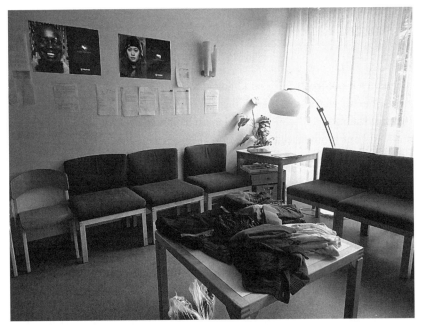

FIGURE 6.3. The waiting room at Dr. Fritz's charity clinic. In addition to its humanitarian medical care, Dr. Fritz's clinic provided some social-work services. Donated clothing is folded neatly on the table, available for clients to take as needed.

she lost both her job and her health insurance. Only then did she reach out for help, through the Catholic church she attended. A clergy member recognized Rose's "deservingness" (Huschke 2014b) and referred her to a Catholic charity providing services for "women in distress." This organization then took Rose under their wing, arranging emergency housing, legal aid, and perinatal care with a medical charity serving the uninsured (almost all of whom are irregular migrants).

Rose returned to the medical clinic for regular checkups, relieved that someone was taking care of her in her late pregnancy and even after the birth. Dr. Fritz, the director of the charity clinic, issued Rose a Mutterpass and carefully noted a thorough series of federally mandated prenatal tests and checkups. Dr. Fritz is a tough, no-nonsense woman, an effective physician and administrator who has won prizes for her charity work. She distanced herself from the touchy-feely nature of "do-gooders," explaining: "*My motivation is neither political nor starry-eyed idealism . . . I'm also no friend of grand statements such as 'Ever since I was a child, I . . .' Nah, that's not my thing.*"

Nonetheless, she shared a critique of medicalized childbirth with what Durand (2004) describes as the contemporary German organic-food middle class.[18] In an interview conducted several months after Rose's baby Serge was born, Dr. Fritz told me that she was not pleased about the mandatory nature of prenatal care. *"They have to endure this technological medicine, which is obviously by far not as pronounced in other countries. Especially in Africa . . . pregnancy is not treated like an illness."* Dr. Fritz worried that her African patients, having witnessed many "natural" births "in the village," would find the medicalization of childbirth alienating. But it was not so for Cameroonian migrant mothers like Rose, who come from urban settings; as women who had not yet borne children, they would not have been allowed to view a birth *au village*. Rose and other migrant mothers relished the highly regulated perinatal care offered, indeed *required*, through the German health and child-welfare system. Although they worried about being reported to Youth Protection Services if they missed an appointment, Rose and other mothers praised the *"thorough"* series of pediatric checkups tracked through their child's bar-coded pediatric- checkup booklet.

Serious marital dispute placed both Fanny and Rose in multiple layers of emotional, social, medical, and legal risk. These risks affected both the women's access to health care and their immigration status, threatening to thrust them into the category of illegal migrant. Fortunately, Fanny and Rose worked through decentralized social-service organizations—a private language school offering federally mandated integration courses and a Catholic charity—to make use of the legal resources of a new legal community.

Conclusion

If German state law acted like Spittler's Leviathan, we would expect its shadow would make Cameroonian migrant mothers turn to the legal culture and dispute mechanisms that they carried with them in their suitcases. But something happened in transport, and in the interaction of a legal culture "from home" with a new legal and bureaucratic environment. Cameroonian migrant mothers continue practices they learned in Cameroon when they are creative with the law (e.g., proxy marriage) and in their mistrusting attitudes toward the agents of state law. But there are discontinuities as well, when women turn to that very Leviathan for help.

Law sets parameters of migrant women's everyday experiences of making families—the restricted pool from which to choose partners, the occasional instrumentalization of romantic relationships, the recognition of only certain types of marriage and only certain types of kin as "family," and the resulting absence of supportive kin at crucial life-cycle moments. Law contributes to mothers' fear that without discipline their children will go astray and that an intrusive state apparatus will prevent parents' attempts to enforce Cameroonian norms regarding respect.

But law affects African migrants' family life through more than its set of legal norms, urging me to speak of "the shadow of the state" rather than the shadow of the Leviathan. The shadow of the state makes itself felt in Cameroonian migrant mothers' lives through rules, administrative organization, and interpersonal interactions.

The German state sets rules—legal norms—regarding entry, residence, and even migrants' degree of effort toward integration. The complex organization of social control and service provision for immigrants necessitates seemingly unending journeys through a labyrinthine system. The combination of legal rules and the German bureaucratic organizational form affects African migrants' direct encounters with state agents. Rules allow government bureaucrats a degree of discretion, which can be applied either to the benefit or to the detriment of migrant women's goals. Such discretion in the application of legal norms allows for a human side in these encounters but also considerable variation in the way state agents handle women's cases. This variation is further shaped by the organization of work within and between government agencies. Clients' cases are shifted from jurisdiction to jurisdiction. Combined with heavy caseloads, this limits the ability of caseworkers, such as Frau Amt, and clients, like Maimouna, to develop lasting relationships. In situations like Constance's run-in with Youth Protection Services, the consequences of cursory, formalized encounters can be devastating.

Migrant women's social relationships are an important part of managing life under the shadow of the state. Some of these relationships are fleeting and largely instrumental, such as the relationship between caseworkers and their clients. Other relationships are formed through more lasting bases of identification, such as the circuits formed in hometown associations. To be able to "fight for your papers" and access both public and private benefits, all migrants are dependent on the information that circulates—often in story form—among their fellow migrants. The undocumented are even more dependent on the help and information that flows through their networks. Through word-of-mouth recommendations, women like Lily, Rose, and Maimouna can access charity clinics, activist networks of medical personnel (Castañeda 2013), and other services for the undocumented. The care provided by these institutions reflects back on the trustworthiness of the person who recommended them.

Using the same affective circuits through which women forge belonging, migrant mothers exchange experiences about the way law affects family making. The cautionary tales they circulate in the course of everyday socializing develop into shared orientations about getting along with the law in a new place. Through founding families and rearing children, women encounter and develop understandings of the law. Migrant mothers develop new strategies that shape their marital and reproductive lives, their obligations to kin, and their child-rearing practices. Mothers' migrant legal consciousness is fresh, emergent, in flux—and an important element in women's efforts to reproduce belonging.

Notes

Chapter One

1. Here and following, all names are pseudonyms. In most cases, my interlocutors chose their own pseudonyms as part of the informed-consent process.

2. Although it uses a different vocabulary, the vast twentieth-century literature on social networks within anthropology and sociology addresses diverse practices of belonging. Network-based concepts of embeddedness, communication, social support, and social capital are most relevant here (Boswell 1969; Coleman 1988; Emirbayer and Goodwin 1994; Granovetter 1973, 1985; Lin 1999; Marsden 1987; Mitchell 1969; Pescosolido 1986, 1992; Portes 1998; Uehara 1990; Valente et al. 1997).

3. Related uses of the term "insecurity" to refer to a combination of political-economic conditions, symbolic meanings, and affect-laden everyday experience include Devisch, De Boeck, and Jonckers' treatment of food insecurity (1995), Ashforth's work on spiritual insecurity (2005), and Robinson's work on the relationship between an ethics of care and global human security (2011).

4. A similar set of questions can be asked of migrants who cross international borders. As we will see in chapter six, belonging is framed in German popular discourse in terms of "integration," loyalty to sending vs. destination countries in terms of discussions over dual citizenship, and the spacialization of basic rights in terms of asylum law and "Fortress Europe."

5. See Abu-Lughod (2008) on the importance of "ethnographies of the particular" as well as the role of friendship in anthropological fieldwork.

6. Local polities in the Grassfields—including both Anglophones of the Northwest Region and Francophone Bamiléké of the West Region—are ruled by sacral chiefs, or what many designate as divine kings (cf. Frazer 1922; Feeley-Harnik 1985). Terms designating these rulers vary by local language (e.g., *mfən* in Bangangté or *fo* in Bafoussam). For simplicity I employ *fon*, for the rulers, and *fondom* for the polity, following common usage among Anglophones and, in public discourse, now increasingly among Francophones.

7. Some Bamiléké respond to public warnings about the alleged risk of Bamiléké domination by referring to themselves as the Igbo or Jews of Cameroon, making metaphoric bridges to other places, times, and peoples considered fatally "problematic."

8. From the colonial to the postcolonial eras, Bamiléké have perceived the state as a threat to reproduction (Feldman-Savelsberg 1999; Terretta 2007).

.

9. Some concentrations of Cameroonians are starting to emerge in the districts of Mitte (esp. Wedding), Reinickendorf, and Lichtenberg.

10. Working through sites and their gatekeepers is known as site-based sampling, a procedure that Arcury and Quandt (1999) consider particularly relevant for medical anthropological research in urban settings. Choosing interviewees based on particular characteristics relevant to the study, rather than seeking a randomly chosen representative sample, is called theoretical or purposive sampling (Oliver 2006).

11. Through the use of italics, I indicate exact quotations from audio-recorded and transcribed interviews. I also render quotations in italics when I am certain that exact words, witnessed through participant observation, were recorded in my fieldnotes. I use regular typeface for quotations taken from interviews that were not audio-recorded, quotations from fieldnotes where I have recorded remembered conversations and thus cannot be certain of exact wording, and for oft-repeated phrases that are not attributed to a specific interlocutor. To capture the tone of speech and migrants' peppering of Cameroonian English or French with German words, I am including both original quotations (in English, French, or German) and—when necessary— their English translations. Where there is no translation, the original quotation is in English.

Chapter Two

1. Petition from the Société des femmes Bomp, UPC Local Committee to the Visiting Mission, received June 25, 1956, TIPET.51894 Section 11 (cited in Terretta 2000, 99 ff.). See also Terretta 2013.

2. Marie-Anne Nsoga to UDEFEC meeting held at the home of Mbok Souzanne, December 6, 1956, Babimbi (cited in Terretta 2000, 101).

3. Highly educated and economically well-placed women of the two self-identified "elite" associations we studied frame their engagement as bringing "development" from the city to their home villages. In contrast, members of hometown associations created by women from impoverished or economically mixed neighborhoods in Yaoundé staged often-nostalgic festivals to bring the warmth and tastes of the village to the city (Feldman-Savelsberg and Ndonko 2010, 387–89).

4. 2,010, according to records of the Federal Statistical Office, and 2,080 in the *Ausländerzentralregister 2012* (Rühl 2014; Dick 2014).

5. On West African women's moral and social considerations in "retiring" from childbearing, see Bledsoe 2002.

Chapter Three

1. Olwig (2002) observes similar processes among Caribbean migrants returning home to celebrate a relative's wedding.

2. Can be glossed as "in the village," or "back home."

3. Eugen Zintgraff, during a 1889 expedition financed by the German Foreign Ministry, was one of the first European explorers to reach the highland Grassfields region of what had just become the German colony of Kamerun (Fardon 2006, 5).

4. In 2012, of 193 new Cameroonian arrivals in Berlin, 153 received temporary residence permits, including 61 (40 percent) for family reunification and 86 (56 percent) for education (Dick 2014).

5. Both Fleischer (2012) and Bledsoe and Sow (2011a, 185) remind us that surveillance and harassment from state authorities suspecting "sham marriages" can erode binational Cameroonian-German marriages. Fleischer's research among recently arrived Cameroonians found more registered marriages and births with Germans than with Cameroonians, concluding that Cameroonians orient their marital and fertility practices toward Germans as a strategy for dealing with restrictive German immigration rules (2012). My research indicates that this orientation may be relatively short-lived, and that longer-term Cameroonian residents of Germany seek out relationships with fellow Cameroonians.

6. In many African locales, care is demonstrated as much through material exchanges as through face-to-face interaction. Coe (2013, 28, 173–94) describes this eloquently for the relation between globally migrant parents and their children living in Ghana; using oral history, Moore and Vaughn (1994, 156–77) describe the materiality of care for wives and their relatives practiced by Bemba men, labor migrants to the Zambian copper mines.

7. Bahouoc in French indicates the fondom near Bangangté, and Bawock in English spelling indicates a fondom in the Bali subdivision of the Northwest Region, founded ca. 1905 through mass migrations within the greater Grassfields region (Chilver 1964). A century later, the ethnicization of politics and politicization of belonging encouraged Bawock to identify increasingly with their Bamiléké origins (Page, Evans, and Mercer 2010, 350). A dispute over boundary drawing and land rights in 2006 and 2007 ended in violence that left 2,000 Bawock refugees camped out on the grounds of the Bamenda Conference Hall, raising concerns about epidemic risk by the Bamenda Health District Officer (Nkematabong 2007).

8. Staying together as a couple is a difficult and complex endeavor, particularly so for those with fewer means and those who migrate under less ideal circumstances. Those facing unstable work under poor or demeaning conditions have a hard time engaging in material expressions of love; they may entertain multiple relationships more or less consciously for a variety of purposes, combining material exchange with affection (Manjoh 2013; Mohrmann 2013).

9. That is, with kin related to her husband. "Affines" are people related through ties of marriage, and include relations between the family of the bride and the family of the groom. In everyday American language they are referred to as in-laws.

10. In a report on reproductive behavior and migration prepared for the Federal Office for Migration and Refugees, Schmid and Kohls note that migrant women's fertility adapts to the norms and values of low-fertility Germany (2011, 5). African women have the highest birthrates in Germany, with 2.6 children per woman (compared with native Germans' 1.3) (2011, 6). The authors note large differences in the fertility of migrant women, based on marital status and educational level (2011, 7).

11. See Ewick and Silbey (2003) for a thorough discussion of the role of circulating narratives in the construction and reproduction of legal consciousness. For Cameroonian migrants, what we might call reproductive consciousness and migrant consciousness are mutually constituted with legal consciousness through women's practices of sharing exemplary tales.

12. During the decade preceding my field research (2000–2009), the mean total protection rate (including entitlement to asylum, refugee protection, and stay of deportation) was 5.02 percent. During 2010–2011 the mean total protection rate was 9.2 percent. Of these, the mean percentage of those granted asylum was 0.29 percent during 2000–2009, and 0.93 percent during 2010–2011 (Gumann n.d., based on sources from the Federal Office for Migration and Refugees, the Federal Statistical Office, and the Federal Police).

13. Eveline reported that some sicknesses (perhaps indirectly referring to HIV-AIDS) can be revealed neither to family nor friends, making it difficult to receive advice, referrals, or material help accessing medications. She suggests searching the Internet for anonymous advice. *"Well, I think that perhaps if you have an illness that you don't want to talk to anyone about, if you already know that there is a certain type of medicine that could treat you (sigh), you can search the Internet. There perhaps the Internet could guide you where you'd have a place to start. Because confiding [in someone], really, it's really not [an] obvious[ly good strategy]. It's really not obvious—this same person might laugh at you tomorrow about this."* (cf. Nzimegne-Gölz 2002; M'bayo 2009.)

Chapter Four

1. See Feldman-Savelsberg and Ndonko (2010) on the situationally specific meanings of "home" as a unit of belonging among members of the urban Bamiléké diaspora within Cameroon.

2. Coe defines repertoire as "a set of cultural resources or frameworks—ways of speaking, thinking, and feeling about family—that mobilize material resources and people in ways that are considered normal and natural" (2013, 5).

3. See Benedict Anderson (2006) on "imagined communities" and nationalism.

4. For comparative material on the educational aspirations that immigrant parents, especially mothers, hold for their children, and the emotional backlash that can result, see the controversy surrounding the notion of Chinese-American "tiger moms" (Chua 2011; Juang, Qin, and Park 2013; Qin 2006; Suárez-Orozco, Todorova, and Qin 2006).

5. I follow parents' lead in using "Cameroonian-ness" as a gloss for what are often more locally, regionally, or ethnically based identities within Cameroon.

6. Medumba is the language of Bangangté, the Bamiléké fondom in which I conducted research starting in the 1980s.

7. Like other Cameroonian immigrant women in Berlin, KemKarine uses the term "chambermaid" rather than "housekeeper," connoting the servitude and sometimes Dickensian conditions of low-level hotel work.

8. Stack (1974) describes a similar dynamic among African American women. Literature on the circulation of children also points out that children connect spatially dispersed women and households. (See, for example, Åkesson, Carling, and Drotbohm 2012; Alber, Martin, and Notermans 2013; Bledsoe and Sow 2011b; Coe 2013; and Goody 2008 [1982] for West African examples; Leinaweaver 2008, 2013, for Latin America; and Parreñas 2005 for southeast Asia).

9. In 2012, 61 percent of new temporary residency visas for Cameroonians were given to students; among women, 56.2 percent of new arrivals came on student visas.

10. Federal law in Germany gives parents a legal claim to a day-care spot for children one year and older, but few states (*Bundesländer*) can meet demand. Berlin is an exception, with ca. 5,000 free spots (Köhler 2013) at some 2,300 day-care centers and an intensive day-care expansion program as of March 2014 (Rautenberg 2014). While there may be waiting lists at particularly sought-out day-care centers in neighborhoods that attract young families, children do find day-care spots within the city, and there are no waiting lists at the level of the state government (Rautenberg 2014). For three years preceding entry into primary school at age 6, children may attend publicly subsidized Kitas free of charge, using vouchers (*Kitagutscheine*) that their parents obtain at their district's Jugendamt (youth welfare office, including child protection services).

11. The transnationally "scattered" families thus created differ from fostering arrangements common within West African countries, in terms of the children's age and the direction of

wealth and status differences between biological parents and caregivers. They also differ from fostering arrangements in which Bamiléké teens leave Cameroon to join distant relatives who have become well established in France (Kamga 2013).

12. Bledsoe and Sow (2011a), among others, suggest that due to difficulties in obtaining appropriate papers allowing African migrants to move into and out of Fortress Europe, more workers and their families remain in Europe for fear of not being able to return. This may well be the case for certain of my interlocutors. Others, though, obtain German citizenship to allow them to travel freely, to improve their professional chances, and to secure a future for their children. In addition to settling more permanently "for the children," they speak of the lack of employment opportunities in Cameroon, and their own growing difficulty adjusting to daily inconveniences in their homeland.

13. See Stoller's work on West African migrants in New York City, who contemplate retiring back to their homelands in Niger, Mali, Senegal, and Guinea (2001; 2014).

14. Unlike American stereotypes of German authoritarian parenting styles—based on social-psychological and historical scholarship on parenting during and immediately following the Nazi era (e.g., Adorno et al. 1950; Koomen 1974) and cinematic representations of early twentieth-century north German families, such as *The White Ribbon* (Haneke 2009)—contemporary middle-class German parenting is markedly antiauthoritarian (Durand 2004).

15. See Hobsbawm and Ranger's edited volume *The Invention of Tradition* for a theoretical elaboration of the notion of invented ritual (1983).

16. Literally, "school cones" or "sugar bags" (Balk 2013).

17. Cameroonian mothers make similar cultural compromises to keep their children Cameroonian, with more collective school rituals as well. For example, once Happi was a schoolgirl, Barbara convinced her to dress up as a Grassfields princess rather than as Princess Lilifee for her school's pre-Lenten Carnival parade.

18. Young boys' interest in trucks and football (soccer) did not generate the same level of bemused disbelief, adding a gendered dimension to immigrant parents' interpretations of cultural difference.

19. Meaning being a child old enough to be *allowed* to start first grade vs. to be *required* to start first grade.

20. The term "racial politics" encompasses three dimensions which, despite being interdependent, each change at a different speed. *Law*, e.g., regarding citizenship, has been stable from 1913 to the Nazi era and then again from 1949 to 1999; we witness significant change since 2000. *Policy*, encompassing administrative directives and practices, responds more dynamically to current conditions. *Cultural schemas*, for a large segment of the German population, may lag behind legal changes, but for other segments of society may change faster than law.

21. "Playing in the Dark *oder die Rassismus-Falle*," at the Werkstatt der Kulturen, Nov 24, 2010, moderated by Dr. Michel Friedman (former vice president of the Central Council of Jews in Germany), with participation of Dr. Iman Attia, Dr. Maisha Eggers, Petra Rosenberg, and Dr. Michal Bodemann, all specialists in education and the sociology of race, and of Muslim, black African, Sinti and Roma, and Jewish background, respectively.

22. Tessy framed her narrative of her daughter's encounter with reference to her own story of suffering from a German professor's discrimination when she was a beginning student, working in his laboratory. Circulating stories of such bias form the basis of collectively held ideas about the difficulties facing black immigrants and how to respond to them with resilience.

23. Hauptschulen teach at a slower pace than the technical and college-preparatory school

tracks. They were established in the 1950s to prepare fifth through ninth graders for vocational education. Formerly the most common educational track, Hauptschulen have become increasingly stigmatized. In Berlin, they were formally abolished and merged with other school forms to establish a new type of comprehensive school called Sekundarschule, starting with the 2010–2011 school year.

24. In contrast to, for example, the discipline of a strict daily schedule or early bedtime; such time-disciplining was highly variable among my interlocutors, following no perceivable pattern.

25. Kamga identifies respect for elders, acceptance of authority, limitations to individual liberty, tireless effort, and balancing group solidarity with competition for individual achievement as core Bamiléké values that contribute to the academic success of Bamiléké teens fostered by kin in France (2013, 133, 141; see also Dongmo 1981; Malaquais 2002; and Warnier 1993 for similar depictions of Bamiléké values transmitted through parenting practices within Cameroon).

26. "Posted" is a common expression, both in Cameroonian Pidgin English and among transnational Ghanaians (Coe, personal comm.), for children being sent to the parents' country of origin for care either by kin or in boarding schools.

27. Verhoef (2005) points out that, although these arrangements are common in the Cameroonian Grassfields region, relations between caregivers and biological mothers work with varying degrees of collaboration vs. conflict over material provision and emotional allegiance, which she characterizes as the joint venture, the ambivalent takeover, and the tug-of-war. Based on research in a provincial city in the eastern region of Cameroon, Notermans (2004, 2013) reveals huge variability in the relations between mothers and the grandmothers who foster their children, emerging from multiple, intersecting trajectories in women's life courses.

28. Anthropologists would call them patrilateral parallel cousins, the sons and daughters of Olivia's father's brother.

Chapter Five

1. On African hometown associations, see Barkan, McNulty, and Ayeni 1991; Englund 2001; Little 1965; Mitchell 1969, 1987; Schildkrout 1978; Shack and Skinner 1979; Tostensen, Tvedten, and Vaa (2000); Trager 1998, 2001; Woods 1994. Hometown associations are well documented in other parts of the world as well, for example among Mexicans in the United States (Orozco and Rouse 2013) and Turks in Germany (Çayğlar 2006).

2. In Germany, Cameroonian hometown associations are *eingetragene Vereine* (e.V.), associations registered through the German administrative court system. Many are also registered at the Cameroonian embassy. Home*places* are usually multiethnic sites, even when one ethnic group or fondom predominates. Some hometown associations are ethnic or—as some of my interlocutors put it—"tribal" associations. In these cases the home*place* stands for common descent and allegiance to an ethnic group. Other hometown associations are "town" associations, bringing together people of common origin as well as people with attachment to a locale through childhood residency. Individuals can potentially join several hometown associations, to which they could be connected via their father, mother, spouse, or a period of residence (for example for schooling). Because of this variability, Mercer, Page, and Evans (2008) prefer the term "home association." I continue to use "hometown association" because of its familiarity in the literature and among my interlocutors.

3. The attributions of others can support belonging to a homeplace through both legal and social-emotional means. The new Cameroonian constitution of 1997 required that Cameroonian

identity cards document an individual's ethnic affiliation (Jua 2005; Mercer, Page, and Evans 2008, 98). Stereotypes about Bamiléké and Anglophones that circulate in everyday Cameroonian discourse and contribute to personal anxiety may drive people to seek security in their homeplace, as Trager (2001) and Smith (2005) have pointed out for similar situations in Nigeria.

4. Many scholars of African migration to Europe pay particular attention to Pentecostal churches as affiliations that draw migrants together (Glick Schiller, Çağlar, and Guldbrandsen 2006; Krause 2014; Nieswand 2010). While charismatic church names proclaim their "international" character (as do anthropologists eager to move beyond "methodological nationalism" (Wimmer and Glick Schiller 2002), these churches in both south-north and south-south African diasporas tend to draw on local affiliations at the national (particularly Ghanaian, see Meyer 1999; van Dijk 2003) and subnational level. As part of my fieldwork, I participated in a Pentecostal church service run by a Cameroonian pastor in Berlin and met a few of its parishioners at later community events. However, I noted too much religious variation among Cameroonian migrant mothers to make churches the center of my research. My interlocutors' involvement in hometown associations was more widespread.

5. *Mɛn fì*, literally "fresh person," is the Bangangté term for newborn.

6. See Boehm 2012 on community-building strategies of Mexican migrant families in New Mexico.

7. Antiphonal greetings of this type are used in association meetings throughout the West Region of Cameroon, among the Bamiléké diaspora within the country, and among the transnational Bamiléké diaspora. The greeting can be used to signal one's entrance and greet those present, or to capture their attention, impose silence, or bring the group to order. The speaker repeats the greeting several times until those assembled are listening attentively. *Ngó* means country or territory, so that *Ngó Ndé* could be translated as "Département du Ndé" (Ndé District). Each time, the others respond *Ngó Koni*, translated literally as "Département de l'amour" (district of love), signaling the solidarity of those present (Ndonko 2014).

8. From "*garçons chauds*"; in American slang, they would be cool cats.

9. See Mugler (n.d.) on cultures of accountability, and Gephart (2006) on the importance of *Geltungskulturen* (validity cultures) in law.

10. The immigrants who are the focus of my research originate from regions of Cameroon where associational life is particularly well established. Although hometown association membership is a moral obligation among migrants within the Cameroonian nation-state, it is common but not obligatory in European cities like Berlin and Paris. But compared to Berlin, Paris can support greater differentiation in associational boundaries and activities because of its distinct city scale (Glick Schiller and Çağlar 2011), its postcolonial relationship with Cameroon, and the size of its immigrant population (Schlee 2011). Fifty-five percent of Cameroonians surveyed in the area surrounding Paris (Île-de-France) report involvement in associational life; proportionately, unmarried men are most represented, followed by married men and married women (Kamdem 2007, 199). In France, Cameroonians form associations at the chiefdom rather than divisional level, allowing for activities such as attempts at language revitalization (2007, 207), visits of fons and nobles using local radio to promote contributions to the development of homeplaces (2007, 218), and large-scale memorial celebrations and meetings of nobility (2007, 242–47).

11. "Good eating" of cooked foods that slide smoothly down the throat contrast with eating that requires biting and chewing with sharp teeth, termed *fed* in Bangangté and *kefala* in Mankon (Bamenda). Fɛd can refer to rough snacking of roasted corn or meat when people are

away at distant farms, but most often refers to witches' cannibalistic eating. Instead of creating unity, fed eating—whether alone or in witches' congeries called *famla'*—is the epitome of antisocial greed (Feldman-Savelsberg 1999, 124).

12. Kohlhagen (2006b) finds the same for participants in Bassa hometown associations among Cameroonians in Berlin.

13. Relationships among (mis)trust, democracy, and migration are subject to debates in sociology, political science, and economics. Paxton (2002) and Putnam (2000) suggest that trust, built in associational life, is essential for effective democracy. Collier controversially contends that migrants from poor countries bring with them mistrust and a lack of "mutual regard" (2013, 63, 83), thus destabilizing wealthier host societies.

14. Cameroonian stereotypes of Bamiléké as the Jews or Igbo of Cameroon draw upon such alleged traits as high achievement orientation, aggressive entrepreneurship, geographic mobility, strong family and ethnic solidarity, and histories of mass victimhood and marginalization.

15. Huschke (2013, chap. 4) turns Granovetter's "strength of weak ties" (1973) on its head to refer to the lack of solidarity among co-ethnics as the "weakness of strong ties."

16. In Bangangté in the 1980s, and even in Yaoundé during the 1990s and early 2000s, these perceived risks included the occult attack of envious witches as well as vulnerability to infection. None of my interlocutors in Berlin spoke of witchcraft, instead mentioning "tradition" and the biomedical risk of infection among newborns with immature immune systems.

17. A pseudonym, indicating that the homeplace serving as a basis for this association is vast, encompassing parts of two Cameroonian provinces ("regions," in a recent administrative change of designation).

18. I met one of my interlocutors at a program sponsored by an initiative to rename these streets; activists were especially concerned about streets carrying the names of former colonial officers known for their brutality (Peters, in Tanzania, then Deutsch Ostafrika) or for their promotion of genocide (von Trotha, during the Herero War in Namibia, then Südwest Afrika).

19. For a critical assessment of sexualization of the black body in the Karneval der Kulturen, see Partridge (2012, 82, 163–64 n. 4).

20. See Nyamnjoh and Rowlands' description of "long periods spent on the phone with relatives to arrange how the funeral will take place," in which migrants not only "want to provide the best for their deceased parents" but also "are equally concerned with their image as 'bushfallers' " (2013, 144).

21. Mothers know that children are socialized in a calm, orderly school setting, and worry that lively and chaotic palavers at associations may be off-putting.

Chapter Six

1. Who exactly "real" Germans are is a matter of public and scholarly debate. Migrants from Poland and the former Soviet Union who can prove their German ethnicity, termed *Spätaussiedler* or resettlers, receive German citizenship automatically (Castañeda 2012, 831). This reflects Germany's "monoethnic" regime of ethnicity, in which "the state seeks to restrict membership in the nation to one ethnic category through discriminatory immigration and naturalization policies" (Aktürk 2011, 118; see also Aktürk 2012) Since a change in citizenship law in 2000, it is now easier for people who are not ethnic Germans to become German citizens. And yet they continue to be referred to either as people with migration background or as "foreigners" (*Ausländer*). Indeed, "foreigner" has become a common equivalent for "ethnic" or "other" (Mandel 2008).

Reflecting Germany's "cosmopolitan anxieties" (Mandel 2008), a recent German right-wing movement (PEGIDA, "Patriotic Europeans Against the Islamization of the West") drew record crowds of 17,500 for a protest in Dresden on December 22, 2014, answered by over 65,000 signatures against the movement collected on an Internet petition in just two days over the Christmas holidays (Deutsche Welle 2014). More recently, participation in weekly PEGIDA demonstrations has fluctuated in response to record numbers of refugees arriving from via the "Balkan route."

2. Compared with 15.9 percent public welfare spending in the United States and 20.7 percent average investment among OECD countries (Giehle 2014).

3. Maurizio Ferraris suggests that even the exchanges and conversations that constitute everyday social relations are documented through receipts, mobile phone records, and text messages (2013).

4. The original quotation, from Bertolt Brecht ca. 1940 during a period of exile in Sweden: "Der Pass ist der edelste Teil von einem Menschen. Er kommt auch nicht auf so einfache Weise zustand wie ein Mensch. Ein Mensch kann überall zustandkommen, auf die leichtsinnigste Art und ohne gescheiten Grund, aber ein Pass niemals. Dafür wird er auch anerkannt, wenn er gut ist, während ein Mensch noch so gut sein kann und doch nicht anerkannt wird." In the author's English translation: "A passport is the noblest part of a human being. It does not come about in as simple a way as a human does. A human can come about at any place, in the most irresponsible way and without deliberate reason, but not a passport. And for that it is recognized [respected], if it is good, whereas the human, no matter how good, may not be recognized [respected]" (Brecht 2000, 7).

5. Some English translations refer to the Ausländer Amt as the immigration office. To capture the connotations of the German term, I use a shortened translation, the "Foreigners Office."

6. Like all names throughout this book, a pseudonym. *Eiche* means "oak" in German, connoting the steadfastness of this experienced German bureaucrat.

7. A pseudonym.

8. Following rules that I learned through my volunteer activities in Berlin, I did not ask my interlocutors about their HIV status, and no one volunteered it. As far as I know, none of the Cameroonian women living in Berlin whom I met were HIV-positive.

9. The full quotation from Sarazin's interview is: "Integration requires effort from those that are to be integrated. I will not show respect for anyone that is not making that effort. I do not have to acknowledge anyone who lives by welfare, denies the legitimacy of the very state that provides that welfare, refuses to care for the education of his children and constantly produces new little headscarf-girls. This holds true for 70 percent of the Turkish and 90 percent of the Arab population in Berlin." Translated by the author, from *Lettre International* 86 (2009), 197–201.

10. See also http://www.gesetze-im-internet.de/aufenthg_2004/__55.html, accessed January 24, 2015.

11. Some of my more critical, activist Cameroonian interlocutors would question the motives of people like Anoush, wondering whether they are helping out of altruism or out of a need to feel good about themselves, and if their help is a hindrance to migrants' independence, self-organization, and self-efficacy.

12. Roth and Wittich's English translation of Weber's *Economy and Society* explains rather than translates Weber's passage, "*Aktenmässigkeit der Verwaltung,*" as: "Administrative acts, decisions, and rules are formulated and recorded in writing, even in cases where oral discussion is the rule or is even mandatory [i.e., prescribed]" (Weber 2013, 219).

13. A pseudonym, translated as Dr. Well-Intentioned, or Dr. Kind.

14. Federally mandated counseling centers for women considering abortion, often integrated into more comprehensive family-planning and reproductive-sexual health centers.

15. A pseudonym, based on the German root for "community."

16. "(1) The care and custody of the person [child] includes the right to consent to a medically not indicated circumcision of a male child, who is not capable of appropriate understanding and judgment, if this circumcision is to be conducted according to the rules of medical expertise. This does not apply if circumcision, even under consideration of its purpose, endangers the well-being of the child. (2) Persons selected by a religion may conduct circumcisions according to paragraph 1 during the first six months after the birth of a child, if they have been specifically trained to do so and if they, without being a physician themselves, are comparably capable of conducting the circumcision" (http://www.gesetze-im-internet.de/bgb/__1631d.html, accessed December 22, 2014, translated by the author.

17. §31 II AufenthG; "Zur Vermeidung 'besonderer Härte,' wie sie z.B. das Festhalten an der Ehe in Fällen häuslicher Gewalt darstellt, ist aber von der Einhaltung der [dreijährigen] Frist abzusehen (§31 II AufenthG)." ["To avoid particular hardship, for example, upholding a marriage in cases of domestic violence, the [three-year] waiting period is to be disregarded"] (Dethloff 2012, 89).

18. Beginning with the ethnographies of Brigitte Jordan (1978) and Robbie Davis-Floyd (1986), a similar cultural, social, and medical critique has dominated anthropological studies of childbirth for over three decades.

References Cited

Abu-Lughod, Lila. 2008. *Writing Women's Worlds: Bedouin Stories.* 15th anniversary ed. Berkeley: University of California Press.

Adichie, Chimamanda Ngozi. 2009. *The Thing Around Your Neck.* New York: Alfred A. Knopf.

Adorno, Theodor W., Else Frenkel-Brunswik, Daniel J. Levinson, and R. Nevitt Sanford. 1950. *The Authoritarian Personality.* Oxford: Harpers.

Åkesson, Lisa, Jørgen Carling, and Heike Drotbohm. 2012. "Mobility, Moralities and Motherhood: Navigating the Contingencies of Cape Verdean Lives." *Journal of Ethnic and Migration Studies* (special issue: Transnational Parenting) 38 (2): 237–60.

Aktürk, Şener. 2011. "Regimes of Ethnicity: Comparative Analysis of Germany, the Soviet Union/ Post-Soviet Russia, and Turkey." *World Politics* 63 (1): 115–64. doi: 10.1353/wp.2011.0001.

———. 2012. *Regimes of Ethnicity and Nationhood in Germany, Russia, and Turkey.* Cambridge: Cambridge University Press.

Alber, Erdmute, Jeannett Martin, and Catrien Notermans, eds. 2013. *Child Fostering in West Africa: New Perspectives on Theory and Practices.* Leiden: Brill.

Alexander, Jeffrey. 2002. "On the Social Construction of Moral Universals: The 'Holocaust' from War Crime to Trauma Drama." *The European Journal of Social Theory* 5(1): 5–85.

Alpes, Maybritt Jill. 2011. *Bushfalling: How Young Cameroonians Dare to Migrate.* PhD diss., University of Amsterdam.

Alpes, Maybritt Jill, and Alexis Spire. 2013. "Dealing with Law in Migration Control: The Powers of Street-level Bureaucrats at French Consulates." *Social and Legal Studies*: 1–14. doi:10.1177/0964663913510927.

Alt, Jörg. 2003. *Leben in der Schattenwelt: Problemkomplex "illegal" Migration.* Karlsruhe: von Loeper Literaturverlag.

Amt für Statistik Berlin-Brandenburg. 2013. *Statistischer Bericht A | 5-hj 1/13, Einwohnerinnen und Einwohner im Land Berlin am 30. Juni 2013.* Potsdam: Amt für Statistik Berlin-Brandenburg. Accessed Nov. 13, 2013.

Anderson, Benedict. 2006. *Imagined Communities.* 2nd ed. London: Verso.

Angu, Walters. n.d. "Born-House Twin." Unpublished description of a painting. http://www.art cameroon.com/site/wp-content/uploads/2011/06/47-born-house-twin1.jpg. Accessed Oct. 2, 2013.

Arcury, T. A., and S. A. Quandt. 1999 "Participant Recruitment for Qualitative Research: A Site-Based Approach to Community Research in Complex Societies." *Human Organization* 58 (2): 128–33.

Ardener, Edwin. 1970. "Witchcraft, Economics, and the Continuity of Belief." In *Witchcraft Confessions and Accusations*, edited by Mary Douglas, 141–60. London: Tavistock.

Ardener, Shirley, and Sandra Burman. 1995. *Money-Go-Rounds: The Importance of Rotating Savings and Credit Associations for Women*. Oxford: Berg.

Argenti, Nicolas. 2007. *The Intestines of the State: Youth, Violence, and Belated Histories in the Cameroon Grassfields*. Chicago: University of Chicago Press.

Asad, Talal. 1973. *Anthropology and the Colonial Encounter*. New York: Humanities Press.

Ashforth, Adam. 2005. *Witchcraft, Violence, and Democracy in South Africa*. Chicago: University of Chicago Press.

Astone, Nan Marie, Constance A. Nathanson, Robert Schoen, and Young J. Kim. 1999. "Family Demography, Social Theory, and Investment in Social Capital." *Population and Development Review* 25 (1): 1–31.

Baldassar, Loretta. 2007. "Transnational Families and the Provision of Moral and Emotional Support: The Relationship between Truth and Distance." *Identities: Global Studies in Culture and Power* 14: 385–409.

Balk, Karin H. 2013. *Die Geschichte der Zuckertüte*. Friedberg: Verlagshaus Schlosser.

Barkan, J., M. L. McNulty, and M. A. O. Ayeni. 1991. "'Hometown' Voluntary Associations, Local Development, and the Emergence of Civil Society in Western Nigeria." *Journal of Modern African Studies* 29 (3): 457–80.

Barth, Frederik, ed. 1969. *Ethnic Groups and Boundaries*. London: Allen and Unwin.

Basel Mission Archives. n.d. *Ärztliche Mission in Kamerun*. Unpublished MS. Basel, Switzerland.

Bayart, Jean-François. 1979. *L'État au Cameroun*. Paris: Presses de la Fondation Nationale des Sciences Politiques.

———. 1993. *The State in Africa: The Politics of the Belly*. London: Longman.

Becker, Gary S. 1993. *Human Capital: A Theoretical and Empirical Analysis, with Special Reference to Education*. Chicago: University of Chicago Press.

Belinga Belinga, Gabriel. 2010. "Bi-national Leben: In einer globalisierten Welt kennt auch die Liebe keine Grenzen mehr." *Africa Positive* 10 (39): 31–32.

Beloe, Elizabeth. 2014. "'Having the Knife and the Yam': zum Umgang mit Geheimnissen in einer Community-basierten Forschung bei Kamerunischen Migrantinnen in Berlin." In *Forschungsethik in der Qualitativen Forschung: Reflexivität, Perspektiven, Positionen*, edited by Hella von Unger, Petra Nariman, and Rosaline M'Bayo, 133–48. Wiesbaden: Springer Fachmedien.

———. n.d. Personal communication. Discussions surrounding the preparation of a doctoral dissertation on Anglophone Cameroonian migrant women's participation in associational life. Berlin: Freie Universität zu Berlin.

Benndorf, Rolf. 2008. *Lebensperspektive Deutschland: Afrikanerinnen und Afrikaner in Deutschland und ihre gesellschaftliche Integration*. Marburg: Tectum.

Bledsoe, Caroline. 2002. Contingent Lives: Fertility, Time, and Aging in West Africa. With contributions by Fatoumatta Banja. Chicago: University of Chicago Press.

Bledsoe, Caroline, and Papa Sow. 2011a. "Family Reunification Ideals and the Practice of Transnational Reproductive Life among Africans in Europe." In *Reproduction, Globalization, and the State: New Theoretical and Ethnographic Perspectives*, edited by Carole H. Browner and Carolyn F. Sargent, 175–91. Durham: Duke University Press.

———. 2011b. "Back to Africa: Second Chances for the Children of West African Immigrants." *Journal of Marriage and Family* 73 (4): 747–62.

Boehm, Deborah A. 2012. *Intimate Migrations: Gender, Family, and Illegality among Transnational Mexicans.* New York: New York University Press.

Borneman, John. 1991. *After the Wall: East Meets West in the New Berlin.* New York: Basic Books.

Boswell, D. M. 1969. "Personal Crises and the Mobilization of the Social Network." In *Social Networks in Urban Situations: Analyses of Personal Relationships in Central African Towns*, edited by J. C. Mitchell, 245–96. Manchester: Manchester University Press.

Bouly de Lesdain, Sophie. 1999. *Femmes camerounaises en région parisienne: Trajectoires migratoires et réseaux d'approvisionnement.* Paris: L'Harmattan.

Bourdieu, Pierre. 1977. *Outline of a Theory of Practice.* Cambridge: Cambridge University Press.

———. 1983. "Ökonomisches Kapital, kulturelles Kapital, soziales Kapital." In *Soziale Ungleichheiten* (Soziale Welt, Sonderheft 2), edited by Reinhard Kreckel, 183–98. Göttingen: Otto Schwartz.

Brain, Robert. 1972. *Bangwa Kinship and Marriage.* Cambridge: Cambridge University Press.

Brecht, Bertolt. 2000. *Flüchtlingsgespräche.* Expanded ed. Frankfurt: Suhrkamp.

Breyer, Insa. 2011. *Keine Papiere—keine Rechte? Die Situation irregulärer Migranten in Deutschland und Frankreich.* Frankfurt: Campus.

Broch-Due, Vigdis, ed. 2005. *Violence and Belonging: The Quest for Identity in Post-Colonial Africa.* London: Routledge.

Brubaker, Rogers. 1992. *Citizenship and Nationhood in France and Germany.* Cambridge: Harvard University Press.

Bundesministerium für Justiz und Verbraucherschutz. 2014. Staatsangehörigkeitsgesetz (StAG) "Staatsangehörigkeitsgesetz in der im Bundesgesetzblatt Teil III, Gliederungsnummer 102–1, veröffentlichten bereinigten Fassung, das zuletzt durch Artikel 1 des Gesetzes vom 13. November 2014 (BGBl. I S. 1714) geändert worden ist." http://www.gesetze-im-internet.de /rustag/BJNR005830913.html. Accessed Jan. 22, 2015.

Caldwell, John C. 2005. "On Net Intergenerational Wealth Flows: An Update." *Population and Development Review* 31 (4): 721–40.

Campt, Tina M. 2004. *Other Germans: Black Germans and the Politics of Race, Gender, and Memory in the Third Reich.* Ann Arbor: University of Michigan Press.

Castañeda, Heide. 2008. "Paternity for Sale: Anxieties over 'Demographic Theft' and Undocumented Migrant Reproduction in Germany." *Medical Anthropology Quarterly* 22 (4): 340–59.

———. 2012. " 'Over-Foreignization' or 'Unused Potential'? A Critical Review of Migrant Health in Germany and Responses Toward Unauthorized Migration." *Social Science and Medicine* 74: 830–38.

———. 2013. "Medical Aid as Protest: Acts of Citizenship for Unauthorized Im/migrants and Refugees." *Citizenship Studies* 17 (2): 227–40. doi.org/10.1080/13621025.2013.780744.

Castles, S. 2007. "Twenty-First Century Migration as a Challenge to Sociology." *Journal of Ethnic and Migration Studies* 33 (3): 351–71.

Çayğlar, Ayşe. 2006. "Hometown Associations, the Re-scaling of State Spatiality and Migrant Grassroots Transnationalism." *Global Networks* 6 (1): 1–22.

Chilver, Sally. 1964. "A Bamiléké Community in Bali-Nyonga: A Note on the Bawok." *African Studies* 23 (3–4): 121–27.

Chua, Amy. 2011. *Battle Hymn of the Tiger Mother*. New York: Penguin.

Coe, Cati. 2011. "What Is the Impact of Transnational Migration on Family Life? Women's Comparisons of Internal and International Migration in a Small Town in Ghana." *American Ethnologist* 38 (1): 148–63.

———. 2013. *The Scattered Family: Parenting, African Migrants, and Global Inequality*. Chicago: University of Chicago Press.

Coe, Cati, Rachel R. Reynolds, Deborah Boehm, Julia Meredith Hess, and Heather Rae-Espinoza, eds. 2011. *Everyday Ruptures: Children, Youth, and Migration in Global Perspective*. Nashville: Vanderbilt University Press.

Cohen, David W., and E. S. Atieno Odhiambo. 1992. *Burying SM: The Politics of Knowledge and the Sociology of Power in Africa*. Portsmouth, NH: Heinemann.

Cohen, Jane Maslow, and Caroline Bledsoe. 2002. "Immigrants, Agency, and Allegiance: Some Notes from Anthropology and from Law." In: *Engaging Cultural Differences: The Multicultural Challenge in Liberal Democracies*, 99–127. New York: Russell Sage Foundation.

Cole, Jennifer. 2010. *Sex and Salvation: Imagining the Future in Madagascar*. Chicago: University of Chicago Press.

———. 2014. "The *téléphone malgache*: Transnational Gossip and Social Transformation among Malagasy Marriage Migrants in France." *American Ethnologist* 41 (2): 276–89.

Cole, Jennifer, and Deborah Durham. 2007. "Introduction: Age, Regeneration, and the Intimate Politics of Globalization." In *Generations and Globalization: Youth, Age, and Family in the New World Economy*, edited by Jennifer Cole and Deborah Durham, 1–28. Bloomington: Indiana University Press.

Cole, Jennifer, and Christian Groes. 2016. "Affective Circuits and Social Regeneration in African Migration." In *Affective Circuits: African Migrations to Europe and the Pursuit of Social Regeneration*, edited by Jennifer Cole and Christian Groes, 1–26. Chicago: University of Chicago Press.

Cole, Jennifer, and Lynn M. Thomas, eds. 2009. *Love in Africa*. Chicago: University of Chicago Press.

Coleman, James S. 1988. "Social Capital in the Creation of Human Capital." Supplement, *American Journal of Sociology* 94: 95–120.

Colen, Shellee. 1995. "'Like a Mother to Them': Stratified Reproduction and West Indian Childcare Workers and Employers in New York." In *Conceiving the New World Order*, edited by F. D. Ginsburg and R. Rapp, 42–58. Berkeley: University of California Press.

Collier, Paul. 2013. *Exodus: How Migration Is Changing Our World*. Oxford: Oxford University Press.

Collins, Randall. 2005. *Interaction Ritual Chains*. Princeton: Princeton University Press.

Comaroff, John L., ed. 1980. *The Meaning of Marriage Payments*. New York: Academic Press.

Comaroff, John L., and Jean Comaroff. 2009. *Ethnicity, Inc.* Chicago: University of Chicago Press.

Coutin, Susan Bibler. 2000. *Legalizing Moves: Salvadoran Immigrants' Struggle for Legal Residency.* Ann Arbor: University of Michigan Press.

Csordas, Thomas J. 1994. *Embodiment and Experience: The Existential Ground of Culture and Self*. Cambridge: Cambridge University Press.

DAAD (German Academic Exchange Service). 2013. *7.908 Euro für ein Jahr*. https://www.study-in.de/de/studium/vor-der-abreise/nachweis-der-finanzierung—11859. Accessed Oct. 3, 2013.

D'Alisera, JoAnn. 1998. "Born in the USA: Naming Ceremonies of Infants among Sierra Leoneans Living in the American Capital." *Anthropology Today* 14 (1): 16–18.

Davis-Floyd, Robbie. 1986. *Birth as an American Rite of Passage*. Berkeley: University of California Press.

Debarge, Josette. 1934. *La mission médicale au Cameroun*. Paris: Société des Missions Evangéliques.

De Genova, Nicholas. 2002. "Migrant 'Illegality' and Deportability in Everyday Life." *Annual Review of Anthropology* 21: 419–47.

Delaney, Carol. 1991. *The Seed and the Soil: Gender and Cosmology in Turkish Village Society*. Berkeley: University of California Press.

DeLoache, Judy, and Alma Gottlieb, eds. 2000. *A World of Babies*. Cambridge: Cambridge University Press.

den Ouden, Jan H. B. 1987. "In Search of Personal Mobility: Changing Interpersonal Relations in Two Bamiléké Chiefdoms, Cameroon." *Africa* 57 (1): 3–27.

Dethloff, Nina. 2012. *Familienrecht*. 30th ed. Munich: C. H. Beck.

Deutsche Welle. 2014. "Thousands Sign Online Petition against German Anti-Islam PEGIDA Movement." Deutsche Welle, Dec. 27, 2014. http://dw.de/p/1EAUI. Accessed Dec. 27, 2014.

Devisch, Renaat, Filip De Boeck, and D. Jonckers, eds. 1995. *Alimentations, traditions et développements en Afrique intertropicale*. Paris: Éditions L'Harmattan.

Dick, Joscha. 2014 (Jan. 13–14). Personal communication. Analysis of information from the Statistisches Bundesamt and the *Ausländerzentralregister 2012*.

Dongmo, Jean-Louis. 1981. *Le dynamisme bamiléké (Cameroun): La maîtrise de l'espace urbain*. Yaoundé: CEPER.

Douglas, Mary. 1970. *Natural Symbols*. New York: Vintage.

Drotbohm, Heike. 2009. "Horizons of Long-Distance Intimacies: Reciprocity, Contribution and Disjuncture in Cape Verde." *History of the Family* 14: 132–49.

Durand, Béatrice. 2004. *Die Legende vom typisch Deutschen: Eine Kultur im Spiegel der Franzosen*. Leipzig: Militzke.

Durkheim, Emile. 1915. *The Elementary Forms of the Religious Life*. Translated by Joseph Ward Swain. London: George Allen and Unwin.

———. 1984. *The Division of Labor in Society*. New York: Free Press.

Edholm, Felicity, Olivia Harris, and Kate Young. 1978. Conceptualizing Women. *Critique of Anthropology* 3: 101–130.

Egerton, F. Clement. 1938. *African Majesty: A Record of Refuge at the Court of the King of Bangangté in the French Camerouns*. London: George Routledge and Sons.

Eggers, Maureen Maisha. 2006. "Die Auswirkung rassifizierter (post-)kolonialer Figurationen auf die sozialen Identitäten von weißen und schwarzen Kindern in Deutschland." In *Koloniale und postkoloniale Konstruktionen von Afrika und Menschen afrikanischer Herkunft in der deutschen Alltagskultur*, edited by Marianne Bechhaus-Gerst and Sunna Gieseke, 383–94. Frankfurt am Main: P. Lang.

Ehrmann, Georg. 2012. "Beschneidung ist Körperverletzung und gehört verboten." *Der Tagesspiegel*. August 13, 2012. http://www.tagesspiegel.de/meinung/andere-meinung/gastkommentar-beschneidung-is-koerperverletzung-und-gehoert-verboten/6837500.html. Accessed March 4, 2014.

Eley, Geoff, and Jan Palmowski. 2008. "Citizenship and National Identity in Twentieth-Century Germany." In *Citizenship and National Identity in Twentieth-Century Germany*, edited by Geoff Eley and Jan Palmowski, 3–23. Stanford: Stanford University Press.

Ellermann, Antje. 2006. "Street-Level Democracy: How Immigration Bureaucrats Manage Public Opposition." *West European Politics* 29 (2): 293–309.

Emirbayer, Mustafa, and Jeff Goodwin. 1994. "Network Analysis, Culture, and the Problem of Agency." *American Journal of Sociology* 99: 1411–54.

Englund, Harri. 2001. "The Politics of Multiple Identities: The Making of a Home Villagers' Association in Lilongwe, Malawi." In *Associational Life in African Cities: Popular Responses to the Urban Crisis*, edited by A. Tostensen, I. Tvedten, and M. Vaa, 90–106. Stockholm: Nordiska Afrikainstitutet.

Evans, Martin. 2010. "Primary Patriotism, Shifting Identity: Hometown Associations in Manyu Division, South-West Cameroon." *Africa* 80 (3): 397–425.

Evans-Pritchard, Edward E. 1976. *Witchcraft, Oracles and Magic among the Azande*. Oxford: Clarendon.

Ewick, Patricia, and Susan Silbey. 1998. *The Common Place of Law*. Chicago: University of Chicago Press.

———. 2003. "Narrating Social Structure: Stories of Resistance to Legal Authority." *American Journal of Sociology* 108 (6): 1328–72.

Eyoh, Dickson. 1998. "Through the Prism of a Local Tragedy: Political Liberalization, Regionalism and Elite Struggles for Power in Cameroon." *Africa* 68 (3): 338–59.

Express 2012. "Nach Kölner Urteil—Der Beschneidungs-Streit: Darum wird er so heftig geführt." *Express (Politik & Wirtschaft)*. Sept. 7, 2012. http://www.express.de/politik-wirtschaft/nach -koelner-urteil-der-beschneidungs-streit—darum-wird-er-so-heftig-gefuehrt,218,17196150 .html. Accessed March 4, 2014.

Fardon, Richard. 2006. *Lela in Bali: History through Ceremony in Cameroon*. Oxford: Berghahn Books.

Farinaud, Médecin Colonel. 1944. Rapport annuel, année 1944. Yaoundé: Cameroun Français, Service de Santé.

———. 1945. Rapport annuel, année 1945. Yaoundé: Cameroun Français, Service de Santé.

Farmer, Paul. 2003. *Pathologies of Power: Health, Human Rights, and the New War on the Poor*. Berkeley: University of California Press.

Fassin, Didier. 2011. *Humanitarian Reason: A Moral History of the Present*. Berkeley: University of California Press.

Federal Ministry of the Interior (Germany). 2014. "Becoming a German Citizen by Naturalization." http://www.bmi.bund.de/SharedDocs/FAQs/EN/Themen/Migration/Staatsang/Erwerb _der_deutschen_Staatsbuergerschaft_durch_Eingbuergerung_en.html. Accessed December 29, 2014.

Feeley-Harnik, Gillian. 1985. "Issues in Divine Kingship." *Annual Review of Anthropology* 14: 273–313.

Feldman-Savelsberg, Pamela. 1995. "Cooking Inside: Kinship and Gender in Bangangté Idioms of Marriage and Procreation." *American Ethnologist* 22 (3): 438–501.

———. 1999. *Plundered Kitchens, Empty Wombs: Threatened Reproduction and Identity in the Cameroon Grassfields*. Ann Arbor: University of Michigan Press.

———. 2005. "Variations in Royal Blue: Bamiléké Display Cloth from Ritual Respect to Ethnic Demonstration." *HALI: Carpet, Textile and Islamic Art* 142: 86–93.

———. 2011. "Fleeting Trust and Braided Socialities: Temporality and Belonging in African Migrants' Reproductive Practices." Paper presented at the Annual Meeting of the American Anthropological Association, Montreal, Quebec, Nov. 19.

———. 2016. "Forging Belonging through Children in the Berlin Cameroonian Diaspora." In *Affective Circuits: African Migrations to Europe and the Pursuit of Social Regeneration,* edited by Jennifer Cole and Christian Groes, 54–77. Chicago: University of Chicago Press.

Feldman-Savelsberg, Pamela, and Flavien T. Ndonko. 2010. "Urbanites and Urban Villagers: Comparing 'Home' among Elite and Non-Elite Bamiléké Women's Hometown Associations." *Africa* 80 (3): 371–96.

Feldman-Savelsberg, Pamela, Flavien T. Ndonko, and Bergis Schmidt-Ehry. 2000. "Sterilizing Vaccines or The Politics of the Womb: Retrospective Study of a Rumor in Cameroon." *Medical Anthropology Quarterly* 14 (2): 159–79.

Feldman-Savelsberg, Pamela, Flavien T. Ndonko, and Song Yang. 2005. "Remembering 'the Troubles': Reproductive Insecurity and the Management of Memory in Cameroon." *Africa* 75 (1): 10–29.

———. 2006. "The Social Management of Fetal and Infant Death: Dual Disruptions to Reproductive Lives and Discourses." *Curare* 29 (1): 7–15.

Feldman-Savelsberg, Pamela, and Sylvie Schuster. n.d. "Revelation and Secrecy: Women's Social Networks and the Contraception-Abortion Process in Cameroon." In *Abortion in Transcultural Perspective.* New York: Palgrave Macmillan (forthcoming).

Ferguson, James. 2006. *Global Shadows: Africa in the Neoliberal World Order.* Durham: Duke University Press.

Ferraris, Maurizio. 2013. *Documentality: Why It Is Necessary to Leave Traces.* Translated by Richard Davies. New York: Fordham University Press.

Finotelli, Claudia, and Giuseppe Scortino. 2013. "Through the Gates of the Fortress: European Visa Policies and the Limits of Immigration Control." *Perspectives on European Politics and Society* 14 (1): 80–101. doi:10.1080/15705854.2012.732390.

Fleischer, Annett. 2012. *Migration, Marriage, and the Law: Making Families among Cameroonian 'Bush Fallers' in Germany.* Berlin: RegioSpectra.

Fonchingong, Charles C. 2005. "Exploring the Politics of Identity and Ethnicity in State Reconstruction in Cameroon." *Social Identities* 11 (4): 363–81.

Fraczek, Jennifer. 2013. "German Circumcision Law Still under Fire." Deutsche Welle online, December 12, 2013. http://dw.de/p/1AXdD. Accessed December 22, 2014.

Frazer, James George, Sir. 1922. *The Golden Bough: A Study in Magic and Religion.* Abridged ed. New York: Macmillan.

Friedman, Lawrence. 1975. *The Legal System: A Social Science Perspective.* New York: Russell Sage Foundation.

Gans, Herbert J. 1962. *The Urban Villagers: Group and Class in the Life of Italian-Americans.* New York: Free Press.

Gephart, Werner. 2006. *Recht als Kultur: Zur kultursoziologischen Analyse des Rechts.* Frankfurt: Vittorio Klostermann.

Gerhäusser, Tina. 2006. "Gefährliche 'No-Go-Areas' für dunkelhäutige WM-Besucher." Deutsche Welle, May 17, 2006. Permalink http://dw.de/p/8UeM, http://www.dw.de/gef%C3%A4hrliche-no-go-areas-f%C3%BCr-dunkelh%C3%A4utige-wm-besucher/a-2024446. Accessed August 6, 2014.

Geschiere, Peter. 1997. *The Modernity of Witchcraft: Politics and the Occult in Postcolonial Africa.* Charlottesville: University of Virginia Press.

———. 2005. "Funerals and Belonging: Different Patterns in South Cameroon." *African Studies Review* 48 (2): 45–64.

———. 2007. "Regional Shifts—Marginal Gains and Ethnic Stereotypes." *African Studies Review* 50 (2): 43–56.

———. 2009. *The Perils of Belonging: Autochthony, Citizenship, and Exclusion in Africa and Europe.* Chicago: University of Chicago Press.

———. 2013. *Witchcraft, Intimacy, and Trust: Africa in Comparison.* Chicago: University of Chicago Press.

Geschiere, Peter, and Josef Gugler. 1998. "Introduction: The Urban-Rural Connection—Changing Issues of Belonging and Identification." *Africa* 68 (3): 309–19.

Geschiere, Peter, and Francis Nyamnjoh. 2000. "Capitalism and Autochthony: The Seesaw of Mobility and Belonging," *Public Culture* 12 (2): 423–52.

Giehle, Sabine. 2014. "Social Security." http://www.tatsachen-ueber-deutschland.de/en/society/main-content-08/social-security.html. Accessed July 23, 2014.

Glaeser, Norbert. 2014 (Aug. 4). Personal communication (Senatsverwaltung für Gesundheit und Soziales, Abteilung Soziales, II A 13).

Glick Schiller, Nina, and Ayşe Çağlar. 2011. "Locality and Globality: Building a Comparative Analytical Framework in Migration and Urban Studies." In *Locating Migration: Rescaling Cities and Migrants,* edited by N. Glick Schiller and A. Çağlar, 60–81. Ithaca: Cornell University Press.

Glick Schiller, Nina, Ayşe Çağlar, and Thaddeus C. Guldbrandsen. 2006. "Beyond the Ethnic Lens: Locality, Globality, and Born-Again Incorporation." *American Ethnologist* 33 (4): 612–33.

Gluckman, Max. 1967 [1955]. *The Judicial Process among the Barotse of Northern Rhodesia (Zambia).* 2nd ed. Manchester: Manchester University Press.

Goffman, Erving. 1959. *The Presentation of Self in Everyday Life.* New York: Anchor Books.

Goheen, Miriam. 1996. *Men Own the Fields, Women Own the Crops: Gender and Power in the Cameroon Grassfields.* Madison: University of Wisconsin Press.

Goldschmidt, Daniel. 1986. "Le Corps chez les Bamiléké de Bandjoun (Cameroun)." Thèse présentée pour le Doctorat en Médecine, Diplôme d'État. Université Louis Pasteur, Faculté de Médicine de Strasbourg.

Goody, Esther. 2008 [1982]. *Parenthood and Social Reproduction: Fostering and Occupational Roles in West Africa.* Cambridge: Cambridge University Press.

Goody, Jack. 1958. *The Developmental Cycle in Domestic Groups.* Cambridge: Cambridge University Press.

Gottlieb, Alma. 2004. *The Afterlife Is Where We Come From: The Culture of Infancy in West Africa.* Chicago: University of Chicago Press.

Granovetter, Mark. 1973. "The Strength of Weak Ties." *American Journal of Sociology* 78 (6): 1360–80.

———. 1985. "Economic Action and Social Structure: The Problem of Embeddedness." *American Journal of Sociology* 91: 481–510.

Graw, Knut, and Samuli Schielke. 2012. "Introduction: Reflections on Migratory Expectations in Africa and Beyond." In *The Global Horizon: Expectations of Migration in Africa and the Middle East,* edited by Knut Graw and Samuli Schielke, 7–22. Leuven: Leuven University Press.

Grosse, Pascal. 2008. "Conceptualizing Citizenship as a Biopolitical Category from the Eighteenth to the Twentieth Centuries." In *Citizenship and National Identity in Twentieth-Century Germany,* edited by Geoff Eley and Jan Palmowski, 181–97. Stanford: Stanford University Press.

GTZ (Federal Ministry for Economic Cooperation and Development), Division for Economic Development and Employment, Sector Project Migration and Development. 2007. *The Cameroonian Diaspora in Germany: Its Contribution to Development in Cameroon*. Eschborn: Deutsche Gesellschaft für Technische Zusammenarbeit (GTZ).

Gumann, Axel. n.d. Personal communication. Data regarding asylum applications and decisions gathered from the BAMF, Statistisches Bundesamt, and Bundespolizei.

Guyer, Jane I. 1987. *Feeding African Cities: Studies in Regional Social History*. Bloomington: Indiana University Press in association with the International African Institute.

Guyer, Jane I., and Samuel M. Eno Belinga. 1995. "Wealth in People as Wealth in Knowledge: Accumulation and Composition in Equatorial Africa." *The Journal of African History* 36 (1): 91–120.

Haneke, Michael. 2009. *Das weiße Band: Eine deutsche Kindergeschichte. (The White Ribbon)*. Wega Film and X Filme.

Herzfeld, Michael. 1992. *The Social Production of Indifference: Exploring the Roots of Western Bureaucracy*. Chicago: University of Chicago Press.

Hirsch, Jennifer. 2003. *A Courtship after Marriage: Sexuality and Love in Mexican Transnational Families*. Berkeley: University of California Press.

Hirsch, Jennifer, and Holly Wardlow, eds. 2006. *Modern Loves: The Anthropology of Romantic Courtship and Companionate Marriage*. Ann Arbor: University of Michigan Press.

Hobsbawm, Eric J., and Terence O. Ranger, eds. 1983. *The Invention of Tradition*. Cambridge: Cambridge University Press.

Hochschild, Arlie R. 2000. "Global Care Chains and Emotional Surplus Value." In *On the Edge: Globalization and the New Millennium*, edited by Tony Giddens and Will Hutton, 130–46, London: Sage.

Hours, Bernard. 1985. *L'État sorcier: Santé publique et société au Cameroun*. Paris: L'Harmattan.

Howell, Signe. 2006. *The Kinning of Foreigners: Transnational Adoption in a Global Perspective*. Oxford: Berghahn.

Hughes, Everett C. 1945. "Dilemmas and Contradictions of Status." *American Journal of Sociology* 50 (5): 353–59.

Hurault, Jean. 1962. *La structure sociale des Bamiléké*. Paris: Mouton.

Huschke, Susann. 2013. *Kranksein in der Illegalität: Undokumentierte Lateinamerikaner/-innen in Berlin. Eine medizinethnologische Studie*. Bielefeld: Transcript.

———. 2014a. "Giving Back: Activist Research with Undocumented Migrants in Berlin." *Medical Anthropology: Cross-Cultural Studies in Health and Illness*. doi:10.1080/01459740.2014.949375.

———. 2014b. "Performing Deservingness: Humanitarian Health Care Provision for Migrants in Germany." *Social Science and Medicine* 120: 352–59. doi:10.1016/j.socscimed.2014.04.046. Accessed November 9, 2014.

Hutchinson, Sharon. 1996. *Nuer Dilemmas: Coping with Money, War, and the State*. Berkeley: University of California Press.

Hutter, Lieutenant. 1892. "Cermonien beim Schliessen von Blutfreundschaft bei den Graslandstämmen im Kamerun-Hinterland." *Wissenschaftliche Beihefte zum Deutschen Kolonialblatte: Mittheilungen von Forschungsreisenden und Gelehrten aus den Deutschen Schutzgebieten* 5 (4): 176–84.

Janzen, John. 1978. *The Quest for Therapy in Lower Zaire*. Berkeley: University of California Press.

———. 1987. "Therapy Management: Concept, Reality, Process." *Medical Anthropology Quarterly* (n.s.) 1 (1): 68–84.

Jindra, Michael. 2011. "The Rise of 'Death Celebrations' in the Cameroonian Grassfields." In *Funerals in Africa: Explorations of a Social Phenomenon*, edited by Michael Jindra and Joel Noret, 109–29. New York: Berghahn Books.

Johnson-Hanks, Jennifer. 2006. *Uncertain Honor: Modern Motherhood in an African Crisis*. Chicago: University of Chicago Press.

Johnson-Hanks, Jennifer. 2007. "Women on the Market: Marriage, Consumption, and the Internet in Urban Cameroon." *American Ethnologist* 34 (4): 642–58.

Jordan, Brigitte. 1978. *Birth in Four Cultures*. Long Grove, IL: Waveland.

Joseph, Richard A. 1977. *Radical Nationalism in Cameroun: Social Origins of the UPC (Union des Populations du Cameroun) Rebellion*. Oxford: Clarendon.

Jua, Nantang. 2003. "Differential Responses to Disappearing Transitional Pathways: Redefining Possibility among Cameroonian Youths." *African Studies Review* 46 (2): 13–36.

———. 2005. "The Mortuary Sphere, Privilege and the Politics of Belonging in Contemporary Cameroon." *Africa* 75 (3): 325–54.

Juang, Linda P., Desiree Baolian Qin, and Irene J. K. Park. 2013. "Deconstructing the Myth of the 'Tiger Mother': An Introduction to the Special Issue on Tiger Parenting, Asian-Heritage Families, and Child/Adolescent Well-Being." *Asian American Journal of Psychology* 4 (1): 1–6. http://dx.doi.org/10.1037/a0032136.

Kaberry, Phyllis M. 1952. *Women of the Grassfields: A Study of the Economic Position of Women in Bamenda, British Cameroons*. London: Her Majesty's Stationary Office.

Kago Lele, Jacques. 1995. *Tribalisme et exclusions au Cameroun: Le cas des Bamiléké*. Yaoundé: Les Editions du CRAC.

Kamdem, Pierre. 2007. *Camerounais en Île-de-France: Dynamiques migratoires et stratégies d'intégration socio-spatiale différenciées*. Paris: L'Harmattan.

Kamga, Monique. 2013. "Stratégies éducatives parentales et méchanismes familiaux de réussite des enfants bamilékés fosterés en France." *La Revue Internationale de l'Éducation Familiale* 33 (1): 129–48.

———. 2014. *Éducation familiale et fosterage*. Paris: L'Harmattan.

Kamga, Monique, and Bernadette Tillard. 2013. "Le fosterage à l'épreuve de la migration: jeunes Bamilékés du Cameroun accueillis en France." *Ethnologie Française* 43 (2): 325–34.

Kanaaneh, Rhoda. 2002. *Birthing the Nation: Strategies of Palestinian Women in Israel*. Berkeley: University of California Press.

Karagianni, Evangelos, and Nina Glick Schiller. 2006. "Contesting Claims to the Land: Pentecostalism as a Challenge to Migration Theory and Policy." *Sociologus* 2 (1): 137–72.

Kelek, Necla. 2012. "Die Beschneidung—ein unnützes Opfer für Allah." *Die Welt*, June 28, 2012. http://www.welt.de/107288230. Accessed March 4, 2014.

Keller, Heidi, Susanne Voelker, and Relindis D. Yovsi. 2005. "Conceptions of Parenting in Different Cultural Communities: The Case of West African Nso and Northern German Women." *Social Development* 14 (1): 158–80.

Kelodjoue, Samuel, Paul Roger Libité, and Eric Jazet. 2012. "Caractéristiques du pays et présentation de l'enquête." In *DHS Final Reports, Cameroon DHS, 2011*, 1–16. Yaoundé, Cameroon and Calverton, Maryland : Institut National de la Statistique Ministère de l'Économie de la Planification et de l'Aménagement du Territoire, Ministère de la Santé Publique and ICF International. http://dhsprogram.com/pubs/pdf/FR260/FR260.pdf. Accessed Jan. 17, 2016.

Kilomba, Grada. 2008. *Plantation Memories: Episodes of Everyday Racism*. Münster: Unrast Verlag.

Kneebone, Susan. 2005. "Women Within the Refugee Construct: 'Exclusionary Inclusion' in Policy and Practice—the Australian Experience." *International Journal of Refugee Law* 17 (1): 7–42.

Köhler, Regina. 2013. "Berlin verfügt über rund 5000 freie Kita-Plätze." *Berliner Morgenpost*, July 30, 2012. http://www.morgenpost.de/berlin-aktuell/article118516431/Berlin-v . . . Accessed March 4, 2014.

Kohlhagen, Dominik. 2006a. "Ni comme 'ici,' ni comme 'chez nous': Le 'nous' des Camerounais de Berlin et l'expression d'un droit en action." *Cahiers d'anthropologie du droit* 2006: 238–98.

———. 2006b. "'Illegale' Migration und Rechtskultur : Beobachtungen aus einer Feldforschung in Kamerun und Deutschland." *Zeitschrift für Rechtssoziologie* 27 (2): 239–50.

Kom, Dorothée. 2011. "Régionalisme, intégration nationale et éducation." In *Regional Balance and National Integration in Cameroon: Lessons Learned and the Uncertain Future*, edited by Paul Nchoji Nkwi and Francis B. Nyamnjoh, 217–28. Bamenda, Cameroon: Langaa Research and Publishing Common Initiative Group.

Konings, Piet, and Francis Nyamnjoh. 2003. *Negotiating an Anglophone Identity: A Study of the Politics of Recognition and Representation in Cameroon.* Leiden: Brill.

Koomen, Willem. 1974. "A Note on the Authoritarian German Family." *Journal of Marriage and Family* 36 (3): 634–36.

Krause, Kristine. 2008. "Transnational Therapy Networks among Ghanaians in London." *Journal of Ethnic and Migration Studies* 34 (2): 235–51.

———. 2014. "Space in Pentecostal Healing Practices among Ghanaian Migrants in London." *Medical Anthropology* 33 (1): 37–51.

Krause, Kristine, and Katharina Schramm. 2011. "Thinking through Political Subjectivities." *African Diaspora* 4: 115–34.

Kuczynski, Robert R. 1939. *The Cameroons and Togoland: A Demographic Study.* London: Oxford University Press.

Kwayeb, Enock Katté. 1960. *Les Institutions de droit public du pays Bamiléké: (Cameroun), évolution et régime actuel.* Clichy-sous-Bois: R. Cavillon.

Laslett, Barbara, and Johanna Brenner. 1989. "Gender and Social Reproduction: Historical Perspectives." *Annual Review of Sociology* 15: 381–404.

Lavie, Smadar. 2014. *Wrapped in the Flag of Israel: Mizrahi Single Mothers and Bureaucratic Torture.* New York: Berghahn.

Leinaweaver, Jessaca. 2008. *The Circulation of Children: Adoption, Kinship, and Morality in Andean Peru.* Durham: Duke University Press.

———. 2011. "Kinship Paths to and from the New Europe: A Unified Analysis of Peruvian Adoption and Migration." *Journal of Latin American and Caribbean Anthropology* 16 (2): 380–400.

———. 2013. *Adoptive Migration: Raising Latinos in Spain.* Durham: Duke University Press.

LeVine, Victor, and R. P. Nye. 1974. *Historical Dictionary of Cameroon.* Metuchen, NJ: Scarecrow Press.

Levitt, Peggy, and Mary C. Waters, eds. 2002. *The Changing Face of Home: The Transnational Lives of the Second Generation.* New York: Russell Sage Foundation.

Lévi-Strauss, Claude. 1969 [1949]. *The Elementary Structures of Kinship.* Translated by J. Bell and J. von Sturmer. Boston: Beacon Press.

Lin, Nan. 1999. "Building a Network Theory of Social Capital." *Connections* 22 (1): 28–51.

Little, Kenneth. 1965. *West African Urbanization: A Study of Voluntary Associations in Social Change.* Cambridge: Cambridge University Press.

Lochner, Susanne, Tobias Büttner, and Karin Schuller. 2013. "Das Integrationspanel: Langfristige Integrationsverläufe von ehemaligen Teilnehmenden an Integrationskursen" (working paper 52). Nuremberg: Bundesamt für Migration und Flüchtlinge.

Malaquais, Dominique. 2002. *Architecture, pouvoir et dissidence au Cameroun.* Paris: Karthala.

Malkki, Liisa. 1992. "National Geographic: The Rooting of Peoples and the Territorialization of National Identity among Scholars and Refugees." *Cultural Anthropology* 7 (1): 24–44.

Mandel, Ruth. 2008. *Cosmopolitan Anxieties: Turkish Challenges to Citizenship and Belonging in Germany.* Durham: Duke University Press.

Manjoh, Priscillia. 2013. *Snare.* Kansas City, MO: Miraclaire Publishing.

Marsden, Peter V. 1987. "Core Discussion Networks of Americans." *American Sociological Review* 52: 122–31.

Mau, S., and H. Brabandt. 2011. "Visumpolitik und die Regulierung globaler Mobilität: Ein Vergleich dreier OECD Länder." *Zeitschrft für Soziologie* 40 (1): 3–23.

Mauss, Marcel. 1979 [1938]. "The Notion of Body Techniques" and "Principles of the Classification of Body Techniques." In M. Mauss, *Sociology and Psychology,* translated by B. Brewster, 97–105 and 106–19. London: Routledge and Kegan Paul.

Mazzucato, Valentina, and Djamila Schans. 2011. "Transnational Families and the Well-Being of Children: Conceptual and Methodological Challenges." *Journal of Marriage and the Family* 73 (4): 704–12.

M'bayo, Rosaline. 2009. "Die Gesundheitsversorgung afrikanischer MigrantInnen—Über die Arbeit vom 'Afrikaherz.'" Berlin: Heinrich Böll Stiftung. http://heimatkunde.boell.de/2013 /11/18/die-gesundheitsversorgung-afrikanischer-migrantinnen-%E2%80%93-%C3%BCber -die-arbeit-vom-afrikaherz. Accessed February 17, 2014.

Mercer, Claire, Ben Page, and Martin Evans. 2008. *Development and the African Diaspora: Place and the Politics of Home.* London: Zed Press.

Merry, Sally. 1990. *Getting Justice and Getting Even: Legal Consciousness among Working-Class Americans.* Chicago: University of Chicago Press.

Meyer, Birgit. 1999. *Translating the Devil: Religion and Modernity among the Ewe of Ghana.* Trenton, NJ: Africa World Press.

Mitchell, J. Clyde. 1969. *Social Networks in Urban Situations.* Manchester: Manchester University Press.

———. 1987. *Cities, Society, and Social Perception: a Central African Perspective.* Oxford: Clarendon Press.

Mohrmann, Marie. 2013. "Berlin als Falle." *Der Freitag.* Blogpost November 11, 2013. https://www .freitag.de/autoren/mariemohrmann/berlin-als-falle. Accessed April 27, 2015.

Moore, H., and M. Vaughan. 1994. *Cutting Down Trees: Gender, Nutrition and Agricultural Change in the Northern Province of Zambia, 1890–1990.* New York: Heinemann.

Moore, Sally Falk. 1978. *Law as Process: An Anthropological Approach.* London: Routledge and Kegan Paul.

———. 1986. *Social Facts and Fabrications:"Customary" Law on Kilimanjaro, 1880–1980.* Lewis Henry Morgan Lectures. Cambridge: Cambridge University Press.

Moore, Sally Falk, and Barbara G. Myerhoff, eds. 1977. *Secular Ritual.* Assen, Netherlands: Van Gorcum.

Mugler, Johanna. n.d. Personal communication. Discussion of paper presented at LOST Colloquium of the Max Planck Institute for Social Anthropology, Halle, 2010–11.

Ndjio, Basile. 2006. "Intimate Strangers: Neighbourhood, Autochthony and the Politics of Belonging." In *Crisis and Creativity: Exploring the Wealth of the African Neighbourhood*, edited by P. Konings and D. Foeken, 66–86. Leiden: Brill.

———. 2009. "Migration, Architecture, and the Transformation of the Landscape in the Bamiléké Grassfields of West Cameroon." *African Diaspora* 2 (1): 73–100.

Ndonko, Flavien. 2014 (May 8). Personal communication.

Ndzelen, Kelen. n.d. "Cameroonian Tradition Born House" blog post. http://visionshakers.blog spot.de/2011/07/cameroonian-tradition-born-house.html. Accessed Oct. 2, 2013.

Nelkin, David. 2004. "Using the Concept of Legal Culture." *Australian Journal of Legal Philosophy* 29 (1): 1–26.

Ngongo, Louis. 1982. *Histoire des forces religieuses au Cameroun*. Paris: Karthala.

Nieswand, Boris. 2010. "Enacted Destiny: West African Charismatic Christians in Berlin and the Immanence of God." *Journal of Religion in Africa* 40 (1): 33–59.

———. 2011. *Theorising Transnational Migration: The Status Paradox of Migration*. New York: Routledge.

Niger-Thomas, Margaret. 1995. "Women's Access to and the Control of Credit in Cameroon: The Mamfe Case." In *Money-Go-Rounds: The Importance of Rotating Savings and Credit Associations for Women*, edited by Shirley Ardener and Sandra Burman, 95–110. Oxford: Berg.

Njikam Savage, Olayinka M. 1996. "'Children of the Rope' and Other Aspects of Pregnancy Loss in Cameroon." In *The Anthropology of Pregnancy Loss*, edited by Rosanne Cecil, 95–109. Oxford: Berg.

Njiké-Bergeret, Claude. 1997. *Ma passion africaine*. Paris: Éditions Jean-Claude Lattès.

———. 2000. *La sagesse de mon village*. Paris: Éditions Jean-Claude Lattès.

Nkematabong, Martin. 2007. "Bali/Bawock Crisis: Medics Pre-empt Epidemic Outbreak!" Cameroon-info.net, from the *Cameroon Tribune*, March 26, 2007. http://www.cameroon-info .net/stories/0,19105,@,bali-bawock-crisis-medics-pre-empt-epidemic-outbreak.html. Accessed Jan. 20, 2014.

Nkwi, Paul Nchoji. 1976. *Traditional Government and Social Change: A Study of the Political Institutions among the Kom of the Cameroon Grassfields*. Fribourg: The University Press (Studia Ethnographica Friburgensia).

———. 1987. *Traditional Diplomacy: A Study of Inter-chiefdom Relations in the Western Grassfields, Northwest Province of Cameroon*. Yaoundé: University of Yaoundé.

Nkwi, Paul Nchoji, and Francis B. Nyamnjoh, eds. 2011. *Regional Balance and National Integration in Cameroon: Lessons Learned and the Uncertain Future*. Bamenda: Langaa Research and Publishing Common Initiative Group.

Notermans, Catrien. 2004. "Sharing Home, Food, and Bed: Paths of Grandmotherhood in East Cameroon." *Africa* 74 (1): 6–27.

———. 2013. "Children Coming and Going: Fostering and Lifetime Mobility in East Cameroon." In *Child Fostering in West Africa: New Perspectives on Theory and Practices*, edited by Erdmute Alber, Jeannett Martin, and Catrien Notermans, 155–76. Leiden: Brill.

Notué, Jean-Paul, and Louis Perrois. 1984. *Contribution à l'étude des sociétés secrètes chez les Bamiléké (Ouest Cameroun)*. Yaoundé: ISH and ORSTOM.

Novotný, Lukáš. 2009. "Right-Wing Extremism and No-Go-Areas in Germany." *Czech Sociological Review* 45 (3): 591–609.

Nyamnjoh, Francis. 2011. "Cameroonian Bushfalling: Negotiation of Identity and Belonging in Fiction and Ethnography." *American Ethnologist* 38 (4): 701–13.

Nyamnjoh, Francis, and Michael Rowlands. 1998. "Elite Associations and the Politics of Belonging in Cameroon." *Africa* 68 (3): 320–37.

Nyamnjoh, Henrietta, and Michael Rowlands. 2013. "Do You Eat Achu Here? Nurturing as a Way of Life in a Cameroon Diaspora." *Critical African Studies* 5 (3): 140–52. doi: 10.1080/21681392.2013.837703.

Nzikam Djomo, E. 1977. *Les rites relatifs à la naissance chez les Feè Feè de Babouantou (Pùàntù)*. Mémoire de Diplôme des Études Supérieures, University of Yaoundé.

Nzimegne-Gölz, Solange. 2002. *HIV und AIDS: Umgang mit Patienten aus Schwarzafrika*. Berlin: GlaxoSmithKlein.

Oguntoye, Katharina, May Ayim/Opitz, and Dagmar Schultz, eds. 2006. *Farbe Bekennen: Afrodeutsche Frauen auf den Spuren ihrer Geschichte*. 3rd ed. Berlin: Orlanda Frauenverlag.

Oliver, Paul. 2006. "Purposive Sampling." In *The SAGE Dictionary of Social Research Methods*, edited by Victor Jupp. London: Sage. doi: http://dx.doi.org/10.4135/9780857020116. Accessed Nov. 1, 2014.

Olwig, Karen Fog. 2002. "A Wedding in the Family: Home Making in a Global Kin Network." *Global Networks* 2 (2): 205–18.

Ong, Aihwa. 2003. *Buddha Is Hiding: Refugees, Citizenship, the New America*. Berkeley: University of California Press.

Orozco, Manuel, and Rebecca Rouse. 2013. "Migrant Hometown Associations and Opportunities for Development." In *The Community Development Reader*, edited by James DeFilippis and Susan Saegert, 280–85. NY: Routledge.

Page, Ben. 2007. "Slow Going: The Mortuary, Modernity, and the Hometown Association in Bali-Nyonga, Cameroon." *Africa* 77 (3): 419–41.

Page, Ben, Martin Evans, and Claire Mercer. 2010. "Revisiting the Politics of Belonging in Cameroon." *Africa* 80 (3): 345–70.

Parreñas, Rhacel S. 2000. "Migrant Filipina Domestic Workers and the International Division of Reproductive Labor." *Gender and Society* 14 (4): 560–80.

———. 2005. "Long Distance Intimacy: Class, Gender and Intergenerational Relations between Mothers and Children in Filipino Transnational Families." *Global Networks: A Journal of Transnational Affairs* 5 (4): 317–36.

Partridge, Damani. 2012. *Hypersexuality and Headscarves: Race, Sex, and Citizenship in the New Germany*. Bloomington: Indiana University Press.

Paxton, Pamela. 2002. "Social Capital and Democracy: An Interdependent Relationship." *American Sociological Review* 67: 254–77.

Pelican, Michaela. 2012. "Friendship among Pastoral Fulbe in Northwest Cameroon." *African Study Monographs* 33 (3): 165–88.

———. 2013. "International Migration: Virtue or Vice? Perspectives from Cameroon." *Journal of Ethnic and Migration Studies* 39 (2): 237–57. http://dx.doi.org/10.1080/1369183X.2013.723256.

Pelican, Michaela, and Peter Tatah. 2009. "Migration to the Gulf States and China: Local Perspectives from Cameroon." *African Diaspora*, 2 (2): 229–45.

Pescosolido, Bernice A. 1986. "Migration, Medical Care and the Lay Referral System: A Network Theory of Adult Socialization." *American Sociological Review* 51: 523–40.

———. 1992. "Beyond Rational Choice: The Social Dynamics of How People Seek Help." *American Journal of Sociology* 97: 1096–1138.

Piot, Charles. 1999. *Remotely Global: Village Modernity in West Africa*. Chicago: University of Chicago Press.

Polke-Majewski, Karsten. 2012. "Urteil: Kein Weg aus dem Dilemma Beschneidung." *Zeit Online*. June 27, 2012. http://www.zeit.de/gesellschaft/2012-06/bescneidung-urteil-koeln/komplettansicht.

Portes, Alejandro. 1998. "Social Capital: Its Origins and Applications in Modern Sociology." *Annual Review of Sociology* 24: 1–24.

Portes, Alejandro and Rubén G. Rumbaut. 2001. *Legacies: The Story of the Immigrant Second Generation*. Berkeley: University of California Press.

Pradelles de Latour, Charles Henry. 1994. "Marriage Payments, Debt and Fatherhood among the Bangoua: A Lacanian Analysis of a Kinship System." *Africa* 61 (1): 21–33.

Putnam, Robert. 2000. *Bowling Alone: The Collapse and Revival of American Community*. New York: Simon and Schuster.

Qin, Desiree Baolian. 2006. "'Our Child Doesn't Talk to Us Anymore': Alienation in Immigrant Chinese Families." *Anthropology and Education Quarterly*. 37 (2): 162–79. doi:10.1525/aeq.2006.37.2.162.

Rabinovici, Doron. 2012. "Im Hintergrund schwelen Kastrationsängste." *Süddeutsche.de*, July 11, 2012. http://www.sueddeutsche.de/kultur/kritik-an-ritueller-beschneidung-im-hintergrund-schwelen-kastrationsaengste-1.1408075. Accessed March 4, 2014.

Rautenberg, Marlies. 2014 (March 5). Personal communication. Director of the Section on Family Policy, Daycare, and Preschool Education, Office for Education, Youth, and Science, Berlin Senate.

Republic of Cameroon, National Institute of Statistics. 2013. *Annuaire statistique du Cameroun: Édition 2013*. Yaoundé: National Institute of Statistics.

Retel-Laurentin, Anne. 1974. *Infécondité en Afrique Noire: Maladies et conséquences sociales*. Paris: Masson et Cie.

Reynolds, Rachel. 2006. "Professional Nigerian Women, Household Economy, and Immigration Decisions." *International Migration* 44 (5): 167–88.

Robinson, Fiona. 2011. *The Ethics of Care: A Feminist Approach to Human Security*. Philadelphia: Temple University Press.

Rolland, P. 1951. *Quelques aspects sociologiques de la vie des Bamiléké de la Subdivision de Bagangte* [sic]. Typescript from the archives of Claude Tardits, dated October 31, 1951.

Rosaldo, Michelle Z. 1980. *Knowledge and Passion: Ilongot Notions of Self and Social Life*. Cambridge: Cambridge University Press.

Rosaldo, Renato. 1989. "Introduction: Grief and a Headhunter's Rage." In *Culture and Truth: The Remaking of Social Analysis*, 1–21. Boston: Beacon Press.

Rowlands, Michael. 1995. "Looking at Financial Landscapes: A Contextual Analysis of ROSCAs in Cameroon." In *Money-Go-Rounds: The Importance of Rotating Savings and Credit Associations for Women*, edited by Shirley Ardener and Sandra Burman, 111–24. Oxford: Berg.

———. 1996. "The Consumption of an African Modernity." In *African Material Culture*, edited by Mary Jo Arnoldi, Christaud M. Geary, and Kris L. Hardin, 188–213. Bloomington: Indiana University Press.

Rudin, Harry Rudolph. 1938. *Germans in the Cameroons: 1884–1914*. New Haven: Yale University Press.

Rühl. Stefan. 2013. Personal communication. Information from the Federal Office for Migration and Refugees [Bundesamt für Migration und Flüchtlinge].

Rumbaut, Rubén G. 2004. "Ages, Life Stages, and Generational Cohorts: Decomposing the Immigrant First and Second Generations in the United States." *International Migration Review* 38 (3): 1160–205.

Sachsenröder, Delphine. 2012. "Körperverletzung oder Gottesgebot?" *General Anzeiger Bonn*, July 14, 2012. http://www.general-anzeiger-bonn.de/news/politik/Koerperverletzung. Accessed March 4, 2014.

Sahlins, Marshall. 2013. *What Kinship Is—and Is Not*. Chicago: University of Chicago Press.

Sammartino, Annemarie. 2008. "Culture, Belonging, and the Law: Naturalization in the Weimar Republic." In *Citizenship and National Identity in Twentieth-Century Germany*, edited by Geoff Eley and Jan Palmowski, 57–72. Stanford: Stanford University Press.

Sargent, Carolyn F. 2011. "Problematizing Polygamy, Managing Maternity: The Intersections of Global, State, and Family Politics in the Lives of West African Migrant Women in France." In *Reproduction, Globalization, and the State*, edited by Carole H. Browner and Carolyn F. Sargent, 192–203. Durham: Duke University Press.

Sarrazin, Thilo. 2009. "Thilo Sarrazin im Gespräch. Klasse Statt Masse: Von Der Hauptstadt der Transferleistungen zur Metropole der Eliten." Interview. *Lettre International* 86: 197–201. http://www.pi-news.net/wp/uploads/2009/10/sarrazin_interview1.pdf. Accessed Jan. 24, 2015.

———. 2010. *Deutschland schafft sich ab: Wie wir unser Land aufs Spiel setzen*. Munich: Deutsche Verlags-Anstalt.

Savelsberg, Joachim J., and Ryan D. King. 2011. *American Memories: Atrocities and the Law*. New York: Russell Sage Foundation.

Saul, Nicholas, ed. 2009. *The Cambridge Companion to German Romanticism*. Cambridge: Cambridge University Press.

Scheper-Hughes, Nancy, and Margaret Lock. 1987. "The Mindful Body: A Prolegomenon to Future Work in Medical Anthropology." *Medical Anthropology Quarterly* (n.s.) 1 (1): 6–41.

Schildkrout, Enid. 1978. *People of the Zongo: The Transformation of Ethnic Identities in Ghana*. Cambridge: Cambridge University Press.

Schlee, Günther. 2011. "Afterword: An Ethnographic View of Size, Scale, and Locality." In *Locating Migration: Rescaling Cities and Migrants*, edited by N. Glick Schiller and A. Çağlar, 235–42. Ithaca: Cornell University Press.

Schmid, Susanne. 2010. With Kevin Borchers. *Vor den Toren Europas? Das Potenzial der Migration aus Africa. Forschungsbericht 7*. Nürnberg: Bundesamt für Migration und Flüchtlinge.

Schmid, Susanne and Martin Kohls. 2011. *Generatives Verhalten und Migration: Eine Bestandsaufnahme des generativen Verhaltens von Migrantinnen in Deutschland. Forschungsbericht 10*. Nürnberg: Bundesamt für Migration und Flüchtlinge.

Schmidbauer, Wolfgang. 2012. "Beschneidung ist nicht harmlos." *Süddeutsche.de*, July 4, 2012. http://www.sueddeutsche.de/wissen/nach-dem-koelner-urteil-beschneidung-ist-nicht-harmlos-1.1401049. Accessed March 4, 2014.

Scholz, Kay-Alexander. 2012. "Circumcision Remains Legal in Germany." Deutsche Welle online, December 12, 2012. http://dw.de/p/160DQ. Accessed December 22, 2014.

Schwarz, Tobias. 2011. "'Bei dauerhafter Verweigerung der Integration . . .': Der Integrationsbegriff in deutschen Ausweisungsdebatten." *Sociologia Internationalis* 49 (1): 53–68.

Schwenken, Helen. 2013. "'The EU Should Talk to Germany': Transnational Legal Consciousness as a Rights Claiming Tool among Undocumented Migrants." *International Migration* 51 (6): 132–45.

Senatsverwaltung für Inneres und Sport, Abteilung Verfassungsschutz. 2007. *Rechte Gewalt in Berlin 2003 bis 2006. Studienreihe "Im Fokus."* Berlin: Verfassungsschutz.

Sewell, William. 1992. "A Theory of Structure: Duality, Agency and Transformation." *American Journal of Sociology* 98 (1): 1–29.

Shack, W. A., and E. P. Skinner, eds. 1979. *Strangers in African Societies*. Berkeley: University of California Press.

Shandy, Dianna. 2008. "Irish Babies, African Mothers: Rites of Passage and Rights in Citizenship in Post-Millennial Ireland." *Anthropological Quarterly* 81 (4): 803–31.

Silbey, Susan. 2005. "After Legal Consciousness." *Annual Review of Law and Social Science* 1: 323–68.

———. 2010. "Legal Culture and Cultures of Legality." In *Handbook of Cultural Sociology*, edited by John R. Hall, Laura Grindstaff, and Ming-Cheng Lo, 470–79. London: Routlege.

Small, Mario Luis. 2009. *Unanticipated Gains: Origins of Network Inequality in Everyday Life*. Oxford: Oxford University Press.

Smith, Daniel J. 2001. "Romance, Parenthood, and Gender in a Modern African Society." *Ethnology* 40 (2): 129–51.

———. 2004. "Burials and Belonging in Nigeria: Rural-Urban Relations and Social Inequality in a Contemporary African Ritual." *American Anthropologist* 106 (3): 569–79.

———.2005. "Legacies of Biafra: Marriage, 'Home People' and Human Reproduction among the Igbo of Nigeria." *Africa* 75 (1): 30–45.

Socpa, Antoine. 2010. "New Kinds of Land Conflicts in Urban Cameroon: The Case of the 'Landless' Indigenous People in Yaoundé." *Africa* 80 (4): 553–72.

Solsten, Eric, ed. 1995. *Germany: A Country Study*. Washington: GPO for the Library of Congress. Ch. 4, Social Welfare, Health Care, and Education. http://countrystudies.us/germany/111.htm. Accessed July 23, 2014.

Sow, Noah. 2008. *Deutschland Schwarz Weiss: Der alltägliche Rassismus*. Munich: C. Bertelsmann.

Spittler, Gerd. 1980. "Streitregelung im Schatten des Leviathan: Eine Darstellung und Kritik rechtsethnologischer Untersuchungen." *Zeitschrift für Rechtssoziologie* 1 (1): 4–32.

Stack, Carol B. 1974. *All Our Kin: Strategies for Survival in a Black Community*. New York: Harper and Row.

Statistisches Bundesamt. 2013. *Bevölkerung und Erwerbstätigkeit*. Wiesbaden: Statistisches Bundesamt. (Via Stefan Rühl. Personal communication, October 2013.)

Stoller, Paul. 2001. *Money Has No Smell: The Africanization of New York City*. Chicago: University of Chicago Press.

———. 2014. *Yaya's Story: The Quest for Well-Being in the World*. Chicago: University of Chicago Press.

Strathern, Andrew J. 1996. *Body Thoughts*. Ann Arbor: University of Michigan Press.

Suárez-Orozco, Carola, Irina Todorova, and Desirée Baolian Qin. 2006. "The Well-Being of Immigrant Adolescents: A Longitudinal Perspective on Risk and Protective Factors." In *The Crisis in Youth Mental Health: Critical Issues and Effective Programs, Vol. 2: Disorders in Adolescence. Child Psychology and Mental Health*, edited by Francisco A. Villarruel and Tom Luster, 53–83. Westport, CT: Praeger/Greenwood.

Süddeutsche Zeitung. 2012. "Muslime und Juden reagieren: Heftiger Widerstand gegen Beschneidungsurteil." *Süddeutsche.de*, July 5, 2012. http://www.sueddeutsche.de/politik/muslime-und-juden-reagieren-heftiger-widerstand-gegen-beschneidungsurteil-1.1402167. Accessed March 4, 2014.

Süddeutsche Zeitung. 2012. "Rabbiner zu Beschneidungsurteil: Schwerster Angriff auf jüdisches Leben Seit dem Holocaust" *Süddeutsche.de*, July 16, 2012. http://www.sueddeutsche.de

/politik/rabbiner-zu-beschneidungsurteil-schwerster-angriff-auf-juedisches-leben-seit -dem-holocaust-1.1410909. Accessed March 4, 2014.

Swidler, Ann. 1986. "Culture in Action: Symbols and Strategies." *American Sociological Review* 51 (2): 273–86.

Tardits, Claude. 1960. *Contribution à l'étude des populations Bamiléké de l'Ouest Cameroun.* Paris: Editions Berger-Levrault.

Taussig, Karen-Sue, Klaus Hoeyer, and Stefan Helmreich. 2013. "The Anthropology of Potentiality in Biomedicine." Supplement 7, *Current Anthropology* 54: S3–S14.

TAZ (Tageszeitung). 2008. *TAZ.de,* "Abschiebeschutz fuer Schwangere," August 20, 2008. http://www.taz.de/1/berlin/artikel/?dig=2008/08/20/a0168&cHash=6fd9a17473/. Accessed October 5, 2014.

Terretta, Meredith. 2000. "Cameroonian Women and the Writing of a Popular Nationalism." MA thesis, Department of History, University of Wisconsin.

———. 2007. "A Miscarriage of Nation: Cameroonian Women and Revolution, 1949–1971." *Stichproben: Vienna Journal of African Studies* 12: 61–90.

———. 2013. *Petitioning for Our Rights, Fighting for Our Nation: The History of the Democratic Union of Cameroonian Women, 1949–1960.* Bamenda: Langaa Research & Publishing.

Ticktin, Miriam. 2011. *Casualties of Care: Immigration and the Politics of Humanitarianism in France.* Berkeley: University of California Press.

Tostensen, A., I. Tvedten, and M. Vaa, eds. 2000. *Associational Life in African Cities: Popular Responses to the Urban Crisis.* Stockholm: Nordiska Afrikainstitutet.

Trager, Lilian. 1998. "Home-Town Linkages and Local Development in Southwestern Nigeria: Whose Agenda? What Impact?" *Africa* 68 (3): 360–82.

———. 2001. *Yoruba Hometowns: Community, Identity, and Development in Nigeria.* Boulder: Lynne Rienner.

Transparency International. 2014. *Country Profile: Cameroon.* Berlin: Transparency International. http://www.transparency.org/country#CMR_DataResearch. Accessed November 1, 2014.

Uehara, Edwina. 1990. "Dual Exchange Theory, Social Networks, and Informal Social Support." *American Journal of Sociology* 96 (3): 521–57.

United Nations, Population Division of the Department of Economic and Social Affairs. 2012. *World Population Prospects: The 2012 Revision.* http://esa.un.org/unpd/wpp/unpp/panel _indicators.htm. Accessed March 8, 2015.

Valente, Thomas W., Susan C. Watkins, Miriam N. Jato, Ariane van der Straten, and Louis-Philippe Tsitsol 1997. "Social Network Associations with Contraceptive Use among Cameroonian Women in Voluntary Associations." *Social Science and Medicine* 45 (5): 677–87.

Van der Geest, Sjaak. 2004. "Grandparents and Grandchildren in Kwahu, Ghana: The Performance of Respect." *Africa* 74 (1): 47–61.

Van Dijk, Rijk. 2003. "Localisation, Ghanaian Pentecostalism and the Stranger's Beauty in Botswana." *Africa* 73 (4): 560–83.

Verhoef, Heidi. 2005. "'A Child Has Many Mothers': Views of Child Fostering in Northwestern Cameroon." *Childhood* 12 (3): 369–90.

Vubo, Emmanuel Yenshu. 2005. "Matriliny and Patriliny between Cohabitation-Equilibrium and Modernity in the Cameroon Grassfields." *African Study Monographs* 26 (3): 145–82.

Wakam, Jean. 1994. *De la pertinence des théories "économistes" de fécondité dans le context socio-culturel Camerounais et Négro-Africain.* Yaoundé: IFORD.

Warnier, Jean-Pierre. 1985. *Échanges, développment et hiérarchies dans le Bamenda pré-colonial (Cameroun).* Stuttgart: Franz Steiner Verlag.

———. 1993. *L'esprit d'entreprise au Cameroun.* Paris: Karthala.

Weber, Max. 1972. *Wirtschaft und Gesellschaft: Grundriß der verstehenden Soziologie.* 5th ed. Tübingen: J. C. B. Mohr (Paul Siebeck).

———. 2013. *Economy and Society.* Translated and edited by Guenther Roth and Claus Wittich. Berkeley: University of California Press.

Die Welt 2012a. "Fast einhellige Kritik am Kölner Beschneidungsurteil." *Die Welt,* June 27, 2012. http://www.welt.de/107280710. Accessed March 4, 2014.

———. 2012b. "Kölner Beschneidungsurteil ist rechtskräftig." *Die Welt,* June 29, 2012. http://www.we.t.de/107303669. Accessed March 4, 2014.

Whitehouse, Bruce. 2012. *Migrants and Strangers in an African City: Exile, Dignity, Belonging.* Bloomington: Indiana University Press.

Whyte, Susan Reynolds. 1997. *Questioning Misfortune: The Pragmatics of Uncertainty in Eastern Uganda.* Cambridge: Cambridge University Press.

Wimmer, Andreas, and Nina Glick Schiller. 2002. "Methodological Nationalism and Beyond: Nation-State Building, Migration and the Social Sciences." *Global Networks* 2 (4): 301–34.

Woods, D. 1994. "Elites, Ethnicity, and 'Home Town' Associations in the Côte d'Ivoire: An Historical Analysis of State–Society Links." *Africa* 64 (4): 465–83.

World Bank. 2013. *Cameroon (Data by Country): World Development Indicators.* Washington: The World Bank. http://data.worldbank.org/country/cameroon. Accessed November 1, 2014.

Yue, Ming-Bao. 2000. "On Not Looking German: Ethnicity, Diaspora, and the Politics of Vision." *European Journal of Cultural Studies* 3 (2): 173–94.

Yuval-Davis, Nira. 2006. "Belonging and the Politics of Belonging." *Patterns of Prejudice* 40 (3): 197–214.

Zambo Belinga, Joseph Maria. 2011. "Equilibre régional, replis identitaires et fragilisation croissante de l'intérêt national: vers un effet 'boomerang' de la politique des quotas au Cameroun." In *Regional Balance and National Integration in Cameroon: Lessons Learned and the Uncertain Future,* edited by Paul Nchoji Nkwi and Francis B. Nyamnjoh, 195–216. Bamenda: Langaa Research and Publishing Common Initiative Group.

Index

Page numbers in italics signify illustrations.